1992

The beginning of *Troilus and Criseyde*, Ms. Morgan 817, fol. 1., Pierpont Morgan Library, New York.

Chaucer's *Troilus and Criseyde* and the Critics

Alice R. Kaminsky

OHIO UNIVERSITY PRESS

Printed in the United States of America by Oberlin Printing Company

Library of Congress Cataloging in Publication Data

Kaminsky, Alice R.
    Chaucer's Troilus and Criseyde and the critics.

    Bibliography: p. 207
    Includes index.
    1. Chaucer, Geoffrey, d. 1400. Troilus and
Criseyde. 2. Chaucer, Geoffrey, d. 1400—Criticism
and interpretation—History. I. Title.
PR1896.K3   821'.1   79-27535
ISBN 0-8214-0428-8

For

JACK, ERIC, and HY

TABLE OF CONTENTS

LIST OF ABBREVIATIONS

AI	American Imago
AN&Q	American Notes and Queries (New Haven Connecticut)
AnM	Annuale Mediaevale (Duquesne University)
Archiv	Archiv für das Studium der Neueren Sprachen und Literaturen
AUBFA	Alexandria University Bulletin of the Faculty of Arts
AUMLA	Journal of Australasian Universities Modern Language Association
BSUF	Ball State University Forum
CamQ	Cambridge Quarterly
ChauR	Chaucer Review
CE	College English
CEJ	California English Journal
CF	Classical Folia
CL	Comparative Literature
CLAJ	College Language Association Journal (Morgan State College, Baltimore)
CR	Critical Review (Melbourne: Sydney)
CSSH	Comparative Studies in Society and History (London)
DA	Dissertation Abstract
DN	Delaware Notes
DQR	Dutch Quarterly Review of Anglo American Letters
EETS	Early English Text Society
EGS	English and Germanic Studies
EIC	Essays in Criticism (Oxford)
ELH	Journal of English Literary History
ELN	English Language Notes (Univ. of Colorado)
EM	English Miscellany
ES	English Studies (Amsterdam)
E&S	Essays and Studies by members of the English Association
Expl	Explicator
GRM	Germanisch—romanische Monatsschrift
HSCP	Harvard Studies in Classical Philology
HudR	Hudson Review
IJES	Indian Journal of English Studies (Calcutta)
In	Interpretations
JAF	Journal of American Folklore
JNMD	Journal of Nervous and Mental Disease
KCUR	Kansas City University Review
LangQ	Language Quarterly
L&P	Literature and Psychology (Univ. of Hartford)

MAE	Medium Aevum
MC	Monthly Criterion
M&H	Medievalia et Humanistica, 1970-new series
McNr	McNeese Review (McNeese State College, Louisiana)
MLN	Modern Language Notes
MLQ	Modern Language Quarterly
MLR	Modern Language Review
MP	Modern Philology
MQR	Michigan Quarterly Review
MR	Massachusetts Review (Univ. of Massachusetts)
MS	Mediaeval Studies
NM	Neuphilologische mitteilungen: Bulletin of the Modern Language Society (Porthania University)
N&Q	Notes and Queries
NYTBR	The New York Times Book Review
NYRB	The New York Review of Books
OJES	Osmania Journal of English Studies
OL	Orbis Litterarum
PAPA	Publications of Arkansas Philological Association
PELL	Papers on English Language and Literature
PLL	Papers on Language and Literature
PMASAL	Papers of the Michigan Academy of Science, Arts, and Letters
PMLA	Publications of the Modern Language Association of America
PQ	Philological Quarterly
PTRSC	Proceedings and Transactions of the Royal Society of Canada, Third Series
RES	Review of English Studies
RPh	Romance Philology
RS	Research Studies (Washington State University)
SATF	Société des anciens texts français
SELit	Studies in English Literature (English Literary Society of Japan)
SFQ	Southern Folklore Quarterly
SHR	Southern Humanities Review
SLit	Studies in the Literary Imagination (Georgia State College)
SMC	Studies in Medieval Culture (Western Michigan University)
SN	Studia Neophilologica
SoRa	Southern Review: an Australian Journal of Literary Studies (University of Adelaide)
SP	Studies in Philology
Spec	Speculum
SSS	Studies in Scottish Literature

SUS	Susquehanna University Studies (Selingsgrove, Pa.)
TLS	London Times Literary Supplement
TRSC	Transactions of Royal Society of Canada
TSE	Tulane Studies in English
TSL	Tennessee Studies in Literature
TSLL	Texas Studies in Literature and Language
UBHJ	University of Birmingham Historical Journal
UCS	University of Colorado Studies
UES	Unisa English Studies
UMPLL	University of Michigan Publications Language and Literature
U Port R	University of Portland Review
URKC	University Review—Kansas City
UWSLL	University of Wisconsin Studies in Language and Literature
WHR	Western Humanities Review
WSLL	Western Studies in Language and Literature (Ankara)
WVUPP	West Virginia University Bulletin: Philological Papers
XUS	Xavier University Studies
YES	Yearbook of English Studies (MHRA)
YR	Yale Review

PREFACE

This study is the result of a life-long interest in both Chaucer and the philosophy of criticism. My investigation of the criticism of Chaucer's *Troilus and Criseyde* not only aims to enlarge our understanding of this poem, but it also attempts to identify and assess the methodology employed by critics who write interpretations of this remarkable work. Such an examination should have paradigmatic value that extends beyond the field of medieval literature.

My concern is mainly with the English and American critiques written in the last thirty years, although I do not ignore important earlier commentary. I have read exhaustively in the areas of Chaucer scholarship and criticism; however, space limitation prevents me from mentioning in the context of my study every item which appears in my notes. The essays and books which are appraised seem to me to be most relevant and most representative of certain crucial positions which make it possible to categorize the various approaches to the criticism of Chaucer's poem. I have tried to exercise the greatest scrupulosity in selecting those passages for quoting that best reveal the essence of a critic's idea. Since the quality of an analysis does not necessarily depend on its length, I sometimes pay more attention to short, interesting essays and merely refer to longer studies, which, in my opinion, have scant critical value.

The Research Foundation of the State University of New York awarded me a grant in 1969 which enabled me to undertake my research for this volume. I wish to thank the Research Foundation and Professors Lillian Herlands Hornstein and Francis Mineka who helped me to obtain this award. I am especially grateful to Lillian Hornstein and Margaret Schlauch, two exceptional teachers, who many years ago sparked my interest in medieval literature. Nor must I forget to mention what I owe to my students who during the past two decades helped me to increase my understanding of Chaucer's poetry. It is not possible to name all the Chaucerian scholars and all the critics whose work I have read through the years, but I wish to acknowledge my indebtedness to their scholarship and critical perception. The following librarians at the Cortland Memorial Library offered me invaluable aid: Lauren Stiles and especially Eileen Williams who, with infinite patience, ordered hundreds of books and articles for me through the inter-library loan system. Finally, I must mention my husband, Professor Jack Kaminsky, without whose support and encouragement this work would not have been written.

"A wise scepticism is the first attribute of a good critic."

James Russell Lowell,
Shakespeare once More

"But where's the man, who counsel can bestow,
Still pleased to teach, and yet not proud to
   know?
Unbiased, or by favor, or by spite,
Not dully prepossessed, nor blindly right;
Though learned, well-bred; and though well-
bred, sincere;
Modestly bold, and humanly severe:
Who to a friend his faults can freely show,
And gladly praise the merit of a foe?
Blessed with a taste exact, yet unconfined;
A knowledge both of books and human kind;
Generous converse; a soul exempt from pride;
And love to praise, with reason on his side?
Such once were critics, such the happy
   few. . . ."

Alexander Pope,
Essay on Criticism

INTRODUCTION

Chapter One

 In this century Chaucer's *Troilus and Criseyde* has received a great deal of attention from scholars and critics. The variety of responses it has evoked is truly remarkable. For every view expressed about the form and meaning of the poem there is an opposite opinion, and for those who prefer mediation, there is always the middle ground. What we have witnessed in recent years in criticism is the relentless subversion of the principle of Occam's Razor which tells us that the best explanation is the simplest one. The proliferation of literary analyses offers the bewildered reader too rich a diet which he cannot digest. Such critical abundance led Susan Sontag to write her diatribe against interpretation; it led David Morse to condemn the "relentless perspectivism, profitably enshrined in endless series of casebooks."[1]

However, to the pluralistic theorists interpretive plentitude is not to be viewed as a malaise of criticism. Ronald S. Crane insists that "we ought to have at our command, collectively at least, as many different critical methods as there are distinguishable major aspects in the construction, appreciation, and use of literary works. The multiplicity of critical languages is therefore something not to be deplored, but rather rejoiced in, as making possible a fuller exploration of our subject in its total extent than we could otherwise attain. . . ."[2] Walter A. Davis has written a critique of various interpretations of Faulkner's "The Bear" to demonstrate the validity of the theory of "radical dialectical pluralism."[3] Presumably Crane and Davis and

other pluralists are not proselytizing for critical chaos. Like
John Stuart Mill, they hope that some kind of Truth will emerge
from the wide spectrum of opinion.

And this brings us to the most crucial issue, "What *is* Truth in
Criticism?" Morris Weitz uses *Hamlet*, the most extensively
discussed work in literature, as a test case to determine whether
the philosophy of criticism can embody the notion of truth as a
viable concept. He concludes that the net result of his
investigation "has been to establish the logical multiplicity of
Hamlet criticism, and consequently, the falsity of the assumption, pervasive in this criticism, that all its discourse is true or
false statement."[4] Criticism, he says, has no defining properties: "The multiplicity of procedure, doctrine, and disagreement
of *Hamlet* criticism incorporates a multiplicity of properties,
none of which is necessary and sufficient. . . . Any claim
about what is primary or relevant or necessary or sufficient in
criticism, consequently, is not a true (or false) statement about
its nature, but an expression of a preference on the part of the
particular critic that he converts into an honorific redefinition
of 'criticism.' "[5]

Similarly, Joseph Margolis contends that critical interpretations are not true or false statements; instead they should
be viewed as plausible or implausible observations.[6] Even more
extreme is Allan Rodway's assertion that all critical theories
are inherently fallacious. He has identified no less than sixteen
logical fallacies in literary criticism and concludes: "Adopt *any*
one standard as your sole criterion of literary merit and you fall
into a fallacy; commit all the fallacies and you near perfection
of method."[7]

It is obvious that Weitz, Margolis, and Rodway utilize the
language of logic and scientific explanation. They believe that
critical inquiry is radically different from scientific inquiry
since literary texts by their very nature elicit a plurality of
unverifiable hypotheses. Crane has expressed this idea
succinctly: "There can be no such thing as certainty in the
interpretation of texts; demonstration is out of the question; the
most we can hope for, if we are lucky, is a high degree of
probability."[8] However, to stress the polarity between criticism
and science is to overlook important similarities in the
procedural logic employed by both critics and scientists. John
M. Ellis observes that "the typical version of the contrast
between science and literary criticism creates a gulf between

the two by dwelling on the precise, observational stage in the one case and the interpretative stage in the other; this results in a contrast between the certainty of science on the one hand, and the judgmental character of criticism on the other. This contrast is quite false; in both cases we find the two stages of observation-making and hypothesis-development." The usual view of a "split" between science and criticism erroneously "relies on a contrast between two stages of a cycle where the whole cycle is common to both fields; the contrast of interpretative judgment to precise observation is a contrast found within both fields, not between the two fields."[9]

Of course, Ellis is not arguing that science and criticism are identical disciplines. He is aware that scientists and critics employ different observational and interpretive techniques. But he maintains that the cycle of investigation for both science and criticism does involve "a circular process of continual refinement" in which the observation of facts leads to a hypothesis, and new observations may lead to a revision of the original hypothesis or to a totally new interpretation. Scientists do not deal with "certainties" and they never rule out further investigation and continual rethinking of any issue. What Ellis says about the nature of scientific investigation is clearly illustrated in the recently published *Encyclopedia of Ignorance* in which major scientists frankly discuss the fallibility of their hypotheses. Critics have not written their encyclopedia of ignorance, although they often expound favorite theories as if they were absolute truths.

Like Ellis, Allen Tate believes that critics should have logical expertise. In fact, Tate believes that it is not possible to write literary criticism today because we no longer study rhetoric, grammar, and logic. Whereas the sciences have a high-powered rationale of their own for the pursuit of truth, the rationale for humanistic study is dead. For Tate this rationale is the art of rhetoric, "the study and the use of the figurative language of experience as the discipline by means of which men govern their relations with one another in the light of truth. Rhetoric presupposes the study of two prior disciplines, grammar and logic, neither of which is much pursued today, except by specialists."[10]

Occasionally some critics display their formal training in logic. John J. Murray and Harold Skulsky have used the symbols of contemporary logic to discuss the meaning of the

"To Be or Not to Be" soliloquy."[11] Schlomith Rimmon has
written what may well be the first book of criticism that prints
truth tables in the introduction. To formulate the principle of
ambiguity in literature, Rimmon introduces a modified symbol
for exclusive disjunction a∧b.[12] But as Tate correctly observes,
few critics today are logicians nor would they want to be. To
them logical analysis debases the coin of artistic and critical
exchange. Thus even Meredith Thompson who has condemned
the fallacious reasoning in Chaucer criticism expresses his
antipathy for the logical bias of critics.[13] He objects to the
"intellectual fallacy" which results from the logical, concise,
precise nature of the scholarly mind which imposes upon the
feeling and imagination of the artist the pedantry of the small
mind. Many theorists agree with Thompson. They maintain
that factual statements are radically different from critical
statements, and they insist that the methods employed to
obtain factual information are not relevant for critical interpretation.

Lionel Trilling is willing to admit that "criticism in its
relation to literary phenomena bears comparison with science
in its relation to natural phenomena. The comparison is
permissible only if it is not carried beyond a certain point."[14]
The point is the point beyond objective, quantitative description. Like the scientist, the critic classifies an object, observes
its particularities, and identifies its form and structure. But
when the critic performs the act of interpretation he leaves the
realm of scientific objectivity. John Reichert is also disturbed
by the extent to which terms like "probability," "causal
inference," and "hypothesis formation" are used in criticism.
What is most important is not the critic's desire to achieve a
scientific ideal, but his ability to convey his *perception* of an art
work. "And that acknowledgement suggests that if criticism
can be usefully studied from the viewpoint of the philosophy of
science, it ought also to be regarded in terms borrowed from the
philosophy of perception. . . . There is a difference between
believing that such and such is true of a given work and
actually perceiving it and responding to it in a way consistent
with that belief."[15] Reichert does not adequately explain what
he means by perception. Since the philosophy of perception is
one of the most important areas of inquiry for the philosophy of
science, it is diffcult to understand why he polarizes science and
perception. What is perception if it defies logical explanation?

Is perception as the "aspect of *seeing as*" a Crocean intuition or a Kantian noumenon? Like E. D. Hirsch, Jr., Reichert believes that it is possible to obtain "objective" or "correct" interpretations in criticism, but he never clarifies the relationship of perception to ratiocination. Note that while Reichert devotes very few pages to a discussion of perception, for the most part he does use the vocabulary of logic, scientific linguistics, and scientific methodology to write his metacriticism, and to formulate his definition of a valid interpretation. In the end he seems to place the highest valuation on such criteria as rational premises, coherence, and consistency, and these are the very criteria which enable him to write a lucid and intelligible analysis.

E. D. Hirsch is another critic who disapproves of the use of the scientific paradigm in literary criticism: "Modern students of literature have objected justly that the analogy of literary science with natural science is as unworkable as it is uninformative. Literature is a subject matter peculiar to itself, requiring its own intrinsic concepts and methods; to treat it in terms of alien concepts is to neglect two central and paramount aspects—meaning and value."[16] But to validate his theory of objective interpretation, Hirsch uses the "Principles of Probability" which are, if nothing else, scientific principles. Furthermore, when he states that "an interpretive hypothesis is ultimately a probability judgment that is supported by evidence,"[17] he is using the very words which define a scientific hypothesis. Thus we see how difficult it is for rational, intelligent critics to avoid or ignore logical and scientific conceptualization.

Not only do some analysts reject the scientific paradigm in criticism, but they also maintain that criticism is inherently subjective. Thus David Bleich writes: "Under the objective paradigm, the first question automatically is, What is it? Under the subjective paradigm, the first question is, What do I want to know? . . . The latter question uses as its criterion of adequacy the satisfaction of the community of askers and of the community of co-askers. In principle, this criterion will allow a superstitious or otherwise irrational answer to prevail; yet if that is what the human community chooses, it can't be helped."[18] Can't be helped indeed! Such solipsistic subjectivity has frightening implications for those who fear irrationality and superstition.

Another subjectivist Cary Nelson has argued for the kind of self-reflexive criticism which is primarily concerned with the ethos of the critic. He writes: "The value of identifying the critic in his criticism is much greater than the value of deciding which theories of literary history are correct and which are not." This is not a satirical or ironic comment. Nelson wants us to believe that "this dialectic between self and other, embedded in the critic's language and method, is really what criticism is 'about.' "[19] However, although he suggests that we should treat a critic as if he were a character in a novel and ask whether he has grown, whether he has changed, Nelson assures us that he does not want to "make criticism more personal. The decision to add personality to criticism usually results in preciosity or hysteria. Rather, we should become attentive to the individual element already present in criticism, the give-and-take of our own ethos in what we read and write."[20]

William Schaefer, the editor of the journal *PMLA* in which Nelson's "Reading Criticism" appeared, noted that one of the readers of Nelson's essay called it " 'touchy-feely stuff,' and, while I am not at all sure what that means, I do think the essay should be touched or felt. . . ."[21] These remarks reveal the extent to which subjective criticism can involve us in *Schwärmerei*. I do not believe that it is the critic's function to make us "touch" and "feel." Touching and feeling are activities that a baby can pursue, with more enthusiasm and less inhibition than an adult. In the broad, non-technical sense of the term *critic*, we are all critics when we judge the quality of a steak or the beauty of a woman. In the professional sense, a critic performs the special function of communicating ideas about a work of art. His ideas may and usually do originate in feelings, but he has to do more than exclaim: "I love, I hate, I pant, I faint." Despite what Geoffrey H. Hartman would have us believe, the critic does not write Literature.[22] He is not a poet, or a dramatist, or a novelist. His role is primarily hermeneutic. His criticism is a form of logical discourse by means of which he makes explicit the hypotheses (interpretations, judgments, conclusions) which he formulates utilizing the evidence of the literary text.

A good critic impresses us for the same reasons that any good thinker impresses us; he is able to relate premises to conclusion in a logically defensible fashion. He does not have the license of the artist to be ambiguous or inscrutable. The critic's *raison d'être* is to make clear what is unclear, to make explicit what is implicit in a work of art. A bad critic believes that "imaginative" incoherence is profundity and idiosyncratic perception is universal truth. He is guilty of obfuscation because the premises and conclusions of his analyses can not be validated in any rational fashion. Tolstoi is a bad critic because his critical premise does not entail the infamous evaluations he formulates about Shakespeare's plays and Beethoven's Ninth Symphony. But even in the pronouncements of good and great critics, we find statements that are questionable, falsifiable, tautological, or illogical. For example, Northrop Frye makes the following crucial observation in his famous essay "Ethical Criticism: Theory of Symbols":

> The study of archetypes is the study of literary symbols as parts of a whole. If there are such things as archetypes at all, then, we have to take yet another step, and conceive the possibility of a self-contained literary universe. *Either archetypal criticism is a will-o'-the-wisp, an endless labyrinth without an outlet, or we have to assume that literature is a total form, and not simply the name given to the aggregate of existing literary works.*[23] (my italics)

The last sentence of this quotation is an exclusive disjunction. In Frye's view, Disjunct A, "archetypal criticism is a will-o'-the-wisp, an endless labyrinth without an outlet" is false, while Disjunct B, "we assume that literature is a total form, and not simply the name given to the aggregate of existing literary works" is true. In an exclusive disjunction, both disjuncts cannot be true, nor can both be false. Thus if I claim that Disjunct B is false, in opposition to Frye who wants me to agree that literature *is* a Total Art, then I would have to affirm that archetypal criticism is false, that Disjunct A is true. Frye's use of the exclusive disjunction makes it logically necessary for me to choose between two irreconcilable alternatives, and thus to either accept or reject the validity of his entire theory. Since I do not believe that literature is a total form, I cannot accept the validity of archetypal criticism. But the fallaciousness of this kind of either-or reasoning is obvious; it is possible to argue that archetypal criticism is valuable even if literature is not a total form.

Then there are the critics who dazzle us with linguistic virtuosity and seduce us into acquiescence. Harold Bloom has offered the fascinating, if somewhat eccentric theory, that "it is only by repressing creative 'freedom,' through the initial fixation of influence, that a person can be reborn as a poet. And only by revising that repression can a poet become and remain strong."[24] Bloom offers the following enigmatic statements as if they were proven facts: "We can define a strong poet as one who will not tolerate words that intervene between him and the Word, or precursors standing between him and the Muse; . . . if any poet knows too well what causes his poem, then he cannot write it, or at least will write it badly; . . . a poetic 'text' . . . is not a gathering of signs on a page, but is a psychic battlefield upon which authentic forces struggle for the only victory worth winning; the divinating truimph over oblivion. . . ."[25] Bloom's notion of *misprision* may be no more than an idiosyncratic hypothesis which does not really explain the complex process of poetic creativity. Furthermore, it may well be a prime example of the genetic fallacy. What he calls his "machine for criticism" involves the use of such terminology as: *zimzum, clinamen, tikkun, tessera, kenosis, daemonization, askesis*, and *apoprades*. If we are not alert, we will accept the hypostatization of these words. We will forget that they do not prove Bloom's theory; they merely describe it.

I have discussed the issues raised in contemporary criticism not only because they are the perennially important ones, but also because it is necessary to make clear at the outset the critical overview utilized in this study of *Troilus and Criseyde*. This overview consists of the belief that a critical statement must communicate meaning rigorously, meaning which is based on the logical relationship of premises to conclusion drawn from the evidence of the text. That such interpretations or evaluations may be less rigorous or "weaker" than scientific statements does not absolve the critic of the responsibility to strive for the verifiable assertion, nor should it in any way impede his capacity to be original and imaginative.

Yvor Winters warns that "unless criticism succeeds in providing a usable system of evaluation it is worth very little."[26] But Northrop Frye disagrees; in his view the task of evaluation belongs to the journalist. He maintains that the task of interpreting the great literary works belongs to the academic critics.[27] Most analyses of *Troilus and Criseyde* are written mainly by academicians, and they seem to agree with Frye, for they rarely evaluate the poem in Yvor Winter's sense of the term. They accept as a proven premise the view that the

Troilus is a masterpiece. Most modern critics echo William M. Rossetti's judgment that *Troilus* is the most beautiful long narrative poem in the English language.[28] Kemp Malone calls it a "monumental work of art, noble in design, ample in scale, and perfected in all its parts."[29] Albert C. Baugh refers to it as Chaucer's "greatest artistic achievement."[30] John McCall describes it as "one of the richest and most challenging poems in the English language," and George L. Kittredge says that "it is the first novel, in the modern sense, that ever was written in the world, and one of the best."[31]

Admittedly, a few negative notes have been sounded amidst the clamor of idolatrous acclamation. Back in 1867 Alfons Kissner wrote concerning *Troilus*: "In Betreff des allgemeinen künstlerischen Werthes hat die englische Nachbildung das italienische Original nicht erreicht: die einheitlich abgerundete Composition ist verlassen und zu einer vieltheiligen, bunten Mosaik geworden; der mit pathetischen und barocken Elementen willkührlich untermischte Styl kann sich mit der ebenmässigen Eleganz des italienischen nicht messen. . . ."[32] Émile Legouis judged *Troilus* to be a "glorieux échec. . . . Auprès de la sûreté aisée de Boccace où se sentent la maîtrise et la race, [Chaucer's] . . . inexperiénce a quelque chose de trouble encore, on dirait presque . . . d'un peu barbare."[33] Mario Praz deplored the fact that Chaucer's "emotional inferiority" made him suppress "those fresh, direct effusions of naive sensual love which give such a juvenile charm to Boccaccio's account. . . . What the Italian had *lived* from within, the English poet *saw* from without."[34] While these opinions might be dismissed as the chauvinistic reactions of "foreigners," the minority view has also been expressed by some English and American critics. To Ian Robinson, *Troilus* is a failure "because the many parts do not cohere into a great whole and much of it is plain dull."[35] Alain Renoir states that *Troilus* is a "rather unimaginative piece of work."[36] John Speirs disapproves of parts of the major love scene in Book III; Marchette Chute thinks that Book V is defective, and both she and Paull F. Baum believe that Chaucer should have written a different ending for the poem.[37]

Troilus is, without question, a remarkable poetic achievement. But it is not a flawless creation, and we do Chaucer a grave disservice if we write about his art with fautous adulation. It will be the aim of this study to identify genuine critical scrutiny which avoids the pitfall of substituting idolatrous commentary for intelligible analysis. The bulk of *Troilus* criticism can be examined in terms of the historical, philosophical, formalistic, and psychological approaches. In the following pages I will attempt to determine the extent to which the hypotheses of each critical approach yield plausible, or correct, or objective interpretations. I turn first to a consideration of the historical approach, the most favored and most widely used method of analysis in medieval studies.

"Bald heads forgetful of their sins,
Old, learned, respectable bald heads
Edit and annotate the lines
That young men, tossing on their beds
Rhymed out in love's despair
To flatter beauty's ignorant ear.

All shuffle there; all cough in ink;
All wear the carpet with their shoes;
All think what other people think;
All know the man their neighbour knows
Lord, what would they say
Did their Catullus walk that way?"

W. B. Yeats, *The Scholars*

"Histories make men wise; poets, witty; the mathematics, subtile; natural philosophy, deep, moral, grave; logic and rhetoric, able to contend."

Francis Bacon, *Of Studies*

THE HISTORICAL HYPOTHESIS

Chapter Two

 In 1940 Percy Shelly objected to the fact that Chaucer had been taken over by the scholars and transformed into a "Field of Research." Except for Virginia Woolf and Aldous Huxley, no poet critics or non-specialists had devoted their attention to Chaucer.[1] Whether he would think that the situation has changed today is hard to judge. However, his clear-cut distinction between scholars and critics is no longer acceptable to us. Years ago the late Arthur G. Kennedy, then Chairman of the Department of English at Stanford, told Yvor Winters that criticism and scholarship do not mix; in fact he advised Winters to give up criticism if he wanted to become a "serious scholar" because his publications were a disgrace to the department.[2] I doubt that any chairman of any respectable department would make such a statement now, and he would probably agree with Cleanth Brooks that "the critic selects from scholarship those things which will help him understand the poem qua poem; in some matters the contribution of the scholar may be indispensable. Literary criticism and literary scholarship are therefore natural allies in their concern to understand the poem. . . ."[3]

A scholar, unlike a critic, is primarily concerned with engaging in the kind of research which enables him to accumulate "facts" which fill up the book called literary history. Therefore, the critic who is committed to the view that a work of art can be understood only in relation to its age and who utilizes the information supplied by the scholar—either of a biographical, textual, linguistic, social, economic, political, cultural, or literary nature—is a historical critic. He works with the hypothesis that criticism has essentially one important goal, that of reconstructing the past to discover what an author really intended to create and to become as it were a contemporary of the author. This is the kind of reconstruction known as historicism, and a good deal of medieval criticism is written by historicists. Among them are the well known spokesmen for this view, C. S. Lewis and D. W. Robertson, Jr. who, while they may offer different interpretations of Chaucer's poetry, agree that they can decipher the secrets of the past as Chaucer meant us to know them.

Thus C. S. Lewis, who believes in the existence of a medieval model of the universe, writes: "I hope to persuade the reader not only that this Model of the Universe is a supreme medieval work of art but that it is in a sense the central work, that in which most particular works were embedded, to which they constantly referred, from which they drew a great deal of their strength." The bookish nature of the medieval mind and the love of system created this medieval synthesis, "the whole organisation of their theology, science, and history into a single, complex, harmonious mental Model of the Universe."[4] Like Lewis, D.W. Robertson believes that the historical critic can form a "workable conception of the intellectual background of a period as a whole so that the various ideas he has to deal with may be considered in perspective," and will enable us to understand the literature better.[5] In this view, the only certain way of understanding Chaucer is to fathom him as a Medieval Mind.

While the establishment view embodied in the essays published by journals like the *Chaucer Review* is mainly committed to the historical approach, non-conformists like Ian Robinson reject the view that we must read medieval literature as if we were living in the medieval period. Robinson says: "Lewis's ambition is to be *sure* he has understood a medieval poem, by seeing it as its original audience saw it; and that we can simply never do. The original audience is as much a construction of our modern imagination as the poem, but, unlike the poem, is not based firmly on a text in a language. We cannot know what people thought of literature in the Middle Ages except from what they say or imply, which isn't much. . . . Many other scholars fall into Lewis's error of not fully recognizing the inevitable pastness of the past and simultaneously not seeing the necessity of present reading."[6] Because we are interested in seeing something as it really is, we emphasize "present reading." Then we can, "if we wish, argue that the poetry *was* the same (or different) in the fourteenth century: but that is a secondary matter. The first fact must remain the present reading of Chaucer—to be sure a present recreation of this part of the past." But then he goes on to confuse the issue by stating: (1) "Any investigation of Chaucer must be, I repeat, historical: we try to see a product of the life of the distant past as in itself it really is"; (2) Criticism must recognize that "Chaucer belongs to the past as well as to the present. . . . "[7] Unfortunately, Robinson does not attempt to reconcile these contradictory observations. He seems to be on the verge of clarifying his position when he states: "Chaucer is the main source of evidence about himself; and so the common characteristic of the practitioners of the historical approaches is that they all prefer something other than the main evidence: which is a failure of, amongst other things, historical method."[8] Finally Robinson insists that "our only hope of reading Chaucer is to stay inside his language . . . by present reading in a language that belongs to our own language."[9] No one would quarrel with the notion that we must study Chaucer's language. But Robinson does not explain exactly how one stays "inside Chaucer's language," nor does he explain how else one could read Chaucer *without* using the "language that belongs to our own language."

There are those who take a less equivocal view than Robinson. They are very certain that concern with history and origins leads critics to commit the genetic fallacy.[10] The defenders of the historical approach reply in kind by accusing those who reject the study of origins of committing the parthenogenetic fallacy. Not to study the original context in which the art work was conceived is tantamount to viewing it as a virgin birth, an immaculate not a real conception.[11] René Wellek, Austin Warren, and Lionel Trilling offer a mediating position which seems to me to make the most sense. Wellek and Warren state:

> The total meaning of a work of art cannot be defined merely in terms of its meaning for the author and his contemporaries. It is rather the result of a process of accretion, i.e., the history of its criticism by its many readers in many ages. It seems unnecessary and actually impossible to declare, as the

historical reconstructionists do, that this whole process is
irrelevant and that we must return only to its beginning. It is
simply not possible to stop being men of the twentieth century
while we engage in a judgment of the past; we cannot forget
the associations of our own language, the newly acquired
attitudes, the impact and import of the last centuries.[12]

Writing about the problem of recreating the Elizabethan
Hamlet, Trilling makes essentially the same point. It is illusory
to think that we can reproduce the Elizabethan view of *Hamlet*.
The real *Hamlet* is a complex creation resulting from what
Shakespeare meant him to be, what his theater audience
thought they saw, what his readers read, and what we now
perceive. The real poem is "the poem as it has existed in history,
as it has lived its life from Then to Now, as it is a thing which
submits itself to one kind of perception in one age and another
kind of perception in another age, as it exerts in each age a
different kind of power."[13]

But what the strict historicist wants to do is to reconstruct
Troilus as it has "existed in one period of history." The crucial
test for the historical hypothesis is whether it can provide the
most reliable means for understanding the poem. To ac-
complish this task the historical critic has examined the
"evidence" uncovered by the scholar concerning the
manuscripts, the sources, the language, and biographical,
social, cultural, economic, and political data.

Robert K. Root studied all the known manuscripts of *Troilus*
and offered his conclusions in a number of important textual
studies. He concluded that the 16 extant manuscripts of *Troilus*
were derived from a single authentic manuscript in Chaucer's
possession, which underwent progressive modification. Root
distinguished three types of manuscripts: the *alpha* versions
which were based on a corrected copy of Chaucer's first
completed form of the poem; the *gamma* versions which were
copies made after Chaucer revised Books I, II, and IV; and the
beta versions which were based on the final copy of the poem,
which included Chaucer's revisions of Books III and IV.
According to Root, "it is possible to determine with a high
degree of certainty the authentic text of *Troilus* so far as its
essential content is concerned, to restore *verbatim* Chaucer's
final version of his poem."[14] But Aage Brusendorff disagreed
with Root. Brusendorff maintained that "all corrected copies
have disappeared, and our present texts are descended from

publishers' copies, which were not revised and which consequently mix up rejected and corrected readings. . . . It may thus be considered perfectly certain that not one of the extant MSS. of *Troilus* has preserved a really authentic text, though no doubt several have handed it down to us in a condition pretty close to that in which it left Chaucer's hand."[15] But despite Brusendorff's refusal to accept Root's view that two versions of *Troilus* exist, Root's theory has prevailed. Thus Daniel Cook advises us to read *Troilus* in Root's edition and to avoid F.N. Robinson's version, presumably because Robinson rejects the unique *beta* readings in Books III and IV of the poem. Cook believes that Root correctly printed the *beta* readings because they represent the revised version. Robinson admits that Root's edition is definitive: "The received text of the *Troilus* in the future is not likely to differ materially from that now printed in his edition." In his new edition of Chaucer's poetry, John Hurt Fisher comments: "One disappointment is that textual criticism has not been able to discern a controlling purpose or consistent improvement in the variations in the manuscripts [of *Troilus*]." This observation seems to reinforce Brusendorff's position. Moreover, I am particularly interested in his judgment that the text of *Troilus* "is in a very peculiar state . . . that in most instances one version was especially close to the Italian original."[16] Obviously, not all textual problems have been resolved, and scholars will continue to search for *the* version which most accurately reflects Chaucer's intention. This involves us in the critical controversy on intentionalism, an issue which will be discussed in this chapter. But now I tentatively accept the generalization that textual scholarship has not unearthed any crucial data which radically affects the interpretation of the poem.

While nobody questions Chaucer's authorship of *Troilus*, some of the most illustrious names in Chaucer scholarship: Root, J.L. Lowes, C. Brown, J. S. P. Tatlock and G.L. Kittredge, have not agreed on the date of the poem.[17] The significance of assigning a date to the composition of a work has critical interest insofar as it enables the critic to make judgments about the nature of an author's creative development. Given their passion for order and classification, scholars like to assign the works of prolific writers to specific periods. Thus we get Shakespeare's Early, Balanced, Overflowing and Final Periods, and Chaucer's French, Italian, and English Periods.

This triplicity is widely accepted as correctly representing
Chaucer's method of composing while under the influence of
different writers, and the *Troilus* is assigned to Chaucer's
Italian Period.

Albert C. Baugh seems to think that the dating problem
concerning *Troilus* has been resolved by Root and Russell in
their "A Planetary Date for Chaucer's *Troilus*," in which they
claim that a rare astonomical happening mentioned in Book II
makes it necessary to date the poem no later than May 1385.[18]
However, Lowes proposes 1382 as the *terminus a quo* because of
what he interprets as a historical allusion to Queen Anne.[19]
More recently John V. O'Connor has joined Tatlock in
contending that the astronomical conjunction mentioned in
Troilus is a mere literary device, and that Book III could have
been written earlier than 1380.[20]

John Lydgate in the Prologue to the *Fall of Princes* said that
Chaucer wrote *Troilus* "in youthe," more specifically "longe or
that he deide." Root rejects Lydgate as an unreliable witness
because Lydgate identified the source of *Troilus* as being
Trophe.[21] So far as we know, Chaucer himself may be an
unreliable witness because he called his source Lollius.[22]
Perhaps *Trophe* is a lost French version of *Troilus*, and
Lydgate's date for the poem is correct and not a blunder as Root
would have us believe. But we no more know the exact date of
Troilus than we know who Lollius was or what Lydgate meant
by *Trophe*. There is no reason why Chaucer could not have
begun to write his poem as a young man; only the preconception that a writer composes his best verse when he is older
makes us peremptorily dismiss Lydgate's view. In the same
way we automatically assume that *King Lear* is the product of
Shakespeare's old age, although he might very well have begun
to compose the play when he was a young man.Future scholars
in the twenty-first century with no knowledge of the dates of
Tennessee Williams' plays might wrongly conclude that *A
Streetcar Named Desire* was the product of his mature years,
and that his recent poor plays were the products of his youth.
We must beware of what I call the dating fallacy, the unwar-
ranted assumption that an artist's best work is the product of
his maturity. If we did know the exact date of composition of
Troilus, then perhaps we could formulate a more valid critical
hypothesis about Chaucer's development as an artist. All we
seem to have the right to say at this moment in time is that

no incontrovertible evidence exists which enables us to date *Troilus* in any apodictic sense.

Of all the evidence used by the historical critic none has been so assiduously investigated as the source material. In his view it is perfectly obvious that if we knew the shaping principle by means of which Chaucer transformed his sources into *Troilus*, we would learn a great deal about his creative powers. Thomas Tyrwhitt is given credit for being the first to notice that *Troilus* is based on *Il Filostrato*.[23] Through the years scholars have uncovered other sources: Boccaccio, *Il Filocolo, Teseida,* and *Genealogus*; Benoit de Sainte-Maure, *Roman de Troie*; Guido de Columnis, *Historia destructionis Troie*; Boethius, *Consolation of Philosophy; Epistles* of Seneca; Ovid, *Metamorphosis, Ars Amatoria, Heroides, Remedia Amoris*; Statius, *Thebaid*; Dante, *Divine Comedy*; Petrarch, Sonnet 88; *Romance of the Rose*; Juvenal, *Tenth Satire*; Alanus de Insulis, *De Planctu Naturae*; Senechal d'Anjou, Beauvau, *Le Roman de Troyle et de Criseide*, and the unknown and mysterious Lollius. At this very moment someone somewhere is industriously discovering other sources Chaucer may have used.[24]

C. S. Lewis, Sanford B. Meech, and Hubertis M. Cummings have concentrated on the most important source, the *Filostrato*.[25] Rossetti's statistical tabulation of Chaucer's borrowings from that Italian poem estimated that Chaucer expanded the 5,704 lines of the *Filosotrato* to 8,246 lines in the *Troilus*, utilizing 2,730 lines from Boccaccio's work.[26] Cummings tried to demonstrate that Chaucer was more dependent upon the *Filostrato* than is usually recognized. He denied that Chaucer's borrowings involved only a little more than one third of the poem. According to Cummings "such an inference is very far from being the truth. Besides the material, borrowed line for line from Boccaccio, there is of course in *Troil.* [sic] much in the way of episode, plot, or characterization, which is taken over into the English work by a less direct method than verbal translation, and which constitutes a far greater indebtedness to *Fil.* [sic] than the actual use of a number of Italian lines, however great. It is really impossible to over-estimate Chaucer's debt in this regard."[27] Cummings maintains that Chaucer actually used more lines than those Rossetti listed because Chaucer used lines two or three times, often repeating the same thought of a literally translated stanza in different words in another stanza. Thus the greater length of *Troilus* is

not so significant in demonstrating Chaucer's originality
through expansion because translations by their very nature
utilize an enlarged vocabulary. It would have been impossible
for Chaucer to translate the *Filostrato* without using more
words than his original source unless he was primarily
interested in summary and reduction. Cummings then concludes with a judgment which is the antithesis of the commonly
accepted view: "The atmosphere of *Troilus and Criseyde* then,
like that of the *Filostrato,* is permeated with the breath of
romance. The defining cosmos of the two poems remains much
the same. The devices of love-lore in Boccaccio's work, its spirit
of southern romance, its erotic exuberance, all are brought into
the English poem. And there they remain very largely in their
own pure essence. It is only Chaucer's maturer spirit, half in
conflict with itself, as it broods with divided feelings over the
folly and beauty of youth, that creates some change in them.
But even the introduction of Boethian philosophy and
Chaucer's instinct for the analysis and enlargement of
character psychologically, do not far succeed in changing the
totality of effect of the *Filostrato,* as its materials and spirit are
fused into *Troilus and Criseyde.*"[28]

Yet while Cummings insists that Chaucer's poem is less
original than it is generally assumed to be, other critics accept
as axiomatic Chaucer's creativity in shaping his source into
what is virtually a new poem. For example, Sanford B. Meech
who has written one of the most detailed comparisons of the
Troilius and the *Filostrato,* comprising a total of 529 pages,
believes that Chaucer's version is clearly superior to Boccaccio's. He examines in exhaustive fashion the action,
characterization, point of view, treatment of time and the
supernatural, and the use of figurative language of the two
works. He concludes that Chaucer's "adaptation" (Meech's
word), by emphasizing the courtly and romantic elements of
the love story and introducing the theme of God's control and
the vanity of human wishes, is more universal a poem than the
Filostrato:

> Attentive   beyond   Boccaccio   to   place   and   time,
> [Chaucer] . . . appears thereby the truer historian, in-
> tegrates his more elaborate version . . . by closer linkage of
> events both temporally and spatially, achieves more of three-
> dimensional realism by sharper visualization of setting and
> action against it, and now glamorizes now minifies the

behavior of the characters through glimpses of nature's pageant. Such supplementation of the original in literal particulars is matched by enrichment of it in figurative associations. Congruent, they refine contrast and broaden its significance, multiply tensions accordingly but organize them into a unity no less powerful than Boccaccio's for being more complex. This unity achieved with much art rests upon unity of spirit.[29]

Meech seems unaware of the critical problem posed by his judgment of "Chaucer's procedures of adaptation"; that is, he seems to be unaware of the significance of the term "adaptation." The title of his book *Design in Chaucer's Troilus* leads us to expect close scrutiny of the formal elements of the poem, but Meech's exclusive concern with the comparison of the *Troilus* and the *Filostrato* has the unfortunate effect of diminishing the achievement of Chaucer, who seems to be no more than a clever adapter. For example, Meech describes how Chaucer uses the imagery of fire, heat and cold. We are further informed that Chaucer uses fewer images of heat than Boccaccio to lessen the impact of sexual passion in *Troilus*. Such analysis makes the reader more keenly aware of the pervasive influence of Boccaccio upon Chaucer, and it leads him to question whether Chaucer's change of imagery necessarily signifies improvement. Above all, it makes the reader more conscious of the role of creativity in a work that is essentially an adaptation at best and at the very least a translation.

Surely aesthetic, if not moral, issues are involved when Chaucer uses Boccaccio and makes no mention of indebtedness. No one has as yet done to Chaucer what Norman Fruman has done to Coleridge. Moreover, even in the face of incontrovertible evidence, it has been difficult for critics to accept the view of Coleridge as a plagiarist. One hard pressed reviewer resorts to the *tu quoque* argument to defend Coleridge on the grounds that writers have borrowed the ideas, plots, and language of other writers for hundreds of years.[30] There would, of course, be no dilemma at all if we simply thought of Chaucer as his contemporary Eustache Deschamps described him: "Grant translateur noble Geffroy Chaucier."[31] But such a designation would be unacceptable to C. S. Lewis who states: "To speak of *Troilus* in the language of the stable as being by *Il Filostrato* out of *Roman de la Rose* would seem to be an undervaluing of Chaucer's creative genius only if we forgot that Chaucer's mind is the place in which the breeding was done."[32] We detect here a very obvious *petitio principii.* We can, according to Lewis, speak of an artist's borrowings without derogating the creative genius of the artist *only if* the writer is a genius. Since Chaucer was a genius, whatever sources he used would inevitably be transformed into superior works of art.

But then who wants to think of Chaucer as a "great translator?" Translators have second class or even third class status in the literary world, and nobody eulogizes them, certainly not with the effusiveness of a Deschamps. John Speirs suggests that we should not be concerned with the question of Chaucer's indebtedness to different sources; instead criticism should work with what exists.[33] The problem is exemplified by Stephen Knight's discussion of several stanzas in the *Troilus* which are translated from Boccaccio:

> Both of these stanzas and those which follow[III, 12, 13-14] are translated fairly directly from Boccaccio . . . but it seems to me that this in no way alters our judgment of them. In the first stanza the poise and balance of Chaucer's English fully create the notion of loftiness and in the second he makes us sense the vigour of earthly love very strongly (more strongly than Boccaccio does in fact). We have no feeling that these stanzas are derivative as we read them. . . .[34]

Knight's attempt to exonerate Chaucer of the charge of authorial theft is a circular defense: "If we didn't know the passage was taken from Boccaccio, we wouldn't know it was derivative." Most Chaucerian critics like Root discuss *Troilus* as an "original poem." But when Tyrwhitt first discovered what the *Troilus* owed to the *Filostrato,* he bluntly described Chaucer's version as a "theft."[35]

Writing about Coleridge's plagiarism, Geoffrey Hartman asks: "Is not every claim to fame or authority, especially in the modern period, shadowed by imposture?" He believes that the plagiarism issue is linked to the "curse of secondariness," of not "finding an original relation which afflicts us still. . . . From Melville through Gide, Mann and Borges the theme of con-man or falsifier is closely linked to that of the artist, and reflects the troubled relations of authorship to authority."[36] I do not think that we can eliminate this "curse of secondariness," but at least we can attempt to categorize correctly. In this connection Alice S. Miskimin's statement is refreshingly straightforward:

"Chaucer, as a translator and borrower from first to last, wrote the first great 'imitations' in English poetry; he then in turn became the subject of imitation, conscious and unconscious, by his immediate heirs and their later successors. The study of *Troilus and Criseyde* reveals both dimensions of Chaucerian imitation; it is the epitome of his own synthetic fiction making, and it became a model, in the Renaissance evolution of the poem, marvelously transformed."[37]

Let us assume that the critic can resolve the moral issue by pointing to the precedent in medieval tradition which tolerates unacknowledged borrowing from sources. But this still leaves unanswered the aesthetic questions raised by the imitative act. If we had never heard of Boccaccio's poem, we could take Speirs' advice, but the *Filostrato* does exist as a perennial source of interest to scholars. For example, Robert P. apRoberts' study of the *Filostrato* shows us how *Troilus and Criseyde* is superior because the latter poem is less sensual and more spiritual.[38] But this is a matter of personal preference rather than aesthetic judgment, for to the modern reader with erotic interests, Boccaccio's version might well seem to be more real and vital. No matter what view we take, the *Filostrato* is a phenomenon that reminds us of *Troilus*.

What shall we call Chaucer's poem? If the *Melibee* in forthright fashion is called a translation, is the *Troilus* a partial translation? It makes a big difference, critically speaking, whether we are dealing with the first, great English poem, or the first, great English translation-adaptation of an Italian-French poem. In relation to no other subject does the historical critic of Chaucer reveal a greater love of paradox, for at the same time that he is busy hunting for sources and finding them in abundance, he keeps insisting that the poem is to be categorized as an "original translation." Note, for example, the following remarks by Kittredge who seems to be unaware of the oxymoronic nature of his discussion:

> Most of . . . [*Troilus*] is original, and the originality is of a high order. Further, if we study the sources of the *Troilus*, we find that its composition involved not only the use of the *Filostrato* and the *Filocolo*, but that the poet drew also from Dante and Petrarch and that he reverted to both Benoit and Guido delle Colonne, to say nothing of his employment of Ovid and Statius and Boethius. Some of these authors are but slightly utilized, but others are drawn upon abundantly.[39]

144, 227

Kittredge's summary of the sources used by Chaucer is accurate enough, although other sources have been discovered that he does not mention. Source hunting is a worthwhile activity when it enables us to distinguish what is borrowed and what is original in a creative performance. I am indebted to those scholars who have revealed the sources Chaucer used in the *Troilus* and who have made it possible for me to make the following judgment. I believe that *Troilus* is essentially a "great adaptation." Such a designation does not denigrate Chaucer's achievement; it merely places it in proper perspective. However, most medievalists will probably continue to describe *Troilus* as an "original poem" because any other label might serve to minimize its artistic worth.

But nothing is as important or as zealously researched in historical criticism as biographical data. The premise is obvious. If we know the author, then we know his work. Therefore, every effort has been made to learn all that we can about Chaucer's life: his youthful experiences, his love affairs, marriage, family, friends, education, and professional activities. We also try to determine how much he was influenced by political, social, religious, cultural, and economic factors in his age. This information is important because it helps us to understand Chaucer's reasons for writing his poetry, and it helps us to correlate purpose with actualization in the content and form of his work.

But while such intentionalism was for many years the favored approach to literary studies, and while it has to this day a privileged status among medievalists, William K. Wimsatt, Jr. and Monroe C. Beardsley wrote their famous essays which made anti-intentionalism fashionable in critical circles.[40] Thus Robert B. Martin states that "it ought to be no longer necessary to insist much upon the error of judging a work largely or wholly by the purposes of the author, for one of the most significant developments in twentieth-century criticism has been the investigation by aestheticians of what Professor Wimsatt has called 'the intentional fallacy.' "[41] But other critics like Mark Spilka, Frank Cioffi, Richard Ellman, Jean Starobinski, L. T. Milic, Dorothea Krook, and E. D. Hirsch reject the notion that intentionalism is fallacious.[42] Instead they seek to determine meaning in a work of art through an investigation of the psyche of the author, and thus for them biographical information is vital. John Ellis has written what seems to me to be the definitive attack on intentionalism,[43] and Wimsatt and Beardsley continue to defend their position with logical acumen.[44] But it is clearly beyond the scope of this work to resolve the controversy. What is relevant is the question of how the historical critic uses biography to shed illumination on Chaucer's poetry.

George Kane has argued that there is a defensible rationale for using biographical information about a writer when it is available, as for example, when the writer himself tells us that he read and was influenced by a certain book. Kane maintains that biographical inference which is unsupported by external evidence is purely subjective. Kane asks whether in the case of poets about whom little or no biographical data exists, and whose writings are the only source of information about their private lives, there is

> any logic, any rationale, by which biographical inference from these works may be safely conducted. Are there tests by which such inference can be checked? To me this seems improbable, even if those poets have written largely or entirely in the first person, and appear to figure, as themselves, in their writings. . . . When we profess to have detected the poet 'revealing himself' in his works, or when we postulate that certain experiences or attributes ascribed by a poet to himself in his writing are autobiographical, we apply only one criterion: our preconception of appropriateness in the particular instance. This could conceivably be wholly correct; it might be fairly accurate; it might be totally wrong. Who is to say? By exercise of selection in our identification of the moments of self-revelation, or of autobiographical attributes, we beg the question: the instance is appropriate because it seems appropriate.[45]

All sorts of interesting questions can be asked when we try to find the real Chaucer in his poetry. Was he corpulent? Was he a poor lover? Did he have a shrewish wife? Did he rape Cecilia? Was he hopelessly in love with a noble woman for eight years? What was his relation to John of Gaunt who may have enjoyed the favors of both sisters, Katherine and Philippa? Was Chaucer a Laodicean? Was he a devout Catholic? Was he a lecher or a saintly figure? How did he manage to maintain the friendship of two mighty opposites like Richard II and Henry IV? Was he a hypocrite, an opportunist, or a remarkable diplomat? We don't know the answers to these questions, and to seek the evidence in Chaucer's poetry is to be guilty of what Kane aptly labels the autobiographical fallacy. This fallacy does not discourage biographers who continue to search for the real Chaucer despite the lack of objective evidence.

Thus in his *Personality of Chaucer* Edward Wagenknecht undertakes the task of seeking the unseekable, the "psychography" of Chaucer. In his introduction Wagenknecht reveals that he is aware of the autobiographical fallacy. But he explains why it is possible to derive Chaucer's personality from his writings:

> [Chaucer] . . . had Shakespeare's largeness and benignancy also and his capacity for accepting the universe; for all his surface irony and skepticism, his depths gravitated profoundly toward belief. We have more personal data for Shakespeare than we do for Chaucer, but here too we are thrown back upon inference from the work for most of what we think we know about the man's character, upon that and upon the impression that the *tone* of his writing makes upon us. In both cases it is well to be cautious about unverifiable assumptions, but a reasonable use of the imagination, informed by knowledge and guided by good judgment, is not to be denied, for there can be no scholarship of any depth without it; as Theodore Roosevelt once remarked, the use of the imagination makes for distortion in historical writing only when it is a distorted imagination. And it is as true in scholarship as it is in religion that while a reverent agnosticism may sometimes be fruitful, a blatant atheism can only make for sterility."[46]

Note that we are asked to accept the *fact* that Chaucer had a "large" and "benign" nature. We find this *fact* in his writings "by a reasonable use of the imagination, informed by knowledge and guided by good judgment." Knowledge in this context seems to be no more than mere inference, yet in some inexplicable way this inference, aided by "undistorted imagination" presumably transforms an assumption into a fact. Wagenknecht is aware that a writer's literary personality is not necessarily his real personality; he may have different faces which he reveals at different times. Admittedly, the only true psychographer is God, "but being men, we must, in some measure, try to think God's thoughts after Him and trace the lines of His creation. . . ."[47]

Wagenknecht then proceeds to show us Chaucer's feelings about cats, dogs, birds, spring, wrestling, books, chivalry, alchemy, children, love, women, religion, war, drinking, etc. Chaucer turns out to be a sweet, balanced, wholesome, tolerant human being, a man who couldn't possibly be guilty of the rape that Paull Baum has the temerity to believe in, for "anyone who can believe the man who wrote the poems we know could possibly have been guilty of committing rape under any circumstances must be capable of accommodating far more complicated and contradictory notions of human character than I can."[48] Obviously Wagenknecht, like Longinus, accepts the view that good men write good books and bad men write bad books.

While Wagenknecht tries to think God's thoughts and reconstructs for us a very admirable Chaucer, another biographer seems to interpret God's thought in quite a different way. George Williams attempts to show that Chaucer is really Pandarus! Williams' entire argument is based on the premise that John of Gaunt was the "enormous brilliant sun of public life around which Chaucer's small asteroid of an official career revolved for more than thirty years."[49] Besides the usual services that would be rendered by a loyal retainer, Chaucer performed the task of marrying the woman Gaunt had seduced, Philippa, and in addition assumed the burden of pretending that Gaunt's and Philippa's child was Chaucer's. John of Gaunt was a noble, loyal, courageous, pious, great person, and it would, says Williams, "have been surprising and even disgraceful of Chaucer not to have esteemed such a man." Therefore, Chaucer should have esteemed him, and the trouble with Chaucerian scholarship all these years is that it hasn't seen Gaunt as Chaucer saw him, and as a result it hasn't seen Chaucer himself. All this is based upon what Williams admits is sheer conjecture. "Let me say at once that, in all probability, no more than four or five people ever knew the truth about matters to be glanced at in the following brief review of a complex situation—and these four or five people died centuries ago, presumably without revealing their darkest personal secrets (if they really had any) to anyone else. Therefore, all we can do today is to guess—and to guess under the clear realization that we may be mistaken in every detail. The question may well be asked whether, under such conditions, guessing is profitable. Perhaps not. Nevertheless, it is intriguing, and just possibly it may hit the mark."[50]

If the secret and private lives of Gaunt and Chaucer were as intertwined as Williams believes they were, and if half of Chaucer's poetry deals with Gaunt and the Gaunt circle, then we have to deal with a rather odd obsession. Since Williams feels free to make wild, unsubstantiated guesses, why not go one step further and describe Chaucer's obsession as homosexual? After all, Williams assures us that Chaucer did not love his wife. Maybe he loved John of Gaunt!

How does Williams interpret *Troilus* in the light of the Gaunt-Chaucer relationship? Well, as one might guess, Troilus is John of Gaunt, Criseyde is Katherine de Swynford, and wonder of wonders, Pandarus is Chaucer himself. Gaunt, a king's son like Troilus, was in love with Katherine, a young widow beneath him in rank, like Criseyde. There is no evidence for Katherine's unfaithfulness. But, reasons Williams, Chaucer was simply forced by literary convention to use this theme even though it did not really relate to Katherine. But because Criseyde represents Katherine, Chaucer apologizes for Criseyde and treats her as kindly as possible. Chaucer probably never read the last two books of the poem to his court audience because they deal with Criseyde's betrayal. While Boccaccio explicitly informs us that Criseyde had no offspring, Chaucer alters the text to say that he is ignorant about this matter. Did he do this because Katherine and her husband Hugh had two children when she began her affair with John of Gaunt? In all likelihood, Chaucer did not want to deny in any explicit fashion the existence of this progeny.

Unlike Boccaccio, Chaucer exalts Hector over Troilus, and this is because Hector stands for Edward, the Black Prince. At that time Gaunt was suspected of wanting to take the throne from Edward's son, Richard II, and any suggestion that Gaunt-Troilus was superior to Edward-Hector would have been virtual treason. Deiphebus must stand for Prince Edmund since Gaunt was on the most friendly terms with him. Katherine took Gaunt as a lover shortly after her husband's death, and this explains why Chaucer apologizes for Criseyde's quick capitulation to Troilus-Gaunt.[51] (Williams does not attempt to deal with the rumor that Gaunt was responsible for the death of Katherine's husband; this would hardly help to support the Troilus-Gaunt identification.)

Unfortunately, as Williams himself admits, we do not have any way of knowing whether Katherine looked like Criseyde. But Williams insists that we do know that Gaunt was physically like Troilus. As for Pandarus, he bears a startling resemblance to Chaucer. Both are diplomats, fixers, practical philosophers, humorists, astrologers, experts on writing, sufferers in love, and sophisticated and shrewd observers of human nature. What Williams neglects to mention is their skill as panders.

Now why did Chaucer choose to write a long poem about Gaunt and his mistress? Williams offers the following reasons: (1) Chaucer wanted to flatter Gaunt. (2) He didn't want Gaunt to forget that Chaucer was involved in facilitating the liaison of Gaunt and Katherine. (3) He tried to excuse Katherine for her temporary defection from Gaunt (that is, assuming there ever was such a defection). (4) He wished to remind Gaunt of what he owed to Katherine, Chaucer, and Philippa, and to beg him not to desert Katherine while on his Spanish campaign.[52]

Williams never faces the implications of what he has written. If and only if what he says about the Chaucer-Gaunt relationship is true, then Chaucer was sorely in need of therapy, for he obviously had a Gaunt father fixation (pun intended). He even married a woman to please Gaunt. Greater love hath no man. Admitting that there is no evidence for his view of the Gaunt and Philippa relationship, Williams, undaunted, uses the *ad ignorantiam*: "Most emphatically, it has *not* been proved. On the other hand, the existence of such a relationship has not been *disproved*, either."[53] Any scrupulous scholar who distinguishes between the use of objective evidence and unsubstantiated fantasying would not tolerate the method of "investigation" employed by Wagenknecht and Williams. These are blatant examples of the worst excesses of the biographical approach to *Troilus*, and they make us understand why the anti-intentionalists have exerted such a strong influence in modern criticism.

John Gardner in his biography of Chaucer makes it very clear at the outset that he is not writing as a historian. In *The Life and Times of Chaucer*, he tells us that he is writing as a novelist and literary disciple, conveying his own subjective impressions of the life of Chaucer. Gardner has not discovered any new or startling information; what he does is to pull together all kinds of miscellaneous data to describe the period in which Chaucer lived, the kings and other people he knew, and the various jobs that he performed for the court. But, as Gardner himself admits, "Strange to say, for all the facts we have about Chaucer's life, we know nothing of what may have been the most intimate part of it."[54] This is why Gardner has to speculate about the "most intimate part" of Chaucer's life.

Gardner offers some interesting theories in a very ingratiating style. Chaucer had sex appeal: "How could a man not conspicuously ugly (as we know from portraits), a man with extraordinary understanding of women (as we know from his poems), a man often praised by those who knew him for his remarkable charm and gentleness, and in later years a man who, as poetry reader in England's greatest courts, stood out as a sort of star performer—how could such a man be anything but attractive to women?"[55] But Gardner does not explain why this sexy Chaucer had to resort to rape or seduction. Gardner accepts the view that Chaucer seduced Cecilia Chaumpaigne: Chaucer, "now forty years old, rich and powerful, more often away from his wife on business for the king than not . . . slipped into bed with a pretty and soft baker's daughter."[56] However, Chaucer and Philippa had "an excellent marriage. . . . [S]ometimes Chaucer lay at night with Philippa's head against his shoulder, listening to her breathing and the breathing of the children . . . and thought, half-smiling in the room's complete darkness, how strange and unpredictable are the ways of this world, and felt the emotion he'd give later to Troilus, a wish that all lovers might fare as well as he. . . ."[57] These are passages which make us feel that we are reading a historical novel.

Gardner's biography offers the reader a peculiar mixture: factual recreation of the events which pertain to Chaucer's external life, and imaginary recreation of the feelings and situations which pertain to his inner life. As long as the reader is aware that the novelist and not the historian is describing Chaucer's intimate life, then he can benefit from this introduction to Chaucer. But Gardner has no more solid evidence for his conjectures than Wagenknecht or Williams, and like them, he often makes the mistake of assuming that it is possible to deduce a writer's character from the nature of his art.

Of all the paths of reconstruction undertaken by the historicist, none has proved to be more appealing than the one which seeks to find the meaning of *Troilus* in the "spirit of the age." Such a search has produced two popular hypotheses: the religious and the courtly love explanations.

D. W. Robertson's exegetical method has been the most

influential of all the religious analyses which view *Troilus* as a Christian poem written by a Catholic in a Catholic age. Robertson adapts Alan de Insulis' view that literature has a nucleus of allegorical significance beneath the surface or literal meaning known as the *cortex*. The tropological, allegorical, and anagogical comprise the three levels of meaning of the nucleus, and they express the cultural and intellectual ideas of the age. These ideals are not, as we might expect, the many and varied beliefs of medieval Christianity, but instead are the ideals associated with one specific doctrine concerning *caritas*, the love of God and one's fellow man, and the repudiation of *cupiditas*, the love of one's self. According to Robertson, this was the essential meaning students were instructed to search for in scriptural and other religious writings of the period, and poets naturally availed themselves of this rich storehouse of symbolism which modern critics simply have to decipher in order to fathom the meaning of most medieval texts. Robertson interprets *Troilus* as a Christian tragedy in which the "three stages of tragic development . . . correspond to the three stages in the tropological fall of Adam: the temptation of the senses, the corruption of the lower reason in pleasurable thought, and the final corruption of the higher reason. . . ."[58] The corruption results from Troilus' substitution of Criseyde for divine grace. Robertson's view will be discussed in more detail in the next chapter on the philosophical approach to *Troilus*. It suffices to point out here that reputable medievalists, such as Morton Bloomfield, E. Talbot Donaldson, Robert Frank, Dorothy Bethurum, Charles Donahue, Theodore Silverstein, and John Lawlor, have very effectively criticized Robertson's exegetical method. A few critics have been quite vituperative. One reviewer in the *Times Literary Supplement* said: "This is a country into which most critics will shudder to follow Robertson. In terms of logic the name of the country is *reductio ad absurdum*."[59] Still another detractor wrote: "The suspect nature of Robertsonian scholarship has been so frequently pointed out, one can only marvel at the persistance of this 'school' and the audience which it seems to attract. Many of its 'interpretations' of Chaucer's works are so very incongruous, one might wonder if Robertson will not soon declare it was all a comic hoax, that we may end by having a good laugh together. But this seems unlikely."[60]

Besides the disciples who accept the Robertson interpretation, there are defenders of his position who recognize the deficiences of this "pioneer effort." Thus while R. Kaske admits that Robertson and Huppé have often erred, more research would reveal them to be correct. "What we need first," Kaske suggests, "is a really prodigious amount of minute, systematic research centered on individual medieval works, with the immediate aim of showing the precise contributions made by the exegetical tradition to the meaning of descriptive details, figures of speech, characters, limited passages, and so on."[61] But what Kaske is asking for is research which will confirm the hypothesis he favors. I do not see how the "really prodigious amount of minute systematic research" can fail to do anything else *but* confirm a hypothesis that is not falsifiable. Crane notes: "There is no way of showing it [the Robertson view] to be wrong with respect to any individual poem to which it is applicable, that is, any serious poem of the Middle Ages written by a Christian author. That is precluded by the assumption that if the message of charity is not explicitly present in a given poem of this class, it, or some 'corollary of it,' will be present allegorically, that is, 'by interpretation' according to rules laid down in the hypothesis itself."[62]

As a working rather than a ruling hypothesis, Robertson's religious interpretation deserves the same kind of attention that other religious analyses of *Troilus* warrant. But whether the essential meaning of *Troilus* is to be found in the religious doctrine of the medieval period remains a highly controversial issue if only because the courtly love hypothesis has been a rival contender as the *Zeitgeist* explanation of the meaning of *Troilus*. It is virtually impossible to pick up an analysis of *Troilus* which does not in some way make use of the courtly love theme. Ever since Gaston Paris introduced the term "Amour courtois" in 1883, it has been used to signify a code of behavior in medieval life and literature. Many have labored to find the origin of this concept—seeking its source in Ovid, Arabic and troubadour poetry, Catharism, Mozarabic lyricism, Bernardine mysticism, the *Romance of the Rose*, Chrétien, and Andreas.[63] But it was unquestionably C. S. Lewis' treatment of courtly love that captivated most readers. The title of his book *The Allegory of Love: A Study in Medieval Tradition* reveals his principal premise. For him courtly love is unquestionably "a medieval tradition," and I do not think it is possible to overestimate the influence of his work upon thousands of graduate students who have read his charming discussion and memorized the characteristics of this code: Humility, Courtesy, Adultery, and the Religion of Love. Lewis' treatment of courtly love in relation to the *Romance of the Rose* and the *Troilus* is based on the view that courtly doctrines in the Middle Ages introduced an innovative view of love which paved the way for the modern romantic notion of love. He tells us unequivocally that in medieval society,

> marriages had nothing to do with love, and no nonsense about marriage was tolerated. All matches were matches of interest, and worse still, of an interest that was continually changing. When the alliance which had answered would answer no longer, the husband's object was to get rid of the lady as quickly as possible. Marriages were frequently dissolved. The same woman who was the lady and "the dearest dread" of her vassals was often little better than a piece of property to her husband. He was master in his own house. So far from being a natural channel for the new kind of love, marriage was rather the drab background against which that love stood out in all the contrast of its new tenderness and delicacy. The situation is indeed a very simple one, and not peculiar to the Middle Ages. Any idealization of sexual love, in a society where marriage is purely utilitarian, must begin by being an idealization of adultery.[64]

Such are the generalizations about marriage and adultery that Lewis unhesitatingly accepts to be factual. That "all matches were matches of interest" does not seem to him to be a statement in need of some kind of qualification. But other writers deny that medieval women actually practiced adultery in the ritualized fashion prescribed by courtly love. Donald R. Howard maintains that the special behavior attributed to courtly lovers, the games at court, the courts of love, songs, and the recital of romances were patterned on "underlying habits of thought," rather than on "actual practice." Howard believes that "this-fantasy-directed behavior took conventionalized and approved forms: *courtoisie*, flirting which came to nothing, 'courting' which ended in marriage, and talk or song about polyandrous and adulterous relationships. Not that fantasy precludes actuality—it is quite possible that courtly affairs of the prescribed extramarital kind may sometimes have been consummated but this would have been an outcome of the entire complex, not its cause."[65]

For Howard the key word is *fantasy*. In his view, courtly love was a game which originated "as a ritualized expression of anxieties about social class and sexuality, and that . . . provided medieval men with a morale-building ideology which assuaged their feelings of guilt and unworthiness."[66] What was it that made them feel guilty and unworthy? The explanation is to be found in the social history of the time. Evidently many unmarried men of the lesser nobility who wanted to marry prosperous and noble women in the twelfth and thirteenth centuries in Germany and France were unable to do so because of the lack of eligible women. As a result of the competition for women, this class of lesser knights created a collective fantasy involving the possibility of extra-marital relationships. These knights lived in a castle dominated by a noble lady who was too high born for them, and they could not hope for sexual union with her. They knew that if they were found guilty of adultery, the lord and husband had the right to kill the lover and his wife. These poor bachelors coped with their impossible situation by investing the high born woman with special symbolic qualities. According to Howard, in their fantasy life, these knights envisioned their noble mistress as "the impersonation of the feudal loyalty in which they . . . [w]ere trained, and the idealization of their adulterous fantasy became 'the glorification of excellence within the compass of guilt.' " Thus courtly love literature reflects the anxieties of knights about acceptance into a society and approval by the authority symbol of that group, the woman; the poems " 'verbalized anxieties of rejection and at the same time helped to allay these anxieties.' "[67]

There isn't, of course, any more objective evidence for this Freudian view than there is for Violet Paget's contention that adultery was actually practiced in the castle or H. Moller's notion that the *domina* was an authority symbol of the maternal superego.[68] It is just as possible to believe that the lady was a Virgin Mary substitute as to believe that she was a superego. None of these hypotheses is convincing, and we can readily understand why in recent years reputable scholars and critics have rejected the notion that courtly love was a medieval phenomenon. Donnell Van de Voort, Kurt Lippman, Justina Ruiz-de-Conde, E. T. Donaldson and H. A. Kelly are among those who have attempted to deliver the coup de grâce to the theory of courtly love.[69] Several years ago at a conference on the subject of courtly love, I heard D. W. Robertson state: "There is no historical evidence for this sort of thing . . . . The study of courtly love, if it belongs anywhere, should be conducted only as the subject is an aspect of nineteenth century and twentieth century cultural history. The subject has nothing to do with the Middle Ages, and its use as a governing concept can only be an impediment to our understanding of medieval texts."[70] Robertson obviously has an axe to grind, but supposedly John F. Benton made an objective judgment at this conference when, speaking as a historian, he concluded:

> . . . I have found no evidence of a dramatic change in social or sexual behavior or outlook spreading through southern France like a plague, later to infect the north from a few centers like the court of Champagne or that of Eleanor of Aquitaine. . . . There was much discussion of love in various forms, and women were frequently honored by poets. Such poetry, we are told, increased the honor and profit of the singer, and in fact the service of ladies (which is hardly the same thing as the worship of women) does not seem to have significantly advanced their legal or social position. . . . The study of love in the middle ages would be far easier if we were not impeded by a term which now inevitably confuses the issue. As currently employed, "courtly love" has no useful meaning, and it is not worth saving by redefinition. I would therefore like to propose that "courtly love" be banned from all future conferences.[71]

In this same vein H. A. Kelly insists that the courtly love doctrine "as 'almost everyone now knows' [is] patently unhistorical." Astounded that the theory gained acceptance in the first place, Kelly suggests that "one reason for its success, no doubt, was the insidiousness of its growth. It began as a small tumor in an essay by Gaston Paris in 1883, and then by rapid . . . metastasis increased its range and its claims."[72] This medical metaphor leads us to expect rigorous scrutinizing of evidence. But what Kelly does is to start with a privileged hypothesis and to employ the same kind of deductive reasoning that defenders of other favorite theories utilize. Thus Kelly interprets selected writings by Ovid, Andreas, Rolle, Gower, and examines statements in the Canon Law, the mystical code, the *Romance of the Rose*, and the *Decameron* to demonstrate his thesis that the medieval world believed in marriage, and so did Chaucer and Troilus and Criseyde who were not courtly lovers but were secretly married.

But the whole question of the relation of evidence to theory is much more complicated than Kelly or the patristic exegetes or the courtly love devotees are willing to recognize. They accept a deductive methodology by means of which they interpret texts to reinforce a favored hypothesis. Moreover, despite Kelly's insistence that the courtly love doctrine is irrefutably wrong, other writers persist in believing in it; for example, Claude Marks in a new study, *Pilgrims, Heretics and Lovers*, and a *New York Times* reviewer of that book write as if they have incontrovertible evidence that courtly love flourished in the Middle Ages.[73] When F. L. Utley wistfully asks, "Must We Abandon the Concept of Courtly Love?"[74] the answer, of course, is no, so long as we understand that courtly love is a hypothesis which helps us to illuminate the meaning of *Troilus and Criseyde* in the same limited way that other theories shed light on the poem.

While the case for historicism has been put quite negatively here, we should not underestimate the value of suspending belief. Thus, for example, when Donald R. Howard writes the following passage with such unqualified assurance, we must be careful not to be bullied into unquestioning acquiescence:

> My theme is that this man [Chaucer], whom we feel that we know, is a real and living presence in his works, and that his presence in them is what makes them interesting and good. I present this not as a corollary of any humanistic or existential principles, but as a fact. I say that we are interested in the fictional narrator, the rhetorical workings of irony, the method of creating illusion and reality . . . not because they are devices, but because everywhere *in* and *behind* them lies Chaucer the man. . . . I say that this is the point which various analyses of "narrator" and "persona" have really proved.[75]

But this is precisely what has not been proved. Chaucer is dead, and we have no objective, verifiable method of ascertaining whether the nature of the man who wrote the *Canterbury Tales* and the *Troilus* can be equated with the nature of the narrator or characters in his poetry. All that we can do is to make highly conjectural judgments which satisfy our preconceptions of what a great artist should be like as a human being. He should be kind, loyal, intelligent, witty, and moral. Surely the millions of readers who believe that the author of "Mending Wall" must be a very compassionate, friendly man would be shocked to learn that Robert Frost was "cold," a "tyrant," a "coward," and a "liar." These are the words used by David Bromwich to characterize Frost as a man. Reviewing the latest biography of Frost by L. Thompson and R. H. Winnick, Bromwich writes: ". . . [A] more hateful human being cannot have lived who wrote words that moved other human beings to tears. Filled with hate and worth hating. . . . one feels that to stand in the same room with a man about whom one knew a quarter of the things one now knows about Frost would be more than one could bear."[76]

While in the case of Frost we at least have correspondence, and the evidence of family and friends, extensive research through the years has failed to discover the kind of primary information which would enable us to fathom the "real" Chaucer. We have learned a great deal about his age, and official documents offer some interesting facts about his "external" rather than his "inner" life. We have acquired a higher level of linguistic comprehension which makes the act of reading *Troilus* more enjoyable. But many questions have not been answered definitively. When was Troilus written? Who was Lollius? What specific source did Chaucer have before him when he wrote the poem? What manuscripts are based on the holograph? To what extent was he influenced by Catholic and courtly love doctrines? If, after all his effort, the historical critic can define the limitations of his knowledge, he will be more apt to formulate reliable judgments. He will avoid unsubstantiated and reified generalizations, and he will display a healthy respect for the intellectual activity which relates evidence to theory.

Those who write about the philosophy of *Troilus* usually employ the historical approach. Relatively few offer non-historical readings. In the next chapter I will examine the philosophic analyses of the poem to determine the extent to which the privileged historical hypothesis has enabled critics to derive a consensus from the wide diversity of opinion.

"O Socrates plains de philosophie Seneque en meurs. . . ."

Eustache Deschamps, *Ballade for Chaucer*

"Also who was hier in philosophie to Aristotle in our tonge but thow?"

Thomas Hoccleve, *De Regimine Principum*

"The noble Philosophical poete in Englissh"

Thomas Usk, *The Testament of Love*

"He fixed his eyes upon the road before him, not upon the world to come. He was little given to abstract contemplation."

Virginia Woolf, *The Pastons and Chaucer*

THE PHILOSOPHY OF *TROILUS*

Chapter Three

 No one writing about *Troilus* has ever suggested that it is difficult to understand the plot of the poem. A handsome young man falls in love with a beautiful woman; they have an affair which makes them blissfully happy. Forced to separate by events beyond their control, the woman betrays her lover by becoming the mistress of another man. The lover then dies in battle, assuring us after he has died that love on earth is a vain pursuit while love of God is eternally rewarding. But what has required a great deal of explanation is the meaning of this relatively simple story.

One of the favorite means of conveying to the modern reader the significance of what has been written in the past is to discuss the meaning of a work in philosophical language. Such language can transcend the barriers erected by the passage of time and provide the universal basis for understanding and appreciation. The philosophic approach to criticism deals with the ideas expressed in a literary creation, ideas which all the other elements such as plot, characterization, style and structure combine to produce. In relation to *Troilus* this means grappling with the question of what the famous, unhappy love affair tells us about the important philosophical issues Chaucer *intended* to dramatize. Obviously the historical reconstructionists believe that they can extract from the *Troilus* the true nature of Chaucer's philosophy. But they do not agree as to what the *true nature* of that philosophy is.

The stanzas that make up the epilogue in *Troilus* seem to be

primarily responsible for this state of affairs. Without the
epilogue, the meaning of the poem would be more readily
accessible. But the epilogue divides readers into two groups:
those who consider it to be the concluding ideational commentary, and those who regard it as an irrelevant appendage which
destroys the artistic effect of the poem. To complicate matters
even further, those who believe that the epilogue contains the
most significant philosophical statement concerning the
essentially religious theme of *Troilus* have different and often
contradictory views of the meaning of the epilogue.

The ending has been viewed as consisting of the last twelve,
or seventeen, or eighteen stanzas. A quick glance at the content
of these stanzas readily reveals the truth of Baum's judgment
that they contain a "medley of . . . different subjects, shifting
back and forth from grave to gay."[1] In lines 1786 to 1792
Chaucer bids farewell to his poem—"Go, litel bok, go, litel myn
tragedye"—and reveals his desire to write a comedy before he
dies. He also uses what F. N. Robinson calls the "envy-
postscript" in deprecation of envy of the great poets. In the
next stanza (1793-1799) Chaucer expresses the hope that his
poem will be copied correctly and properly understood. The
lines 1800 to 1806 which describe Troilus' death at the hands of
Achilles are taken from Boccaccio. Troilus' ascent to the eighth
sphere is described in lines 1807-1813. The next two stanzas
(lines 1814-1827) relate how Troilus listened to the harmony of
heavenly music, and how he came to despise the blind lust of
this wretched world, and to delight in the happiness of heaven.
The anaphora in lines 1828-1834 reminds us that Troilus' love,
nobility, and worthiness ended in death—"Swich fyn."
Chaucer then urges "yonge fresshe folkes" to give up worldly
interests and turn instead to the love of Christ who will not
prove false (1835-1848). Chaucer condemns the pagans for their
religion and their gods, Apollo, Jove and Mars (1849-1855). In
the last two stanzas of the poem Chaucer dedicates his work to
"moral Gower" and "philosophical Strode" and ends with a
prayer to the Trinity.

Thus while it is obvious that the epilogue has a "medley of
different subjects", the one subject it ends with is a typical
medieval invocation to the "Lord," "Crist," and "mayde and
moder." The Christian coloring of the epilogue has led to a
variety of religious interpretations of *Troilus* based on the

premise that the philosophy of the entire poem becomes explicit in the last twelve stanzas.

Perhaps the most popular approach is the one which emphasizes the influence of Boethian thought. The foremost exponent of this view is B. L. Jefferson who in his *Chaucer and the Consolation of Philosophy of Boethius* paved the way for endless discussions of the Boethian influence on Chaucer. Jefferson maintained that it was particularly strong in the *Troilus*, which contains the highest number of verbal borrowings, totalling 268 lines. Furthermore, the Boethian philosophy influenced Chaucer's conception of the characters and their actions. Jefferson's study offers us an interesting example of a philosophical interpretation which is historically oriented. Whereas Meech and C. Schaar have tried to show what Chaucer owes to Boccaccio, Jefferson tries to show what Chaucer owes to Boethius.

Boethius was a Christian Roman philosopher; his "golden book" the *Consolation of Philosophy* was translated into almost every European language. Although Hermann Usener considered Boethius to be an essentially derivative, second rate thinker, E. K. Rand judged Boethius to be the "most original philosopher of Rome, except for St. Augustine."[2] The famous story of how the *Consolation of Philosophy* was composed is very touching and dramatic. Unjustly imprisoned for political reasons, the scholar Boethius wrote before he died his famous dialogue which deals with such topics as the nature of God, providence, destiny, fortune, free will, evil, happiness, the bond of love, and the nature of truth.

Boethius believed that an eternal God dispenses his rule through Providence; his Divine Reason controls the universe absolutely and benevolently. The chief minister of Providence is Destiny, and Destiny controls Fortune and Chance. Providence operates through the "bond of love" which links all of the universe together in harmony. Fortune is allegorized as a goddess who is responsible for the mutability of existence since she gives men power, riches, fame, and sensual pleasures, and then takes them away, dropping men on the famous allegorical wheel from prosperity to adversity. Sometimes she makes unhappy men happy, but this is a rare phenomenon. Although she works capriciously, Providence requires her to produce adversities to make men strong and to reveal their true friends.

Destiny is responsible for carrying out the wishes of Providence. Thus Providence is the means by which God involves himself in human affairs.

One of the most interesting issues discussed by Boethius concerns the concept of evil. Why, he asks, if God is just and good and powerful does he permit evil to exist in the universe? Why does he permit the innocent to suffer? Dame Philosophy makes Boethius understand that evil does not really exist because there is nothing in the universe which has the power to oppose God, the highest good and the most powerful. Furthermore, those who are supposedly evil are not human, and they are really less happy when they receive punishment than when they do not. The other interesting question concerns God's foreknowledge and free will. Boethius is assured by Dame Philosophy that free will can be reconciled with God's foreknowledge. It is, of course, axiomatic that God has foreknowledge, but the problem arises as to whether such foreknowledge necessitates events to happen, or whether the necessity is the cause of God's foreknowledge. The answer is that God is not limited by time but has the power to experience the past, present and future as an eternal present. But God's knowledge of what is to happen does not necessitate the event and therefore does not limit man's free will. There is a kind of necessity involved in observing an act, but it is a *conditional* necessity, and such actions in the daily lives of men are to be distinguished from *simple* necessity which produces the natural and universal laws of the universe.

As for the issue of happiness, the Boethian position is essentially the *contemptus mundi* view. All that man thinks will bring him happiness in this life—riches, honors, empires, glory, pleasures, veneration, power, fame, and joy—are mere earthly and transitory things and generate only false happiness while true felicity is to be sought in the highest good which is God.

Even this cursory summary of Boethian thought should explain why a modern theological student would prefer the more profound Thomas Aquinas. But the dramatized form of Christian consolation imaginatively evoked by Boethius has a special kind of appeal even for the present day nullifidian. Small wonder then that Chaucer devoted his energies to his translation of *Boece.* According to Jefferson, Chaucer's thought was so influenced by Boethian philosophy when he wrote the *Troilus* and the *Knight's Tale* that the basic Boethian conceptions of Fate and Felicity determined Chaucer's attitude toward the subject matter of *Troilus*. It offered him the opportunity to depict "a capital example of the sudden reversal of Fortune's wheel, and an unusually interesting example of human falseness or lack of steadfastness of wordly felicity, and of human affairs directed to a predetermined end by a relentless fate. . . ."[3]

Jefferson then goes on to make an analysis of the poem to show that Troilus and Criseyde are the victims of a conglomeration of circumstances over which they have no control, that their tragedy is a tragedy of fate, destiny, necessity, and that Troilus himself as the fatalist of the play is to be equated with Boethius while Pandarus often assumes the role of Dame Philosophy. Even Criseyde in his view turns out to be a philosopher, for she is the only character who has "the intellectual discrimination" to know all the time that the happiness she and Troilus share is a false one. This explains why she is false; if the world is false, how can she be expected to be true? So not only the ideas of the poem but also the characters of the work are also philosophical. "Indeed," says Jefferson, "so philosophical a poem is *Troilus*, so much does it abound in Boethian passages, so much does it illustrate the truth of the Boethian teachings, that it is possible even to suppose that Chaucer translated the *Consolation* for the express purpose that *Troilus* might be the better interpreted. . . ."[4] Whether the poem and its characters are as philosophical as Jefferson would have us believe is a moot question. But his contention that *Troilus* is a deterministic tragedy is a view that some critics accept.

In Chapter II Jefferson treats Troilus' speech on fate and free will as a translation of a part of *The Consolation*. What Chaucer adds to these lines in which Troilus tries to reconcile the issue of God's foreknowledge and man's will are verses which, far from expressing Troilus' acceptance of the notion of predestination, make it clear that he is totally confused about the issue and leaves it up to the "clerkes" to decide:

> "But natheles, allas! whom shal I leeve?
> For ther ben grete clerkes many oon,
> That destyne thorugh argumentes preve;
> And some men seyn that, nedely, ther is noon,
> But that fre chois is yeven us everychon.

> O, welaway! so sleighe arn clerkes olde,
> That I not whos opynyoun I may holde."
> > (IV, 967-973).

Now if Troilus is a philosopher, he is clearly a very confused one!

While in this scene Troilus may be playing the role of a Boethius trying to understand the problems by asking all the relevant questions, he does not, like Boethius, argue for the existence of free will. Jefferson notes that although Chaucer bases such discussions on the *Consolation of Philosophy*, he does not always adopt its conclusions, and he clearly does not accept the Boethian doctrine concerning the reasons for the existence of evil or free will. That Chaucer should invariably, and often humorously, refer these topics to the "clerkes" "perhaps bespeaks his own point of view. And it would, indeed, be in accordance with his characteristic sanity of thought for him to see that these questions were beyond the sophistries of the philosophical schools. If the question of free will remains an open one in his mind, he is unique among the mediaeval writers who discussed this subject, and who might have had some weight with him. Boethius, Bradwardine, St. Augustine, Jean de Meun, and Dante all took sides one way or another on the problem."[5] We can only ask after reading this conclusion, why Chaucer, who never made up his mind about free will, should have written the kind of fatalistic tragedy that Jefferson describes in Chapter IV of his book. There he seems to forget about what he writes in Chapter II about Chaucer's noncommittal attitude towards determinism.

But the most influential essay on the issue of Boethian determinism is Walter Clyde Curry's "Destiny in Chaucer's *Troilus*," for almost every writer who discusses Chaucer's relation to Boethius mentions Curry's analysis. Curry states "that the common fortunes of Troilus and Criseyde are caused by Nature-as-destiny and hence by God, who is the author of Nature; . . . [Chaucer] suggests . . . that the special, individual fortunes of the protagonists are directed by the destinal power inherent in the movements of the erratic stars. But he nowhere postulates a more definite system of destinal forces. Still one is made to feel—by means of reference to this or that planet, by striking suggestions of destructive influences hanging over the doomed city of Troy, and by mysterious intima-

tions of tragedy announced by dreams, oracles, and divina-
tions—that the days of Troy are numbered and that the cloud
of fate hovering over Troilus and Criseyde will presently over-
whelm them in the general disaster."[6] Curry is aware that there
seems to be some confusion in the poem between the influence
of the planets, the influence of the gods and goddesses, and
the Boethian bond of Love. But he assures us that the mythological references are mere poetic devices and what Chaucer
has really wanted to demonstrate is "how the destinal urge
emanating from the erratic stars combines and intermingles
with that having its source in Nature-as-Destiny."[7]

Troilus is clever because he is a fatalist and recognizes the
significance of Destiny, Fortune, Venus, and the Chain of
Love. On the other hand, Criseyde, whom Jefferson calls the
only philosopher in the poem, is not so bright because she is
not a fatalist. Criseyde

> is philosophically shortsighted and is apparently ignorant
> of the relations of Destiny to God and Fortune; or her concep-
> tion of Fate (if she has one) is so dim and limited that she
> does not realize the futility of human struggles against what
> God has ultimately planned. Or perhaps she is so superficial
> in her thinking and so conventional that she actually places
> no faith in her father's prognostications regarding the doom
> of Troy; or maybe her feminine childishness is responsible
> for the supposition that, in hoodwinking her father into be-
> lieving his own prophecies false, she may be averting the
> city's destruction altogether.[8]

In other words, Criseyde has a limited intelligence because she
dares to "oppose her puny strength" and cleverness and wit
against Fortune. Troilus, on the other hand, is brighter. After
an emotional struggle which is revealed in the monologue on
predestination, he tries to see whether there is any logical
escape from fate, and he comes to the wise conclusion that God
rules by necessity, and that men have no free will. Curry
maintains that Troilus is happy when he is a fatalist. But even
in his sad moments when he examines the premises of his
philosophy, he still is a consistent fatalist. In this monologue
Chaucer deliberately ignores the Boethian free will solution to
emphasize the significance of fate as the most powerful element
in the poem. In the manner of Sophocles and Shakespeare,
Troilus is a great tragedy, embodying a sublimity with a

struggling protagonist whose doom is inevitable and whose action is controlled by a stern necessity.

However, Curry is bothered by that fact that the characters do seem to influence each other. So he adds a third destinal force. To nature-as-destiny and the erratic stars, he adds the Boethian *anima mundi*, which Chaucer translates as "some soul." This represents the influence of one soul upon another. "In a certain mediate sense, moreover, the character of an individual himself constitutes one of the 'movable things' to which cleave the disposition and ordinance of destiny. For a character, with the stamp of Nature and of the stars upon it at birth, is itself responsible in large measure for whatever fortune it suffers." The man who does not use free will in controlling his emotions "finds himself presently without free-choice in the guidance of his actions when the power of the stars descends upon him or when he comes in contact with the destinal force inherent in other people's influence."[9] In the end Troilus also is taken to task for being a limited thinker. Although he has a philosophic mind, and although he understands the role of destiny in human affairs, he is a deficient character because he does not exercise his free will by trying to control his emotions.

Curry seems to think that he can resolve the basic contradiction in his analysis by equating destiny and free will, but to stipulate arbitrarily that a term which means *hot* also means *cold* is to involve oneself in linguistic difficulties and to nullify the significance of all defined terminology. First Troilus is a fatalist, and then he is reprimanded for not exercising his free will, which does not exist in Chaucer's poem except that we are assured that free will is really a form of predestination. It does not seem to me necessary to comment any further on this argument; it reveals how critics can make dunces out of intelligent writers. For if what Curry says about the poem's philosophical content is true, then the only conclusion a reader can draw is that Chaucer had a very feeble mind.

But assessing the nature of the Boethian influence in *Troilus* is an insatiable preoccupation of Chaucerian critics. While T. A. Stroud does not see any "unit-to-unit correspondence" between the *Troilus* and the Boethian work, he suggests that Troilus be viewed as a "Boethius," who is controlled by the wheel of Fortune and its alternations, rather than by Philosophy, but who learns in the end that youth should avoid the wheel of Fortune and love the Savior who is superior to the pagan gods. In Stroud's view, Troilus, like Boethius, undergoes a philosophical quest.[10] John P. McCall tries to show that there is a unit-to-unit correspondence between the two works. In fact, he contends that Chaucer imitated the five-book structure of the *Consolation*; the formal and thematic design of the *Troilus* reflects the structured argument of Lady Philosophy.[11] Thus in Book I, Boethius is led by Lady Philosophy to disclose the sources of his suffering. Similarly Troilus, wounded by Cupid, succumbs to Fortune and is led by Pandarus to disclose the source of his wound. Both are thus suffering from the same illness and need physicians to heal them. But to describe Troilus' love agony and Boethius' existential *angst* as similar illnesses is like claiming that there is no difference between a cold and cancer. McCall himself seems to recognize this difficulty, for he hastens to admit that the two works have only very "broad likenesses" and develop along diametrically opposed lines. Pandarus, the spokesman for worldly matters, aims to satisfy Troilus' worldly desires and thus makes him completely subject to Fortune, whereas Lady Philosophy, the spokesman for spiritual affairs, wants to teach Boethius to control his passions and desires through reason and free will to find eternal happiness in God. Troilus' soliloquy shows his doubts about free will and his inability to resist the control of Destiny, whereas Dame Philosophy shows Boethius the need for confidence in human freedom and the rightness of God's rule. In Book V of the *Consolation* Dame Philosophy reveals to Boethius how man can, through the rational agencies of free will and reason, find eternal happiness in God, whereas Troilus is kept in bondage till his death through his blind adherence to the irrational principle of determinism. This is what makes the *Consolation* a comedy, for the main character finds truth and happiness at the end; and this is what makes the *Troilus* a tragedy, for the main character does not find truth or happiness at the end. According to McCall, *Troilus* is, therefore, best defined as a historical tragedy which dramatizes a "man's systematic subjection to Fortune."

On the other hand, John M. Steadman believes that Troilus does find truth, or the consolation of philosophy, in "amor divinus." Steadman contends that Chaucer uses Boethian ideas throughout the *Troilus* to prepare the reader for the *contemptus mundi* theme of the epilogue. Steadman is primarily interested in showing how the flight stanzas of the epilogue, which reveal Troilus standing at the "threshhold of heaven," are integrally related to the Boethian insertions in Books III and IV and to the Christian coloring of the poem. "Without the two Boethian insertions, the intellectual judgments that Troilus makes in the flight stanzas might seem inconsistent with his character as Chaucer had portrayed it earlier; by inserting these passages the poet has laid the necessary foundations for the insights of the flight episode. The Boethian insertions function as preparation (parasceve) for the flight sequence, investing it with verisimilitude, consistency, and probability."[12]

Accepting without question the Boethian deterministic context of the romance, Steadman describes the *Troilus* as a story of love transformed into an "exemplum of false felicity." Criseyde's inconstancy is an example of the world's inconstancy. Criseyde is unfaithful like Fortune. "In the solicitude of the lover we find an instance of the Boethian *cura rerum temporalium*, and in his tragic end an example of the false world's brittleness. From his tragedy of secular love Chaucer has drawn the broadest possible *moralitas*: a condemnation that applies not only to the transitory pleasures of the flesh but to all 'thise wretched worldes appetites,' and indeed to the world itself."[13]

H. R. Patch also believes that the final moral of the *Troilus* is the same as that of the *Consolation*. But Patch contends that Troilus does realize that determinism is an erroneous philosophy. Although Troilus is a determinist on earth, he changes his view when he gets to his Christian heaven and recognizes that he is responsible for his sins against the court of love and against Christian doctrine for yielding to pleasure. Chaucer had too much common sense to deny the existence of free will, just as the Greek dramatists, Aristotle and the medieval theologians, including Boethius and Thomas Aquinas, believed in man's ability to make certain choices. Chaucer's characters are not mere puppets in the hand of fate; they do think and act as if they have the freedom to make choices. Patch believes that the predestination monologue is one which is used for mere dramatic effect to reveal Troilus' feelings of despair and is not to be interpreted as an intellectual statement of Chaucer's position. He deliberately gives Boccaccio's story a Christian coloring, adopting from Boethius and Dante the description of a Christian Fortuna which does not control by means of a capricious Destiny but through a rational God. The Epilogue specifically interprets the entire story in "Christian terms" and reveals a Troilus who "learns that he has suffered from the consequences of his own choice."

Patch asks how, if the actions of the character in *Troilus* are determined, we can speak of their motivations. Who is to blame if all is determined? "No blame attaches to anybody in this scheme, not even to Calchas. . . ." Yet in the *Legend of Good Women* Chaucer refers to Criseyde's sin, and Troilus talks about her guilt. We must understand Chaucer's intention: "Surely it is a safe principle in criticizing a great work of art to assume that the interpretation in harmony with all parts of the poem is the one nearest to the intention of the author. . . . A great artist knows what he is about, and . . . has a right to be understood on his own terms. In all fairness, in the interpretation of the *Troilus*, how can we reject the Epilogue and deny any Christian meaning in the passages on Fortune?" Can we really believe that "Chaucer intended one meaning for the Christians of his day and another, assuming that they were a different group, for those who liked a kind of pagan tragedy? . . . It is, I believe, an unworthy conception of the nature of art to hold that a writer may adopt for the nonce whatever philosophy has artistic value and play it for its effect as if it meant nothing in particular."[14]

The logic of this argument is easily refutable. For it is an "unworthy conception of art" that limits artistic creativity to the expression of a writer's personal beliefs. Great artists often depict contradictory philosophies to reveal the complex nature of human existence. Shakespeare believed in the monarchic principle, but this did not prevent him from creating a credible Brutus. Thus if we are willing to accept Patch's dubious premise that we can fathom Chaucer's intention, then it is also possible to believe that Chaucer intended to provide us with two irreconcilable meanings for *Troilus*.

Other writers have also argued that Chaucer believes in free will. P. Di Pasquale, Jr. maintains that the tragedy of Troilus and Criseyde is caused by the fact that they rely on Fortune in their pursuit of "Sikernesse," and unfortunately they have not had "the benefit of Christian revelation. Nor have they had the benefit of instruction in Boethian philosophy. . . . Their tragedy is the result of not knowing the things Philosophy teaches Boethius." They do not know what Chaucer

himself tells us in his own poem *Fortune* that "men bring
about their own tragedies."[15]

David Sims also believes that the Boethian influence does not
involve a deterministic outlook in the poem, and he points to the
choice made by the lovers to part as an example of an act of free
will. Sims claims that Troilus' difficulty stems from the fact
that he does not understand the Boethian argument, namely,
that "as knowledge, God's foreknowledge can not determine
the occurrence of anything." Like Boethius, Troilus needed
Dame Philosophy to teach him about "conditional necessity."
"Had Troilus had a Philosophy, not a Criseyde, he might have
seen that what is necessary about a characteristically human
action is not its causation but the 'measure' or the quality that
its true description establishes."[16] I do not understand what
Sims is saying in this sentence, but it is quite evident that those
who argue for free will can talk quite as obscurely as those who
argue for determinism.

A rather interesting argument for the free will principle is
offered by Charles A. Owen, Jr. who, in a refreshing change of
pace, doesn't base his discussion on Boethius and Dame
Philosophy but instead utilizes an aesthetic approach. Owen
maintains that creativity in a poem is effective only insofar as
it evades the *mechanistic*. A world which contains a predetermined cause and effect relationship cannot also contain the
notions of good and evil. "Freedom of the creature . . . is the
ultimate evidence of power in the creator." In other words, the
great artist must create characters who have free will. Owens
then asks, " . . . [H]ow can the author create an existential
freedom for his characters, how can he show them as having
wills independent of his own?" In *Troilus*, the "scenic structure,
the experience of the characters in depth—not only what they
say and do, but their thoughts and feelings, their dreams and
sudden impulses as well—and finally the sense that within the
limits of their capacities they change and develop in an
interaction with each other and with the environment, all these
contribute to the impression of a truly dramatic structure, of an
emergent rather than an imposed form."[17] To achieve this
emergent rather than mechanistic form, to give the illusion
that the characters are free from the author's control, Chaucer
uses the device of the self-characterized narrator and the
pretense that he is dealing with actual events. For example,

speaking of Criseyde's free will, Owens points out that while her return to Troy may have been caused by forces beyond her control, "nothing compelled her to accept Diomede as lover."

Robert P. apRoberts tries to mediate the two extreme positions by insisting that the poem gives us the double view of God's necessity *and* man's free will. "From a divine point of view, the agreement of Troilus and Criseyde to the exchange will occur by necessity; from the point of the lovers, it will occur by their own desires."[18] Thus apRoberts fulfills the expectation we have that in any critical controversy with two opposing viewpoints, someone will try to have it both ways. Peter Elbow argues that since Boethian thought is characterized by contradiction and since *Troilus* is permeated with Boethian philosophy, that therefore *Troilus* is a poem which achieves greatness because it is based on a contradiction. Elbow claims that "by characteristically assuming truth on both sides of the contradiction—Boethius gets further than most thinkers did in overcoming the limitations of language, thought, and the single human point of view."[19] We shall see how Elbow lauds Chaucer for the specific way in which he uses ironic effect in *Troilus* to convey the Boethian principle of contradiction. But does Boethius "get further than most thinkers" in relation to the question of determinism by using the principle of contradiction? Does Boethius really get further than Aristotle, Aquinas, Spinoza, Kant or Hume? Only it seems in the minds of those critics who are *solely* intent upon pairing Boethius and Chaucer as twin philosophers of the medieval age.

Other critics have recognized that to discuss *Troilus* merely as a poetic treatment of the *Consolation of Philosophy* is to do Chaucer a grave injustice. To assume that what influenced him most was one work, that he never read any other philosophers, and that he was so completely controlled by Boethian thought that he wrote a poem to illustrate an ethical philosophy rather than to dramatize what he knew about life is an *a priori* assumption which has never been adequately established. While Chaucer was unquestionably interested in Boethius, and while he did use some of his ideas in *Troilus*, interpretations which attempt to force Chaucer's thought so rigidly into the Boethian mold distort both the meaning and the effect of the poem. No one would ever guess from these analyses that Chaucer read other authors besides Boethius, that he had ideas and attitudes which he obtained just by observing and experiencing life, and that the most delightful scenes in the poem are not philosophical.

Moving away from the confining influence of treating *Troilus* as a Boethian tract, a number of critics have broadened the scope of the analysis to deal with the work as a Christian tract. I say *tract* because in the eyes of many of these writers the "moralitee" of the poem is what interests them. Since Chaucer was a Catholic living in a Catholic age, and since *Troilus* ends with a Christian invocation, it is hardly surprising to find many discussions of *Troilus* as a Christian poem. These are easily classifiable into two main types: those which assume that the *contemptus mundi* theme represents the basic attitude of medieval Christianity and therefore of the *Troilus*, and those which deny that *contemptus mundi* is the representative attitude of medieval Christianity and which interpret the *Troilus* in terms of the more affirmative and relevant ideas of love and plenitude in Christian theory.

As we would expect, D. W. Robertson uses a *contemptus mundi* approach in the specific application of his exegetical method to *Troilus*. In his "Chaucerian Tragedy" he uses quotations from Isaiah, Boethius, John of Salisbury, Peter Lombard, St. Augustine and others, as well as passages from the *Monk's Tale* to demonstrate his thesis. I have noted that Robertson believes that Troilus' three stages of tragic development, "subjection to Fortune, enjoyment of Fortune's favor, and denial of providence—correspond to the three stages in the tropological fall of Adam: the temptation of the senses, the corruption of the lower reason in pleasurable thought, and the final corruption of the higher reason." Such correspondence is revealed "by the emphasis on Criseyde's external attractions in Book I, by the wordly wisdom developed under the guidance of Pandarus in Book II and by the substitution of Criseyde for divine grace in Book III. Books IV and V show the practical result of this process: confusion, despair and death. Troilus becomes one of those who *cry for sorrow of heart* and who *howl for grief of spirit.*"[20]

Since Robertson is one of those who denies the existence of courtly love, it is easy for him to ignore it completely and to develop his Biblical analogy with *Troilus*. Robertson says:

> . . . Chaucer's *Troilus* follows in its general outline the pattern of Chaucerian tragic theory. Troilus subjects himself

to Fortune by allowing himself to be overcome by the physical attractions of Criseyde. His fall is an echo of the fall of Adam. When his senses are moved, he proceeds to indulge in "pleasurable thought," allowing his lower reason to be corrupted as he cooperates with Pandarus in deceits and lies. Once his object is attained, he substitutes the grace of Cupid as manifested in Criseyde for providence, thus corrupting his higher reason and turning away completely from "love celestial." Not only is his relationship with Criseyde "up-so-doun," but the "regne" of his mind is inverted too. His "capability and godlike reason" are neglected, so that he becomes, like Nabugodonosor," a "beast, no more." And as a beast he is completely at Fortune's mercy. There is thus a remarkable logic in the events of Chaucer's tragedy, an intellectual coherence that is rooted firmly in Christian doctrine and Boethian philosophy. The tragedy of Troilus is, in an extreme form, the tragedy of every mortal sinner.[21]

Thus Robertson transforms Troilus from an admirable Boethius into the sinner Adam, makes Criseyde the deceitful exemplar of the fallen Eve, and changes the noble "Dame Philosophy" Pandarus into a prototype of the Satanic figure.

Since I have already noted the objections to Robertson's special brand of criticism, I will not repeat them except to note what Meredith Thompson has written specifically about Robertson's view of *Troilus*.

> Chaucer was evidently a good fourteenth century Christian, interested up to a point in certain doctrinal questions, concerned considerably over abuses in the church. But beyond that, as everyone except the Robertson "school" knows, he is the great secular, the humanist whose breadth of affirmation is of itself a renaissance and foreshadows a greater. Symbolism and allegory are elements especially in his earlier works, but it is the "cortex" which more and more mattered to him, the teller of tales. To represent *all* his works primarily as religious and moral exempla is to shift focus away from supreme narrative art and cause serious distortion. To represent *Troilus and Criseyde* as a proselytizing of the more morbid aspects of monkish asceticism, especially as regards human love—out of whatever motive or myopia—is shameful.[22]

It is, of course, possible to argue that Thompson is himself guilty of working with an unproven hypothesis about

Chaucer's "affirmative humanism." But putting aside the question of Thompson's preferred view of Chaucer, Thompson has quite rightly criticized the excesses of the Christian-clerical interpretation.

Of course, Robertson is not the only Christian interpreter of Chaucer. There are others who ride the Christian hobby-horse, not with as much allegorical fury, but with sufficient intensity to make one wish that they would slow down. For instance, there is Eugene E. Slaughter who goes to school not to St. Augustine, but primarily to St. Thomas Aquinas. Slaughter maintains that the Christian doctrine of Grace motivates the "internal action of Troilus, and to a less extent, Criseyde." As for Pandarus, he is to be viewed as "a kind of priest of Love, an implement of gratuitous grace, by which one man cooperates with another in leading him to god. Who would deny that in Love Pandarus encompasses faith, wisdom, knowledge, healing, working of miracles, prophecy, discerning of spirits, kinds of tongues, and interpretation of speeches?"[23]

Obviously D. M. Robertson would deny this, for lo! his Priest of Satan has become the Priest of Love! To arrive at this sanctification of Pandarus, Slaughter has provided the reader with a detailed definition of Grace, buttressed by references to St. Thomas Aquinas. Christian Grace, he tells us, is external and internal, sanctifying and gratuitous, operating and cooperating, prevenient, subsequent, and sacramental. The beginning of the poem is, he assures us, filled with ecclesiastical ideas. Pandarus hears Troilus' confession "with a kind of absolution." Troilus is converted to the religion of Love which indicates the operating of sanctifying grace. In lines 187, 213, 225 and 220 he appears as an unbeliever and is guilty of presumption in the religion of love. "If a parody or extension of Christian doctrine can be understood here, this presumption, arising directly from pride, is an inordinate trust in divine mercy or power, the hope of obtaining glory without merit or pardon without repentance. It is conformed to a false intellect. It is contrary to the virtues of hope and charity and the sin of despair. It is the sin against the Holy Ghost, because by it a man despises the Spirit which might withdraw him from sin."[24] So Troilus' sin ends up being a sin against the Holy Ghost. When Troilus is converted to Love, the providential change is good because God cannot cause sin and indeed Troilus is ennobled by his love. The passions of love and despair are discussed as theological passions and Despair, related to Grace, is not a sin in Troilus because it is a passion. Slaughter concludes:

> The imitation of Christian grace and its associated notions contributes much to the extenuation of earthly love in *Troilus*. Love is god, who causes good but cannot cause sin. Since he is irresistible in moving Troilus's will by grace, Troilus's love appears to be good, and the results of it are increased virtue. The effect is a tone of religious love and devotion that infuses Troilus's endeavor and excites in the reader a serious concern for the hero's high purpose in love. Now, of course, this is specious. And irony, which varies in intensity from one passage to another, attaches to the god of Love and his power. Dispraise and the sorrows of love appear frequently. The epilogue condemns wordly vanity. But the apparent justification of earthly love by several means—among them the doctrine of grace—give consequence to the action of Troilus and Criseyde, which from the point of view of the epilogue is insignificant. *The prologue, therefore, heavy with ecclesiastical figures, is the best approach to the poem. There, by an intermixing and blending of emotions and standards, and a fusion of religious forms, Chaucer presents earthly love as though it were reconciled to God.*[25]   (my italics)

Whatever else Slaughter may be saying in this passage (I do not understand what the "this" refers to in "this is specious"), he clearly seems to be saying that in a poem of more than eight thousand lines, the most important part is the prologue. If we were to accept his view and the views of those who consider the epilogue to be the most significant part of *Troilus*, we could then pay less attention to what happens between the prologue and the epilogue! But then who would read *Troilus*? Despite Slaughter's categorical rejection of the importance of the epilogue, the meaning and significance of the ending have to be analyzed. Recognizing this fact, various critics have offered interesting interpretations of the epilogue.

James L. Shanley presents a Christian interpretation in a more moderate and rational fashion.[26] He admits at the outset that the *Troilus* is not a philosophical poem like *Paradise Lost* or the *Divine Comedy*. Instead he argues that *Troilus* is shaped by Chaucer's philosophy in the same way that Fielding's view of the goodness of natural man shapes *Tom Jones*. Chaucer retold this narrative in the light of certain Christian values.

The characters in the story suffer because certain events are fated, but they are also responsible for certain actions. Troilus suffers not because he places his trust in a woman, but because he chooses to place his trust for perfect happiness in that which is "temporary, imperfect, and inevitably insufficient." In other words, Chaucer revealed in his poem what his medieval audience would have understood and taken for granted, for their religion and philosophy taught them that no matter how wonderful the things of this earth seem they are not adequate, and the individual bears the responsibility for attaining heavenly, eternal bliss. To buttress his remarks about the nature of the medieval outlook, Shanley concludes by referring to various authorities: Etienne Gilson, Dante, Thomas à Kempis, and St. Augustine. The epilogue gives full expression to the meaning of Troilus' sorrow in terms of the Christian tradition; earthly love can never be as sufficient as heavenly love.

Still another interesting attempt to account for the so-called discrepancy between the context of the poem and the epilogue is Alexander J. Denomy's contention that the *Troilus* contains two moralities. He sees the context of the poem as dramatizing a courtly love theme which would have been considered heretical and immoral to the medieval Christian. In fact, the courtly notion of love had been condemned on March 7, 1277 by Archbishop Tempier at Paris. Among the 219 propositions which he denounced as being opposed to Christian orthodoxy were those relating to courtly love principles which preached the ideal of the irresistibility of love as the sole source of human worth. Chaucer, reasoned Denomy, probably knew about this condemnation, and he must have been aware of how dangerous it was to write a courtly romance, and "of the risk of an accusation . . . of heresy."[27] Unlike Andreas Capellanus, who provided courtly love with a logical and philosophical basis, Chaucer merely used courtly love as a background for telling his story. But both he and Andreas felt the need to recant. Chaucer's epilogue contains his retraction in its disapproval, condemnation, and repudiation of courtly love, and its firm reiteration of his Christian faith. Here, and in the retraction to the *Canterbury Tales*, Chaucer tried to salve his Christian conscience and to avoid official displeasure for dealing with themes that the church considered to be heretical.

These writers agree that Chaucer utilized some form of the

contemptus mundi theme to placate his Christian conscience for dramatizing forbidden or suspect subject matter in his love story. However, such an approach is too simplistic and ignores the complex nature of the species *homo sapiens*. Chaucer was a Catholic, but he was also a lot of other things as well: soldier, business man, traveller, husband, politician, reader, thinker, and, most important of all, *artist*. It is difficult enough to generalize about what modern Catholics think about the Pope, the celibacy of the priests, birth control, and abortion. While the Ecumenical Council exonerated the Jews of the charge of murdering Christ, we do not really know how many Christians have accepted this exoneration. How then can we know what Chaucer thought about Archbishop Tempier's condemnation. In 1272 Pope Gregory X warned all good Christians not to tell ritual stories about the murder of Christians by Jews, yet what else is the "Prioress' Tale" but a ritual murder story? Did Chaucer know about the Pope's Bull and was he therefore committing a heretical act by telling such a tale, or is it more likely that he probably never read the Bull or Archbishop Tempier's condemnation? How many well informed priests in our own age are thoroughly familiar with all the inter-pretations of church doctrine promulgated by the Papacy?

But even if Chaucer knew all the decrees of the church, it is unlikely that he would have accepted *every* tenet of the Christian religion any more than a modern Christian does. Furthermore, the universally quantified sentence, "*All* people in the Middle Ages were Christians" does not accurately reflect the reality of life in that age. Drawing essentially upon primary sources in which the medieval people "speak for themselves," Mary Edith Thomas observes: "That the popular mind was not so submissive and uncritical as has been supposed is apparent in the literature, in which a surprising number throughout Christendom expressed considerable freedom of thought, questioned dogmas, the doctrine of immortality, the efficacy of the sacraments, the justice of divine will, and the very existence of God."[28] She reminds us that this was also G. G. Coulton's judgment, who described the age as one which induced a state of mind which was "as definitely sceptical as the scepticism of the eighteenth century or of our own day."[29] And she also refers to Mary Morton Wood's conclusion that "contemporary writers did not regard their own age as an age of faith." Medieval England had its share of skeptics, agnostics, heretics, and atheists. There was the elderly nun who committed suicide because of the despair of disbelief. There was the rationalist priest who examined and repudiated the doctrines of the Scripture like a twentieth-century skeptic. There was Pope Boniface VIII who didn't believe in immortality; about the medieval peasants Gautier wrote that many of them "do not fear God any more than they do a sheep, and would not give a button for the sacred commands of Holy Church. . . . They have little belief and little faith." Pierre Cardinal Matheolus and William Rufus refused to believe in an unjust God; Walsingham, the Monk of St. Albans, described his contemporaries in London in 1392 as the "most unbelieving in God." Other churchmen like Bonaventura and the Bishop of Paris condemned the teachers of philosophy for propagating heresies at Oxford, Cambridge, and Paris. In 1270 the Bishop of Paris listed 12 counts against the universities. Agnellus, after listening to debates at Oxford, moaned: "Woe is me, woe is me! Simple brothers enter Heaven, while learned brothers dispute whether there be a God at all!" Then there were the disappointed believers who lost their faith when so many devout Christians were killed in the Crusades fighting for a God who permitted Saracens to kill Christians. And in literature itself there is the famous unorthodox passage in *Aucassin et Nicolette* which extols the World, the Flesh and the Devil rather than the Kingdom of Heaven.[30] Thus to argue that Chaucer would have had to accept orthodox Christian doctrines *because* he lived in a Catholic age is a suspect kind of *post hoc* reasoning. No one who has read Chaucer's poetry could accuse him of having a dull, passive, plodding, unimaginative mind.

It is necessary, therefore, to look more closely at *Troilus* and the epilogue to discern what is really in the poem without being hampered by *a priori* conceptions about what Chaucer must have meant because he was a Christian, either in a Boethian or Augustinian sense. The Church supposedly taught men to mistrust the joys of this world, to have contempt for its transitory pleasures, and to wait for the eternal joys of Heaven. The question that arises is not merely whether men really lived as the Church specified, but whether the Church ever told them to live this way. The *contemptus mundi* theme has been one of the omnipresent generalizations in medieval studies so that we wonder if it is really possible to describe the actual psychological attitudes of a person in the fourteenth century toward this world and the next.

But some analyses of the philosophy of *Troilus* are based upon a broader conception of the nature of medieval Christianity. Jean Leclercq once refused to participate in a symposium on the *contemptus mundi* theme in the spiritual tradition of the west because "ce thème ne m'est jamais apparu comme un élément dominant, obsédant, comme une donnée fondamentale et qui explique tout, dans la spiritualité des moines du moyen âge."[31] Derek Brewer has also noted that the *contemptus mundi* view "was never exclusive nor uncontested. The Biblical emphasis on God as creator, the influence of the 'School of Chartres' and (in the thirteenth century) of Aristotle, and also, no doubt, normal human instincts, were opposed to it. . . . From the concept of God as creator and from His perfection was deduced the perfection of the world (even though man himself, in Adam's sin, had partially corrupted that perfection). The natural world itself might therefore appear, under certain conditions, as an object fit not for contempt but for study and delight."[32]

Edmund Reiss reminds us of the Christians of the Middle Ages who did not believe in a dichotomy between the body and the soul, or the world and God. In fact, according to *Romans* (1:20), the way to a knowledge of God is through his visible creation. St. Augustine argues that since the world is created by God it is therefore Good. In the *Confessions* he states: "Even those things that are subject to corruption are good"; and in the *Enchiridion* he writes that "every being, even a corrupt one, in so far as it is a being, is good." St. Thomas Aquinas carries this idea one step further when he contends that since we must love all men in order to love God, then even sinners, who are men even when they sin, must be loved even though their sins should be hated. St. Thomas says: "Out of the love of charity with which we love God, we ought to love our bodies also." The famous distinction between the active and the contemplative life further exemplifies this view. Though, according to Christian philosophy, the contemplative existence has the greatest merit, in the words of St. Gregory, "Those who desire to possess the fortress of contemplation must first of all train in the camp of action. . . . Without the contemplative life, it is possible to enter the heavenly kingdom if we do not neglect the good actions we are able to do; but we cannot enter without the active life, if we neglect to do the good we can do." In other words, the active life is necessary for salvation; this world is not to be regarded with contempt but with the understanding that, in the words of St. Thomas Aquinas, "each individual creature exists for the perfection of the whole universe. Furthermore the entire universe with all its parts, is ordained towards God as its end, inasmuch as it imitates as it were, and shows forth divine goodness, to the glory of God. . . . Thus it is evident that divine goodness is the end of all corporeal things."[33]

According to Reiss, Troilus does not accept the conclusions of medieval Christianity that man has free will, and he subverts the thought of Boethius by refusing to take responsibility for his actions. The famous speech on predestination reveals Troilus' inability to understand the world or his relation to God. Either he embraces love to the exclusion of all other concerns, or he rejects love completely. He has the same extreme reactions when he is dead, for he looks down upon this world and expresses contempt for all of its values. He reverses himself and embraces the *contemptus mundi* view, despising all earthly things, and feeling scorn for those who weep for him. In other words, Troilus is guilty of the either-or fallacy; he makes the mistake of assuming that there are only two ways of looking at life; it is either good or bad. But rejection of the world is not necessary for the attainment of otherworldly bliss. Even the contemplatives in Dante's sphere of Saturn express their concern and love for God's earthly creatures. Whether Troilus attains salvation is questionable. But the whole tone of his concluding speech is marked by hate, and none of the supposed serenity and bliss of heavenly salvation is revealed in his words. It is possible for a pagan Trojan to be saved—witness Ripheus in the sphere of Jupiter in Dante—and Troilus' "lighte goost" is described as going blissfully to the spheres and hearing the "hevenyssh melodie," but his final resting place is not in the spheres but "ther as Mercurye sorted hym to dwelle." And in this connection Reiss parts company with most of the commentators when he maintains that "the resting place" is not clearly described. It may be the ogdoad, the place beyond the moving spheres, the traditional abode of the souls of virtuous pagans, or it may be Hades. "In view of what Chaucer writes four stanzas later, when he condemns 'payens corsed olde rites' (1849) and refers to Jove, Apollo, Mars and 'swich rascaille' as they (1853) including—it would seem, Mercury—it is hardly likely that Mercury would, in Chaucer's view, be leading souls to Paradise. Still, even apart from the connotations of Mercury here, the passage showing Troilus going to the spheres distinctly implies that the bliss, the 'pleyn felicite/ That is in hevene above' is still 'above' Troilus. That which he now knows to exist for the saved is not apparently, his; little wonder that he is bitter."

Reiss then proceeds to offer an interpretation of *Troilus* which discards the traditional view that Chaucer utilizes a *contemptus mundi* philosophy in the poem. When Troilus in the epilogue begins to despise this wretched earth and condemns its "blynde lust," he is not acting as Chaucer's spokesman but is speaking for himself. Troilus in Book I is a naive and foolish young man, and even when he is heroic we do not take him too seriously. He doesn't really know what he is doing in Books II and III, and in Book IV he becomes pitiful. For Troilus does not really understand life and lacks wisdom. "Furthermore, although he hears the 'hevenyssh melodie,' he does not participate in it—his inner laugh is not part of it. The joy of heaven, traditionally revealed to all those freed from the body, is never really his or seen in him."[34]

Moreover, Reiss continues to reason, if Troilus were saved, the poem would be a comedy in Dante's sense, and not a tragedy as Chaucer himself labels it. The poem is a tragedy because Troilus dies in despair at losing love, and the puzzling lines with their bitter anaphora can be explained as revealing Troilus' frustration:

> Swich fyn hath, lo, this Troilus for love!
> Swich fyn hath al his grete worthynesse!
> Swich fyn hath his estat real above,
> Swich fyn his lust, swich fyn hath his noblesse!
> Swich fyn hath false worldes brotelnesse! (V, 1828-1832)

Far from revealing the emphatic disgust that Chaucer feels about this world, a disgust which negates in one stanza the opposite feeling expressed in the preceding hundreds of lines in the poem, these lines reveal *Troilus'*, not *Chaucer's* bitterness. The general irony inherent in all the passages disappears in the last stanza in Chaucer's concluding words to the "yonge fresshe folkes," for when Chaucer, not Troilus, advises the young to love Christ he is in effect urging them to love also the

meaningful beauty of this world. He offers hope, not despair.
These are very different from the words of Troilus in the
spheres. "Troilus looks at what is inadequate, and, seeing only
the inadequacy, condemns the thing itself. Chaucer—in the
voice of the narrator—goes beyond the inadequacy, though
recognizing it, looks to what is ideal, and praises this." We
should love Christ because his love is superior to the pretended
loves of this world and Christ in heaven is superior to Troilus
because Christ 'nyl falsen no wight.' "[35] Thus Reiss' adroit
interpretation conceives the meaning of the poem to be more in
harmony with the view of medieval Christianity as a less
ascetic religion.

Reiss offers a convincing argument for the view that church
doctrine did not require the medieval Christian to live as if he
hated the world. Logically, the *contemptus mundi* position is
difficult to maintain, given the premise of God's goodness and
perfection. For if the earth is God's creation, it has to be good;
otherwise as a sorry place, this earth diminishes God's stature
who is by definition incapable of creating imperfection. But
Reiss' analysis of *Troilus* depends on the premise often
expressed by various critics that Troilus' views in the poem are
not Chaucer's views. And as we have seen, it is possible on the
basis of such an assumption to argue for or against the free will
or deterministic or *contemptus mundi* themes in the *Troilus*.

Various attempts have been made to reconcile what seem to
be disparate Christian themes in *Troilus*. Peter Heidtmann
believes that while medieval Christianity regarded Troilus'
love of Criseyde as sinful, as a love which degraded Troilus to
the level of a beast, Chaucer was not bound by doctrinal
considerations as a poet. Therefore, Chaucer felt that he could
disregard the Church's teachings on love and sex and
dramatize love as an ennobling experience in the context of his
poem.[36] E. Talbot Donaldson contends that the complex
morality of *Troilus* involves the paradox of Troilus' strong love
of this world, along with his Christian rejection of it. The poem
tells us that we must make the best of a world which we love and
enjoy and which we must inevitably and ultimately hate.[37] But
Peter Dronke takes Donaldson and other critics to task for
stressing the mood of despair and disgust in the five "Swich
fyn" lines. Dronke claims that in the epilogue Chaucer is
emphasizing what he stresses throughout the poem, "the
divine dimension of human love." The language of love in

Troilus, III has affinities with the language of redemption. Love on earth may be "unstable" but it is not "illusory," as Donaldson claims, and Dronke ends his discussion by using the authority of Boethius to buttress the opinion that Chaucer in *Troilus* reaffirms Boethius' view that it is good to seek happiness in earthly things.[38]

Despite the diversity of opinions expressed about the nature of the philosophic theme in *Troilus,* all the critics referred to in the preceding pages base their conclusions upon the same three assumptions: (1) the *Troilus does* have a philosophy; (2) it is possible to identify the kind of philosophy it expounds by reading the poem in conjunction with what Chaucer is supposed to have assimilated from the philosophers and theologians he read; and (3) the philosophic ideas in the *Troilus* are profound. Even those who minimize the importance of the epilogue are willing to admit that the poem expresses ideas which reflect philosophic concerns. These ideas may be specious, muddled or derivative, but their presence gives the work an added dimension of meaning.

But Paull Baum believes that philosophical and moral confusion is so pervasive in *Troilus* that it reveals artistic confusion. Baum admits that Chaucer made some improvements in adapting Boccaccio's tale, but

> it is to be feared that he did not thoroughly explore the consequences of the alterations and improvements which he added. By making Pandarus so different and Criseyde so different he assumed responsibilities for the outcome which he may be thought to have shirked. In Book V he faced a dilemma, looked about for other helps, fell into contradictions and almost seems to have lost interest. He certainly subjected the Book to no careful revision. If we can trust the text (IV, 26-28) he expected to finish the poem in four books, but instead prolonged the story with Troilus' sentimental excesses of pity and pathos as though he could not bring himself to face the final disaster. And at the end he quite threw up his hands crying 'All is vanity'—which is *not* the moral of his fable.[39]

Troilus, in Baum's view, consists of several dualisms involving pagan and Christian beliefs, worldly and heavenly love, conventional and courtly love ethics, as well as literary conventions and realism, determinism and free will. The epilogue is a miscellaneous patchwork medley which reveals Chaucer's hesitation, not to say confusion, and contains

the offhand reference to Dares for martial details; the apology
for Criseyde; the leavetaking of his poem; the translation of
Troilus to the Fixed Stars (or perhaps the Moon) and his
sudden awareness of Christian *felicite* in Heaven, followed
immediately by his being turned over to Mercury; the
exhortation to all young people to love only Jesus; the
sarcastic dismissal of the whole story as ancient paganism;
the half-serious dedication to Gower and Strode . . . and the
wholly serious prayer to Christ and the Trinity. He has
finished a romantic tale of simple, sensuous, and passionate
love, with an ideal lover betrayed by a weak faithless heroine.
The mixed elements remained soluble until now, when he
looks back and is not too confident. It is too late to admit
embarrassment, but he can at least end with a smiling
deprecatory gesture to the benighted heathen and with a
genuflection to the High Altar. . . .[40]

Baum even offers a suggestion as to how Chaucer *should*
have ended his poem. He could have replaced the scene in
which Troilus laughs in heaven with one in which he has a
"beautified" true vision of Criseyde. This would have been both
consistent and logical, the final glorification of love and yet an
ending that would be pious enough to satisfy all Christians.
Just as Dante's Beatrice led him to the final vision of beatitude,
so Criseyde might have become for Troilus "the symbol,
purified of its human dross, of that merging of earthly and
heavenly love which transcends our limited experience and
ennobles by the imagination both mind and spirit. For Troilus
the love which betrays here below would become an approach, a
guide, to the divine love; Criseyde forgiven and transfigured
would become 'la gloriosa donna della mia mente.' This would
have been the rightful climax and just reward of Troilus'
devotion to his God."[41]

Criseyde a "gloriosa donna?" One can only marvel at Baum's
temerity in offering such a suggestion. I have taken the trouble
to present here what Baum calls a "gratuitous grace-note" not
because I think it deserves serious consideration—it is after all
absurd to tell a dead author how he should have ended his
poem—but because it reveals how strongly Baum feels that the
epilogue is a mistake. He disagrees with Lawrence, Kittredge,
Robinson, and Chesterton that a repudiation of earthly love
takes place in the epilogue, after 8000 lines are devoted to
showing its value. He makes short shrift of Chesterton's
contention that Troilus found happiness at last in a Christian

rather than in a heathen world. As Baum puts it: "That is to say, Troilus, son of the King of Troy, should have delayed a few centuries, until after the Crucifixion: he should simply not have been a pagan, for no pagan can find happiness."[42] Never do Troilus or Criseyde feel or express the view that their love is immoral; only modern moralists take such a position. No false God of Love has betrayed Troilus, and in the end Chaucer merely has Troilus say that he despises the transitory nature of this wretched world, but he does not specifically forbid the love of mortals; he does not actually state that men should give up the love of humankind. Chaucer could not have meant that all people should give up earthly love and turn to love of God. Nothing in Christian theology makes that demand. "Is it possible that he did not express himself clearly? [sic] or that in saying the conventionally expected he gave way to a little too much enthusiasm? Life *is* a vanity fair, but not altogether. Criseyde did her poet a greater wrong than she did her lover if she betrayed him into generalizing her weakness into a pattern of all women." Thus Baum seems to be saying that if Chaucer is really generalizing at the end of the poem about how all people should live, he has expressed not a truth but a foolish observation. What Chaucer really did do is described by Baum in the following colorful metaphor.

> He went back to Boccaccio and transposed Boccaccio's exciting, heady tale into something unattempted yet in English prose or rhyme; and when it was framed in the sophisticated assumptions of *amour courtois*, it became almost impossibly complex. But he gave it all he had. He ran full sail before the wind, pennons flying—and then found himself on a lee shore. He had, for a time, the best of both worlds, sacred and profane; he kept them weaving and unweaving with a dazzling success. What wonder then if having poured his libation to Venus he saw fit to light a candle to the Holy Trinity. But this is far from being a repudiation of the ethics of Courtly Love. It is more like a way of saying that "ancient Troy and modern England are different and you must not think that I advocate Trojan mores for young people nowadays."[43]

Baum doesn't want to call the poem a failure and so he temporizes in the end with a metaphor which is curiously ambiguous and which seems to imply that Chaucer tried but didn't quite make it. "Is it possible," asks Baum, "that Chaucer did not express himself too clearly?" Baum's answer seems to be a rather hesitant yes. Chaucer understood pity and comedy but not tragedy in the Aristotelian sense. Chaucer's moral could not have been what modern critics have attributed to him because then "philosophical" Chaucer would have to be regarded as a rather mediocre thinker. He tried to do something quite complex and couldn't quite handle it.

Obviously, the *Troilus* epilogue has been a baffling phenomenon because many readers seem to feel that it obfuscates rather than clarifies the meaning of the poem. According to Tatlock, "The feeling in the Epilog is in no way foreshadowed at the beginning or elsewhere; it does not illumine or modify; it contradicts. The heartfelt worldly tale is interpreted in an unworldly sense. [Chaucer] . . . tells the whole story in one mood and ends in another."[44] Elizabeth Salter maintains that "the final answers given by Troilus do not match the intelligence and energy of the questions asked, the issues raised."[45] Dieter Mehl agrees: "Die rigorose, ungemilderte Schlussmoral kommt für die meisten Leser überraschend, weil sie ein sehr viel einfacheres Weltverständnis voraussetzt als alles, was vorangegangen ist, nicht etwa, weil sie in einem inhaltlichen Widerspruch dazu steht."[46] While the Christian interpretation of the Epilogue makes *Troilus* a very moral poem, it does not explain why Chaucer himself did not think so, for he included it among the "translacions and enditynges of worldly vanitees" for which he asked to be forgiven. Furthermore, he confused the issue when he wrote in the G Prologue to the *Legend of Good Women* that his *Troilus* was supposed to further the cause of love:

> Ne a trewe lovere oghte me nat to blame,
> Thogh that I speke a fals lovere som shame.
> They oughte rathere with me for to holde,
> For that I of Criseyde wrot or tolde,
> Or of the Rose: what so myn auctour mente,
> Algate, God wot, it was myn entente
> To forthere trouthe in love and it cheryce,
> And to be war fro falsnesse and fro vice
> By swich ensaumple; this was my menynge.
>   (456-464)

In concluding this survey of the various views of the philosophy of *Troilus*, I offer the following nonhistorical observations. Whenever a poem by an established writer inspires different and contradictory interpretations, most critics, unlike Baum, rarely attribute the difficulty to the author himself. It seems fairer to accept the *a priori* assumption that such an artist *always* knows what he is doing. Most of the great classics are studied with a kind of fawning, idolatrous attitude. Sometimes a T. S. Eliot goes *à rebours* and judges *Hamlet* to be a thing of shreds and patches even though virtually all critics judge it to be an eloquent masterpiece. But great artists are not necessarily philosophers or profound thinkers, and it is possible that some works contain shreds and patches which cannot be sewn together in any satisfactory fashion. No one word is more carelessly used in literary analysis than *philosophical.* All that a writer has to do is mention the subject of God, destiny, or free will, and he is automatically dubbed Sir Philosopher, and thousands of words are used to explain his *philosophy.* Many people think about the so-called philosophic issues but that doesn't make them philosophers any more than people who add their grocery bills are mathematicians. Artists are naturally sensitive and imaginative creators, but they are not necessarily philosophers in the technical sense of the term. Long ago Thomas Hoccleve, writing about Chaucer, asked:

> Also who was hier in philosophie to Aristotle in our tonge but thow?[47]

What this statement reveals is that Hoccleve did not really know his Aristotle. When Deschamps called Chaucer a "Socrates plains de philosophie," he was also making an outrageous comparison, for nowhere in the entire corpus of Chaucerian poetry is there any kind of sustained analytic probing of the kind Aristotle and Socrates are famous for. Despite the efforts of many writers to transform Chaucer's borrowed lines from Boethius into original gems of wisdom, I must agree with Tatlock who wrote that Chaucer "was not fertile in his original thinking. . . ."[48] There is no evidence in *Troilus* of a philosophical mind analytically probing the complex issues of existence. Instead we get sporadic references to favorite topics: fate, free will, providence, and sometimes a half-humorous referral of these problems to the "clerkes." Perhaps Lounsbury made too harsh a judgment when he stated that Chaucer's knowledge was neither deep nor accurate,[49] but clearly from a philosophic viewpoint his thought was essentially derivative.

Of course, it has been argued that Christian elements in Troilus are sufficient to make the poem deserve the label philosophic. But Christians are not necessarily philosophers, any more than most Catholics are analysts like Thomas Aquinas. Then there are those who believe that the Christian ideas in *Troilus* are expressed in the spirit of Pascal's Wager in the same way that the Retraction of the *Canterbury Tales* is merely a last minute safeguard for salvation—if it does exist. Critics like Roger Sherman Loomis and Aldous Huxley believe that Chaucer had his skeptical moments. Thus Huxley claims that at times Chaucer "doubts even the fundamental beliefs of the Church. . . . It would not be making a fanciful comparison to say that Chaucer in many respects resembles Anatole France. Both men possess a profound love of this world for its own sake, coupled with a profound and gentle scepticism about all that lies beyond this world."[50] Obviously neither G. K. Chesterton nor Robertson would concur with this opinion. It is generally assumed that Chaucer was a sincere Catholic and that his epilogue offers a specific religion as the means of resolving the dilemma of existence. It is in effect an act of proselytizing for Catholicism. But this makes the *Troilus* a religious poem; it does not necessarily make it a philosophical poem.

The reader who turns to the criticism of Chaucer's poetry before reading *Troilus* might justifiably assume, given the superabundance of essays which attempt to describe Chaucer's indebtedness to Boethius, St. Augustine, Thomas Aquinas, Dante, Thomas à Kempis, Alain de Lille, Macrobius, Bernardus Silvestris, and other medieval writers and theologians, that *Troilus* is essentially a religious tract. Donald W. Rowe has written a book which offers a Christian interpretation of the poem based on the *discordia concors* theme in medieval thought. *Troilus* is, in his view, "a harmony of contraries." The characters are "distorted images" of a Perfect Good. Rowe concludes his religious, symbolical interpretation with the following statements:

> Though Chaucer created *Troilus and Criseyde* to be a sacramental revelation of God, through his dramatization of his narrator's limitations, he confesses his own limitations

and his own conviction that if his poem does reveal God and move men to love Him, the credit for that must be given to God. In the end, the last of last analyses, for Chaucer, God is all in all. Men can only write poems which, if vivified by God, will move the lover of poetry to reject the music of poetry for heavenly harmony. Until that end, the poet returns to writing poetry.[51]

Can this really be the only end of Chaucer's poetry? Is he first and foremost a preacher. I do not think so.

Even the brilliant novelist John Gardner does not escape the pitfall of what Charles Muscatine has aptly described as the "excessive braininess" of exegetical analysis. Gardner does not find the meaning of *Troilus* in "a *harmony* of contraries"; what the poem reveals to him is "the inherently tragic contrast between the many and the one (unity and diversity) of Neoplatonic thought as it comes down through, among others, Macrobius, Boethius, Aquinas, and Dante."[52] But *Troilus* is not a great poem because it contains the Neoplatonic philosophy of unity and diversity. And no amount of philosophic "overkill," even when it is launched with the virtuoso skill of the author of the *Sunlight Dialogues,* can convince us that *Troilus* has survived because of its Christian doctrine. It is a superior poem for the same reason all great poems become classics; they univeralize ideas in an inimitable style so that they become meaningful to men in all ages.

Robert W. Frank, Jr. judges *Troilus* to be "complex, complex . . . the most complex medieval English poem on love that we possess."[53] Its pattern "is of an elaborate oxymoron" with asserted but unresolved contradictions. That it is *essentially* oxymoronic might be debatable, but most readers would agree that it is complex. Since there are too many significant elements in this poem which the philosophic approach ignores, it must be judged to have limited value. Nor does the historical emphasis supply us with a "correct" or "objective" philosophic interpretation. Other approaches might prove to be more illuminating. The formalistic analysis is surveyed in the following pages. It is primarily concerned with the genre, structure, language, and style of *Troilus* and favors the use of close reading or *explication de texte* in both historical and nonhistorical readings of the poem.

"Form is the Cage and Sense the Bird.
The Poet twirls them in his Mind,
And wins the Trick with both combined."

Henry Austin Dobson, *The Toyman*

"It is only after long experience that most men
are able to define a thing in terms of its own
genus, painting as painting, writing as writing.
You can spot the bad critic when he starts by
discussing the poet and not the poem."

Ezra Pound, *A, B, C, of Reading*

THE FORMALISTIC APPROACH TO *TROILUS*

Chapter Four

 In 1963 Robert O. Payne observed that "there is very little (indeed, too little) in any current Chaucer criticism of the close verbal and structural analysis which is characteristic of those New Critics of twenty or thirty years ago."[1] The truth is that the New Critics rarely worked with long poems and they achieved their best results with short poems. It is, therefore, hardly surprising that relatively less *explication de texte* is available for the study of *Troilus*. The key word here is *relatively*, for explications of this poem have been offered with greater frequency in recent years. No one has as yet written a book which explains every line in *Troilus*, but the proliferating verbal and structural analyses can be construed as comprising some kind of formalistic approach.

Formalism has been so closely identified with the New Criticism that it no longer seems necessary to distinguish these terms. But Aristotle was one of the earliest formalists; Boris Tomashevsky, Boris Eichenbaum, Roman Jakobson, Tzvetan Todorov, and Roland Barthes belong to the Russian and French schools of formalistic criticism. However, we usually associate formalism with the English and American New Critics—T. S. Eliot, I. A. Richards, Allen Tate, John Crowe Ransom, William Empson, and Cleanth Brooks—who stress the notion that the poem itself, not the author of the poem or what influenced him, should be the prime concern of the critic. This view rejects the traditional emphasis of historical criticism, reasserts the primacy of the text, and insists upon close textual analysis.

The formalists have also objected to personal or subjective readings which produce the affective fallacy. In the correct kind of reading such terms as ambiguity, complexity, paradox, irony, tension and texture are used to illuminate the subtleties of the text. This does not mean that ancillary information is automatically excluded; historical and linguistic information is often employed to provide supplementary documentation for an interpretation.

Those who object to this critical approach condemn it for being narrow and inadequate as a means of analyzing discursive poetry like Thomson's *The Seasons* or Milton's *Paradise Lost*. They accuse formalism of producing its own fallacies: the conventional fallacy which results from underestimating the real significance of historical convention in the creation of a work of art; the objective fallacy which ignores the author and substitutes the critic's presence; the exhaustive fallacy which mistakenly assumes that the exhaustive examination of every detail in a literary work will reveal its unity and aesthetic grandeur.[2] The historicists have objected to the illusionary nature of a type of explication which can only pretend that it does not go outside the poem when actually any work that is in need of explanation has to have something brought to it from the outside, whether it is merely the personal experience of the reader or his special knowledge. However, despite such criticism, the formalists continue to exert an inestimable influence on literary study. While they have not replaced the historically oriented critics of *Troilus*, they warrant special attention for their analyses which discuss *Troilus* in relation to genre, point of view, irony, ambiguity, structure, and style.

It would seem to be quite important to have a clear idea of the kind of poem we are analyzing. But like almost everything else connected with *Troilus*, determining its genre does not seem to be an easy matter. It has been called a psychological novel, an epic, a romance, a tragedy, a comedy, a tragi-comedy and a martyr play. In other words, it lends itself to a variety of classifications.

The least valid of all the classifications seems to be the one which describes the poem as a psychological novel. E. G. Sandras, E. De Sélincourt, G. L. Kittredge, R. K. Root, W. P. Ker, J. Masefield, and F. Prokosch refer to it as the first great novel, and in more recent studies J. Speirs, M. Mudrick, D. I.

Grossvogel, and J. I. Wimsatt also discuss it as a novel.[3] Perhaps what they mean is that the extensive narration in Troilus is something *like* narrative art in the novel, and the characterization is reminiscent of the realistic techniques employed in the novel as distinct from those used in the romance. But it is not possible to see how the issue is clarified by calling a poem a novel, and while we may have some vague notion of what we mean by the oxymoron *poem-novel*, blurring the distinction between the two forms doesn't help to give us a clearer view of the genre of the *Troilus*.

Those who write about the poem in relation to the epic form usually hesitate to label it categorically as an epic. Thus Bertram Joseph admits that *Troilus* "may not be exactly what we should call an epic today. . . ."[4] Although he points to certain epic elements in the poem—Troilus is a heroic knight; Criseyde is a lovely heroine; Pandarus is a loyal friend; the heroic setting is peopled with heroic personages—Joseph does not really concern himself with the technique of the epic as a special form. He states that the characters have epic qualities, but his essential preoccupation is with the code of courtly behavior.

Daniel C. Boughner also finds "epic elements of grandeur" in the poem: the invocation, the mythological allusions, the atmosphere of high antiquity, the Trojanization of the setting, and the use of astronomy and astrology. These elements are characteristic of the high style, and Chaucer was influenced by Virgil, Dante, and Boccaccio. It is important to remember that Chaucer "belongs to that illustrious company of excellent poets visioned by Dante, who body forth grave subjects in a style not merely ornate, but sublime; for he undertakes to write . . . of moral philosophy in so majestic a form that nothing could be uttered for the instruction of mankind more powerful."[5] But the philosophy of Boethius, and Fortune as the Agent of Divine Providence, as well as the address to the Trinity at the end exalt the poem and make it a tragedy. The five books of the poem suggest the five acts of a drama, and Chaucer himself is a kind of tragic chorus. To confuse the issue even more, Boughner, in the last sentence of his analysis, calls the poem "a high romance of universal appeal ennobled by certain epic features. . . ."

· Other discussions of the genre of *Troilus* deal with it as a romance or a tragedy. Karl Young denies that Chaucer transformed Boccaccio's romance into a novel of real life. Instead, Young insists that *Troilus* is a medieval romance set in a "magical nowhere." By medievalizing and archaizing the old story Chaucer did not involve himself with recreating contemporary actuality, but he did add glamour and strangeness to the locale. Young lists the following as strong evidence for his view that Chaucer deliberately changed Boccaccio's story into a romance: (1) the scene in which Criseyde asks, "Who yaf me drinke?" is very obviously derived from romantic legends; in fact, it is a line that is probably borrowed from the *Romance d'Eneas*; (2) Criseyde has none of Griseida's hearty sensuality; she has instead the tender "circumspection" of Ydoine, Fenice, Lydaine, and the Dame de Fayel. The major love scene is crudely sensual in Boccaccio, but it is highly romanticized in Chaucer. The sensuality of Boccaccio becomes childlike innocence in Chaucer's poem. Even the objection that Pandarus nullifies the effect of the romance and makes the *Troilus* seem like a fabliau can be readily answered, for the romances, Young reminds us, have comic relief precedents which can be found in the jesting Duenna of the *Romance of the Rose* and Kay in *Ywain*. Indeed what is surprising is the abundance of realistic, contemporary scenes in romances, and even the most fantastic ones have at least one scene which recalls the spirit evoked by Pandarus' actions. The narratives of Jean Renart and Flamenca are remarkable for the way in which they depict actual contemporary views of life and for the way in which they avoid fantastic elements. Young insists upon calling the *Troilus* a medieval romance, even though, he says, we may at certain restricted moments admit that *Troilus* reminds us of a modern psychological novel.[6]

Another tendency is to view the poem as a drama. Sometimes *Troilus* is discussed as a poem which contains dramatic elements; sometimes it is defined as a special kind of drama. While Samuel L. Macey denies that *Troilus* is either a comedy or a tragedy, he points to the dramatic elements in the poem: the obvious division into five parts, and the many dramatic scenes which parallel the "front elevation of a Greek temple with its five openings and pyramidal superstructure." The structure without unity of time or place is, however, closer to Shakespearean than Greek drama. But it is important to note that *Troilus* cannot be a tragedy. Why? *Troilus* cannot be tragic since it is a Christian poem and Catholics cannot write tragedies. The ending of *Troilus* is like that of a martyr play rather than a tragedy because the epilogue has no tragic fall but rather the knowledge of a heavenly reward. Thus while Chaucer's religious convictions enabled him to use tragic elements, his ending is not, as Robertson insists, perfectly within the limits of the tragic concept. "My thesis is not, of course," says Macey, "that Chaucer built his work on what were for him virtually nonexistent dramatic rules nor, for that matter, that he was influenced by the vastly inferior 'theater' of his day. I feel rather that like Leonardo da Vinci, who produced sketches regarding ballistics and flying machines in advance of the necessary progress in technology, Chaucer too, with an analogous use of genius, was unable to envisage the dramatic requirements of a theater not yet in existence."[7] Depending on one's interpretation of the play, one can, however, see the play as being a courtly love martyr play or as a religious martyr play. But note Macey's last comment: Chaucer, like Shakespeare, "has provided us with a drama of real life, a drama giving not merely aesthetic pleasure because of the alignment of structure with content, but a drama also from which may be drawn a message that is fleshly or spiritual, local or universal, in accordance with the eye of the beholder or the perspective of the critic."[8] So what began as a discussion of dramatic elements ends up as a discussion of realistic drama from which *any* moral can be drawn.

Unlike Robertson who, as we have seen, regards *Troilus* as a theological tragedy, R. Mayo categorizes the poem as a "personal tragedy."[9] To defend this position, Mayo rejects the views of Lowes, Kittredge, and Curry that the poem has a strong sense of Trojan doom overhanging it and that therefore *Troilus* is also a tragedy of Troy as well as of Troilus and Criseyde. Books I–III offer sprightly romantic comedy. While Fate or doom is emphasized in Books IV and V, it is the doom of the lovers not the doom of Troy that is paramount. The fate of Troy is not an affective force in the story. There are seven references to destiny in Book I, six in Book II, four casual ones in Book III, and while there is concern with Troy in Book IV, Troilus is primarily interested in his own life. The Trojan War is not a sustained theme of Trojan destiny but serves as an indistinct background for the love story. Thus *Troilus* is a personal tragedy. Neither an epic nor a novel, it is as Karl Young has pointed out, a romance. "Let us not make . . . [Chaucer] write like Thomas Hardy and Emily Brontë too."[10] But notice how Mayo's genre distinctions also get blurred. In the end, for Mayo *Troilus* is both a romance and a personal tragedy.

Willard Farnham believes that *Troilus* is a tragedy with a structure that is similar to that of the Hannibal story in Boccaccio's *De Casibus* except that it has to do with love rather than affairs of state. The theme of *Troilus* is revealed in this view through a structure of rising and falling action which teaches the tragic hero the De Casibus lesson, "the lesson that no man has the power by will, by action, or even by merit, to secure himself in any wordly possession, and that therefore such a possession is worthless from the beginning."[11] Criseyde as portrayed in the *De Casibus* tragedy is a worldly possession of *Troilus* and is expected to leave him like youth, or wealth, or power. This is why Chaucer is so lenient with her, for she is the symbol of the instability and untrustworthiness of the world. And furthermore, Troilus' tragedy is intertwined with the tragic doom of Troy. The particular achievement of Chaucer is his use of Boccaccio's *De Casibus* in which Chaucer shows that "a story of serious misfortune gains enormously in force of tragic import when it is plotted at greater length than that of any story in the *De Casibus* or the *Monkes Tale* and with more leisurely attention to the details of setting, dialogue, and action."[12]

Now it is to Farnham's credit that he recognizes that there is more to the *Troilus* than the simple *De Casibus* tragedy, a tragedy with a contempt of the world theme. He sees the implicit contradiction in the poem between an affirmation of worldly love and scorn of that concept. This paradoxical feeling is characteristic of other Renaissance figures such as Bacon and Petrarch. Chaucer contradicts himself when he first advises his readers not to scorn love, for the worthiest men have been ennobled by it, and then at the end he advises his readers to avoid such love. He makes the philosophy of the story deterministic, but then he creates characters who act virtually as if they had free will. For this reason his tragedy is not equal to the status of the great tragedies which recognize the role of both fate and free will. Furthermore, Chaucer does not universalize the love story. He preoccupies himself too much with the individualized emotions of Troilus and Criseyde rather than with "widening of the fable to give it participation in a universal drama of struggling forces, in a drama pitting right against wrong, or duty against desire, or one good against another good. . . ." In fact, he seems to be approximating in his genius the reaches of Shakespearean comedy. "Perhaps the ethical depths reached by the greater tragic poets were waters which Chaucer would have had neither inclination nor ability to sound, even if models of their kind of tragedy had been available to him."[13] Thus Farnham comes to the conclusion that although *Troilus* is not the best kind of tragedy, its greatness is probably to be sought in its adaptation of Shakespearean comedy. He even speaks at one point of the serio-comic spirit of *Troilus*. In his view, it is a tragedy with comic elements in the most important portions of the philosophic and thematic stanzas. Nevill Coghill has a similar view of the genre of the poem: "Tragi-comedy is a kind of vision we associate most readily with the genius of Shakespeare, but it was Chaucer who discovered it. It is a kind of writing in which a hidden philosophic seriousness underlies the smiling account of human behavior, the tears and the buffoonery, and gives them a secret direction. Only at the end of the journey do we realize where we have been taken."[14]

Monica E. McAlpine also deals with the tragedy and comedy of *Troilus*, but she does not use the terms in a Shakespearean sense. She argues that Chaucer was primarily influenced by Boethian genres. She maintains that Chaucer rejected the *De Casibus* notion of tragedy, and instead utilized the Boethian genres of comedy and tragedy which she extrapolates from the *Consolation*. Boethian tragedy "consists essentially of the inner degradation of a person caused by the free commission of an evil act," while Boethian comedy "consists in the inner moral enhancement—Boethius would say divinization . . . of a person caused by the free commission of a good act."[15] Criseyde's story is dramatized as Boethian tragedy, and Troilus' story is dramatized as Boethian comedy. The narrator misnames the poem because *Troilus* is obviously both a Boethian tragedy and comedy. At the outset McAlpine states her view that *Troilus* is a theologically orthodox, Christian poem with both Troilus and Criseyde represented as characters who are contaminated by original sin. But Troilus is a Boethian comic hero because he experiences the agony and triumph of being free; he is not fated like the *De Casibus* hero. Unfortunately, he is a pagan, and so his insight is limited:

> In Troilus—a hero whose theory is inferior to his practice—
> Chaucer gives us a precise representation of the situation of
> the pagan who shares all the richness of his humanity with
> the Christian but is without the aid of Christian revelation to
> interpret it. In the perspective of that revelation, pagan
> wisdom is not wrong, but it is seriously incomplete. . . . In
> short, pagan wisdom does not know that the world is
> redeemable, and in that respect Troilus' [final] speech
> constitutes one of the last acts of betrayal in the poem, because
> only the Christian vision *can* be entirely faithful to the world
> and its goods and their potential for redemption.[16]

Baum and other critics have objected to this view of Troilus'
limited paganism, but McAlpine even goes so far as to state: "If
Troilus had been a Christian, he might have made a confession
of love in which, like Dante in another comedy, he would have
traced the fire of his love for God to its origin in the fire of his
love for a woman. . . ."[17] Both Baum and McAlpine believe
that Criseyde could have functioned as a kind of Beatrice. But
for McAlpine a Beatrice is meaningful only in a Christian
context whereas for Baum, as we have seen, she can provide the
pagan Troilus with insight into divine truths. In the end
McAlpine seems to equate the comedy of Boethius with the
comedy of Dante.

By devoting one chapter to the discussion of the tragedy of
Criseyde, and another chapter to the explication of the comedy
of Troilus, McAlpine sets up an artificial cleavage which has
the effect of transforming one poem into two separate entities.
She tries to extrapolate poetic genres from the philosophy of
Boethius, but they are, after all, what she herself calls
"hypothetical genres." Like McAlpine, Helen S. Corsa also
deals with both the tragic and comic elements in the *Troilus*.
But when Corsa refers to the comedy in the first three books, she
uses the word in a secular rather than a religious sense. What is
comic is humorous. Like Farnham, she characterizes the poem
as a tragedy in which the last two books depict the unfolding of
tragic events. She considers the wheel of Fortune and the
concept of Fate to be two different principles. It is Pandarus
who is the Agent of Fortune. Both Fate and Fortune can make
for tragedy or comedy, but Pandarus' activity is comic. His love
of love makes for joy and when there is no more joy there is no
more comedy. ". . . Comedy in the figure of Pandarus . . . accounts for most of the tragic effect of Chaucer's poem. . . ."[18]

Pure comedy is particularly evident in Book II in the interplay between uncle and niece. There is gaiety and laughter in their interchanges, and without Pandarus Criseyde would not have yielded to Troilus. There are sharp exchanges of wit in this book as well as social "busy-ness" which make for the social comedy. But it is Pandarus who generates the tragedy to come. Book II is predominantly a story of happiness fulfilled. Pandarus is primarily involved with the Flesh while Troilus has both physical and spiritual interests. The comic activity of the vulgar Pandarus is transformed into the lyric beauty of the love scene. Even Troilus' fainting does not detract from the exaltation of the love scene which is initially humorous but which ends with an emphasis on spiritual, earthly, and divine love. But there is no humor in Books IV and V, and no joy. While some have seen some comedy in the lines in which Troilus looks down and laughs at the world and while this may seem to trivialize the tragic seriousness of the poem, the epilogue actually underscores the intensity of the tragedy.

Corsa unequivocally states that the first three books are comic. However, she makes no attempt to define what she means either by comedy or tragedy and takes for granted the fact that the reader will somehow intuit her view of what these terms mean. Nor does she attempt to reconcile the use of both comedy and tragedy in the poem; so that while she is talking about the comic elements, she is at the same time assuring her readers that what she is ultimately talking about is a tragedy.

Only Mark Van Doren discusses *Troilus* as "Pure Comedy." He describes the poem as the "finest instance in narrative poetry of the comic genius at work." Admitting that Chaucer labels the *Troilus* a tragedy, Van Doren maintains that Chaucer misnames it and "who can doubt that he knows it?"[19] Van Doren, with such an observation, forewarns us that he sees no categorical imperative in the historical approach. His analysis is exceptional because it is the reaction of a critic who is unconcerned about the facts of history that might require him to read a poem in a special way. Van Doren responds to *Troilus* with the heightened sensibility of a modern poet. First he offers his definition of Comedy:

> Comedy has no beginning and no end. Its field is the middle distance where riddles are not resolved. Consequently its works are long, since anything that is endless must be long.

> Wit and tragedy may be short, and indeed they had better be,
> or we shall not accept them. But humor, the soul of comedy,
> will not be dictated to. The soul of tragedy, as Aristotle
> observed, is plot, is action, and there comes a time when we
> know what the action meant. Humor means itself. It
> distributes itself everywhere through the work it graces; it is
> in the style, the digressions, the asides, it is in fact the whole
> long body of that work.[20]

In such comedy truth is more important than narrative, and its
truth is always inconclusive, for the comic spirit doubts at the
same moment that it hopes. Whereas in tragedy we learn
through the action in time of the flaw in a hero's knowledge, the
comedy makes us aware of the flaw at the outset. The smile of
the comic poet comes from the pity of an ancient understanding: "Comedy is old, it has seen all this before. It is not weary,
but it is wise. Its laughter expresses a mind not vacant but if
anything too full. Not, however, too full for feeling. . . .
Chaucer is committed to nothing except the pity of understanding, the laughter of a perspective so loud and wide that
cruelty dies out before a sound arrives."[21]

The view of life that Chaucer "brings to ground" is what is
usually associated with the courtly love doctrine, namely, the
view that love is the most important thing on earth, and that it
is nullified if it is not secret. Van Doren does not believe that
Chaucer wishes to condemn love. He sees what is credible in
courtly love and what is true to man's experience. He knows
that love is a private affair, but he thinks that his thoroughly
conventional lovers make too much fuss over their reputation.
"It is natural for lovers to want to be alone. That is enough for
Chaucer. The rest is rubbish." But the comedy of the poem is not
to be sought in any particular passages, in Chaucer's remarks
to the reader, in the character of Pandarus "that older Mercutio
to a still more youthful Romeo. It is not alone in the devious, the
seductive Criseyde. In nothing can it be alone, for comedy is
social, and occupies all of the available air. The comedy of
Troilus and Criseyde is in the tone of the whole, a tone so
delicately maintained that if we hear it at all we understand the
legend that comedy is divine: the gods know best how, when,
and why to smile."[22] It is true that Troilus' heart is broken, that
Criseyde is grief-stricken and even Pandarus expresses doubts
about what his act of friendship has produced. It is also true
that Chaucer has thrown in laments, songs, hymns, and still he

has written a comedy, not a tragedy. "An envelope of sun surrounds even the darkest portions of his scene. It is a sun that dries the tears from metaphor, that substitutes the speech of men for poetry's vapors."[23]

Chaucer pretends he is a historian. But he always offers long explanations of why he is not long, expecting us to see the joke. Since the comic spirit is not committed, it cannot take seriously even a hero and heroine, and his way of criticizing exaggeration is to exaggerate still further, till even fate sounds funny. (Note that Curry's fate becomes Van Doren's joke.) Chaucer is the best friend the lovers ever had, better even than Pandarus, but Chaucer will not spare them any more than he would his enemies. For even though the lovers think they are special, we understand they are flawed human beings. Chaucer is "discursive because he is skeptical; to the comic genius everything is partly true and he is its priest, its garrulous vicar who in a minute can find his attention turned to something else of equal interest. Not that Chaucer is a holy fellow. . . . The reverence of Chaucer is for all that is, not for this or that person, god, or thing. The comic spirit is not committed, and cannot take seriously those who are. . . . Because it respects all things it respects nothing too much. The comic spirit is just, and loves the world entire."[24]

Van Doren's poetic eulogy of Chaucer as a comic genius is a refreshing analysis mainly because it corrects the distortions of the plethora of somber readings of *Troilus* which ignore its humor. But since Van Doren does not refer to the epilogue, he leaves the reader with the uneasy feeling that he is himself guilty of distortion.

This survey of various attempts to define the genre of *Troilus* is very clarifying. It reveals that Troilus is a comic tragedy with romantic and epic elements. Undaunted, Alan M. F. Gunn, who has categorized *Troilus* as a polylithic romance, states that it is "historical, amorous, tightly organized, chivalric, comic, elegiac, tragic, pathetic, philosophical, psychological. . . . allegorical, problematic, ironic, quasi-realistic, myth-oriented."[25] From a logical point of view, this is a model tautology; since it includes everything, it can hardly be falsified. We may well ask, "What is it that *Troilus* is not?" and agree with Northrop Frye "that the critical theory of genres is stuck precisely where Aristotle left it."[26]

Quite a number of interesting attempts have been made to

establish the relationship between Chaucer's authorial presence and the total meaning and effect of the poem. Reading some of these analyses gives me the impression that neither Troilus nor Criseyde nor Pandarus is the crucial character, but that Chaucer looms over the scene, dominating as a kind of protagonist historian. Chaucer's authorial comments were carefully tabulated by H. Lüdeke who, like many a German scholar, was deluded into thinking that mathematical tabulations help to establish aesthetic judgments. Lüdeke actually counted the first person point of view expressions and found that they constitute 2.47 percent of the total lines in Book I, 3.36 percent in Book II, 4.34 percent in Book III, 1.18 percent in Book IV, and 3.9 percent in Book V. About two hundred and ninety lines are given over to the first person address by the author.[27] Morton Bloomfield has calculated that roughly 12 percent of the lines of the first book belong to the commentator; these include all the lines which are not necessarily in the first person, but which are clearly to be attributed to the authorial voice.[28] But the reader does not really need such statistics to realize that the author of the poem intrudes in much the same way that Victorian novelists like George Eliot, Dickens and Thackeray appear in their novels. The question raised by such intrusions has assumed an important dimension in some of the criticism of the poem. Chaucer's authorial presence has been taken by some to indicate involvement and by others detachment; it has been very carefully analyzed with the conclusion reached that Chaucer superimposed a kind of Jamesian point-of-view consciousness upon the structural patterning of the poem. When the modern reader picks up a George Eliot novel and finds the action of the story interrupted by the author's commentary on social and ethical themes, he bluntly calls such interruptions digressions, fascinating as they may be as revelations of the writer's attitude toward her characters and events. It used to be possible to think of Chaucer's role in this way. He was merely employing what the medieval rhetoricians would have called *digressio* to comment on the action and fill out his story in a conventional manner. But a number of analyses in recent years have made a very highly sophisticated artist, and as a result his use of point of view has been found to contain the most remarkable subtleties of a highly self-conscious artist whose intrusion into the story has the effect of turning him into an important, if not the most important, character in the story. This is the position of Morton Bloomfield in an often referred to article entitled "Distance and Predestination in *Troilus and Criseyde*": "Chaucer takes pains to create himself as a character in his poem and also to dissociate this character continually from his story."[29]

The title of Bloomfield's article seems to promise a discussion of Chaucer's philosophy, but Bloomfield is actually presenting one of the seminal analyses of Chaucer's use of point of view. Chaucer, he notes, at the outset assumes the role of historian. Throughout the tale, he continually reminds us that he cannot change his story. He is in all the crucial portions of the poem speaking in his own person directly to us and maintaining a distance from the actual events. This effect of distance between Chaucer as a character and his story is achieved by temporal, spatial, aesthetic, and religious emphases. The greatest emphasis is temporal distance as Chaucer the narrator reminds us again and again that the events he is recording are part of the past; at the same time he constructs dialogue and lively conversation in the everyday living of his characters which serve to contrast his writing in the present and his story in the past.

Chaucer also makes use of spatial distance by giving us a "shifting sense of nearness and farness." Either we see events through close proximity to the characters or are deliberately removed from them in space. This technique Bloomfield likens to the process of continually inverting the telescope, which serves to increase our sense of space and which can be compared to depth perspective in painting. As a cultural relativist, Chaucer stresses both chronological and geographic variability. For example, Troilus' translation to the "eighth sphere" is a prime example of this spatial distance where he joins Chaucer in looking down at this "litel spot erthe."

As for aesthetic distance, Chaucer achieves this by continually distinguishing between the story he tells and by playing the role of commentator. He always keeps before the reader the fact that he is the narrator, and he comments on the difficulties that he faces as a narrator, bemoaning his bondage to the facts of the story. He seems to be continually regretting the events which require him to describe Criseyde's betrayal; he says, "the storie telleth us," "I fynde ek in the stories elleswhere," "men seyn—I not." "The piling up of these phrases here emphasizes the struggle of the artist-narrator against the brutality of the facts to which he cannot give a good turn. As a faithful historian, he cannot evade the rigidity of decisive events—the given."[30] The differentiation, then, that is made between Chaucer the narrator and what is narrated makes for the aesthetic distance.

Then there is the matter of religious distance, for Chaucer never puts Christian sentiments into the mouths of his pagans. His pagans may be aware of God and the moral law, but they do not know about the truths of revealed Christian religion as Chaucer clearly does. It is true that he plays down his own Christianity until near the end of the poem: the religious barrier between his own views and those of the characters is made clear. Although Chaucer in the introduction tells us he is telling a tale which he cannot alter, in other words that he is a victim of historical determinism, it is not until the end that we can fully understand how Christianity helps him to escape this entanglement.

It is Chaucer's use of distance and aloofness which is the "artistic correlative to the concept of predestination. *Troilus and Criseyde* is a medieval tragedy of predestination because the reader is continually forced by the commentator to look upon the story from the point of view of its end and from a distance. The crux of the problem of predestination is knowledge. So long as the future is not known to the participants in action, they can act as if they were free. But once a position of distance from the action is taken, then all can be seen as inevitable."[31] Probably Chaucer was a predestinarian very much in the manner of Bishop Bradwardine, but whatever he actually believed, the source of the inner tension of the *Troilus* stems from Chaucer's awareness of necessity as a historian and his sympathies as an artist and man. In the end, Chaucer reconciles the artist and the historian through a Christian solution in the love of the God who becomes man and whose trinity is unity and unity is trinity.

Bloomfield's conclusion is hardly novel, and it might be more convincing if it were possible to accept the premise of detachment or distance as the basic role of the commentator. However, such a premise is not accepted by other writers who seem to have quite different views of the nature of Chaucer's involvement. For example, Dorothy Bethurum, who has examined Chaucer's role as narrator in his shorter love visions as well as in *Troilus*, comes to an opposite conclusion about

Chaucer's attitude. She notes that in the *Book of the Duchess*, the *House of Fame*, the *Parliament of Fowls*, and in the *Prologue* to the *Legend of Good Women*, he uses the mask of the Fool, what he "hit upon as the ideal reflector of life's extravagances, and he could have found none better. He is the ancestor of Swift in presenting these idealizations through a dullard who can not understand or respond. Through his pose he keeps the true comic spirit, maintaining the *ewige kleine*. It does not condemn the ideal, but marks it as pretty far from normal human experience."[32] But Bethurum contends that Chaucer's attitude of detachment and ignorance undergoes change in *Troilus*, and despite the fact that he keeps insisting upon his lack of involvement in love and upon his reliance upon "myn auctour," he is more deeply involved in the story of Troilus and Criseyde than in any other of his stories. Love moves Chaucer deeply, and in *Troilus* "his identification with his characters is so complete that he cries out in pain as the story moves to its sad end."[33] While Chaucer pretends to be detached, he is actually identifying with his subject, and the whole poem may be read as an exemplum written in honor of the religion of Love. Bethurum speaks of Chaucer's "imprisonment in the story." He had indeed the same freedom as any artist to treat history as he wished. But he chose to write about the conditions under which a woman betrays her lover. "The effect of Chaucer's insistence on his lack of freedom is that he maneuvers himself into exactly the position of the reader, and his intense involvement is that of the fascinated reader or hearer, knowing how the story must end and dreading to see Troilus sign his soul out to the Grecian tents where Criseyde lay that night." Just as Dante has it both ways by showing God's justice and yet expressing his pity for man, so Chaucer has it both ways by showing the ideal vision of love and then offering his "sober realistic comment on it." As narrator Chaucer contrasts polarities of book and experience, and love of this world and God. "From his appreciation of *both* worlds comes his incomparable poise."[34]

But Donaldson takes the most extreme view. He describes the involvement of the narrator as "wildly emotional." Criseyde "is seen almost wholly from the point of view of a narrator who is so terribly anxious to have us see only the best in her, and not to see the worst even when it is staring both us and him in the face, that when he is afraid we will see something he doesn't want us to see, he plunges in to muddy up the water so that we can't see anything clearly. Indeed, in order to understand Criseyde properly we should first have to send the narrator to a psychoanalyst for a long series of treatments and then ask him to rewrite the poem on the basis of his own increased self-knowledge."[35] The narrator, in Donaldson's view, is the living dominant reality in the poem, and what is most important is that he loves Criseyde "with something of the avuncular sentimentality that Dickens lavishes on several of his more intolerable heroines." It is the narrator who makes Criseyde's characterization complex. Because he loves her he will excuse her and while he is forgiving her he gives us reasons to dislike her. Chaucer in his own person interferes with the work of his narrator:

> At some of the moments when his narrator is striving most laboriously to palliate Criseyde's behaviour, Chaucer, standing behind him, jogs his elbow, causing him to fall into verbal imprecision, or into anticlimax, or making his rhetoric deficient, or making it redundant—generally doing these things in such a way that the reader will be encouraged almost insensibly to see Criseyde in a light quite different from the one that the narrator is so earnestly trying to place her in.[36]

Donaldson also turns to the narrator to explain what the epilogue means. Through the narrator Chaucer offers at the end not only the moral that human love and everything human is unstable and illusory, but also the complex qualification of that moral. The narrator who suffers an "internal kind of warfare," who is devoted to Troilus, to Pandarus, and above all to Criseyde, has been reluctant to find that their happiness comes to nothing. To avoid this seemingly simple conclusion,

> he has done everything he could. He has tried the epic high road; he has tried the broad highway of trite moralization; he has tried to eschew responsibility; he has tried to turn it all into a joke; and all these devices have failed. Finally, with every other means of egress closed, he has subscribed to Troilus' rejection of his story. . . . Once having made the rejection, he has thrown himself into world-hating with enthusiasm. But now the counterbalance asserts its power. For the same strong love of the world of his story that prevented him from reaching the Christian rejection permeates and qualifies his expression of the rejection.

> Having painfully climbed close to the top of the ridge he did
> not want to climb, he cannot help looking back with longing at
> the darkening but still fair valley in which he lived; and every
> resolute thrust forward ends with a glance backward.[37]

Having his narrator behave in this way Chaucer achieves a
meaning only great poetry can have. The ending of poem
makes us aware of Christ's mother and a heaven that is
attainable through human experience.

Still another view of the narrator is offered by Allen T.
Gaylord, who claims that the "avuncular" Chaucer is also the
narrator-actor who uses the strategy of entrapment. Gaylord's
interpretation depends entirely on the premise that Chaucer
wrote his poem for a specific kind of audience, and then he read
it to them to "trap them" into accepting his belief that divine
love is preferable to profane love. While Gaylord admits that
the narrator is not always talking to a special age group, "a
most significant section" of the listeners is "noble, interested in
love, and young." Gaylord says "that it is possible to consider
Troilus as specifically shaped, with affectionate malice
aforethought, for a very special audience of young nobles,
about whom we know very little; but it is also possible, and, for
us, surely preferable to say that the form the poem takes is a
rhetorically fitting and artistically appealing snare to engage
first the sympathy and then the understanding of any hearer or
reader whose 'youth' is not naturally inclined toward
Reason."[38]

Thus our very clever Chaucer is represented as providing for
the dynamic structure of the poem by playing a very special
kind of game. He uses a medieval type of structure employing
rhetoric and dialectic and building continuously to a total
vision of order and harmony. The "trap" is intended for the
reader as much as for the fictional listener. "It is only that the
modern response, when finally the trap has sprung shut, has
been with some pain to suggest either that the whole thing was
not really sporting or that the trap was not really there at all."[39]
Perhaps the trap is not "fair," but to recognize its role is to share
with Chaucer a sense of delight in his "pardonable double
dealing" and ironic method of expression.

So the double-dealing Chaucer comes before his audience of
lovers, who are young in heart if not necessarily in age, and
establishes a relationship with them as their representative
voice; he is not writing in praise of the god of love but he is

mainly concerned with the condition of his followers. He is actually preparing the "tender trap" for those who are servants of the god of love, hoping to lead them to self-understanding. This trap is not one that operates through unpleasant, mechanical means; it is supposed to operate by making the young lovers in the audience realize what the older ones and Chaucer have known from the very beginning. In other words, the trap is effective only to the degree that the audience supplies the moving parts, and Chaucer's conclusion becomes a confirmation of what they have begun to think.

Chaucer has to establish a relationship between his audience and Troilus. The audience is made to gradually change its identification with Troilus. As it grows wiser the hero loses his insight. At the end, Chaucer allows Troilus to attain vision and Chaucer appeals to the "yonge fresshe folkes." He uses the sense of history to show that Troilus is a part of the present and the past, and no different from any modern lover. How should the lovers in his audience who have heard Troilus speak of the joys of love and then have witnessed his destruction react when his vision has at least been "restored, completed and elevated? It is at this point that the jaws of Chaucer's trap spring tenderly shut." Now he turns to the audience of young lovers addressing them as audience for the last time: "Swich fyn hath, lo this Troilus for love!" For the sly old man has in effect invited them "to identify their service of the god of Love as something fundamentally pagan, which is as close as Chaucer comes to calling it the service of the Devil. It asks them not to give up the world but to live in it like Christians." This is a strange ending for a poem of love, but considering the author's intent, the "most perfectly logical."[40]

But as we have already noted, other critics do not agree that the ending is "most perfectly logical." For example, from a philosophical point of view, Reiss judges the ending to be illogical unless we distinguish between Chaucer's and the narrator's point of view. S. Nagarajan goes even further than Reiss and contends that the narrator's point of view is simplistic, extreme, and unwise, while to Gaylord the Chaucer who asks his readers to give up love and live like Christians is compassionate, brotherly, and charitable. To Nagarajan the Chaucer who offers such advice would lack a "first rate intelligence." For the moral of the *Troilus*, which reflects an unsophisticated, simple-minded view of the world, is to be attributed to the narrator, not to Chaucer.

Nagarajan rejects the opinion of A. T. Gaylord, and R. M. Durling who equate Chaucer's wisdom with the narrator's wisdom.[41] The narrator tells us that Troilus is the Faithful Lover *par excellence*. He placed Criseyde under an intolerable strain of loyalty. There were extenuating circumstances which explain her behaviour, for she knew that Troy was doomed. Furthermore, Troilus lived with a hopelessly ideal, false view of love; namely, that it is unchanging. He worshipped Fortune and his love was subject to Fortune. But he learned the true lesson that since real love, which is the love of God, is not subject to Fortune, so we must all love God. Such a philosophy, says Nagarajan, is "extremely characteristic of an un-sophisticated mind." If we must take the conclusion as "the moral endorsed by Chaucer, not only are we obliged to stand the poem on its head, but we provoke the question whether all human love shares the characteristics of Troilus' love so that the alternative to it is fairly represented as celestial love."[42] Nagarajan insists that Chaucer understood the danger of generalizing Troilus' experience into two alternatives, and Chaucer used the narrator to provide the reader with the kind of critical detachment that enables him to distinguish between the dramatic sincerity of the narrator and the personal sincerity of the poet. "The tone of the narrator varies greatly in the poem. He appears as a well-meaning, rather simple person, somewhat child-like in his lack of sophistication. Sometimes he is enthusiastic, sometimes grave, sometimes exhortatory, sometimes naively remonstrative with his audience not to be unreasonable in their demands, sometimes he is laborious in his explanations. Chaucer manipulates him skilfully to shift the lights of the story."[43] The so-called "wisdom" of the epilogue is that of the narrator. There is no reason for assuming that it is Chaucer's.

Like Nagarajan, Murray F. Markland argues that the narrator's voice is not Chaucer's voice. The narrator has a "fuzzy" mind and is not a discriminating man, and his "point of view amused Chaucer and is supposed to amuse us. We are to see that it is beside the point and to laugh at the posturing required to maintain it."[44] But we are not to agree with the narrator. We are to see—as he does not—that his moral vision is irrelevant, that he is being a little stuffy in insisting on it. "Those seventeen stanzas—in what they say, in their maunder-ing, in their divergence and catching up, in their solemn morality, in their solemn simplicity—are absolutely consistent with the character of the narrator. Their seeming rejection of all that has been said results less from moral conviction than from moral timidity, less from surety than from doubt, less from singleness of sight than from ambivalence."[45] The inept, disorderly ending then characterizes a narrator "who superimposes on the logic of the events (the story as given him) his own vision of the consequences of such action." And this ending is made up of several endings. "It is as if the tentative narrator is doing an excess of the right things to protect himself. Like a departing guest, he says good-by again and again, finding it difficult to go. . . . And watching that fussy narrator fumbling to a close does not give to the story of illicit love a 'high level of moral elevation' which would be a rejection of the story, but a high level of comic humanity."[46] The disorder of the epilogue is deliberate, artistic disorder by means of which in the voice of a narrator, Chaucer ridicules the views which would deny the meaningfulness of human love.

Whether in the end any of, some of, or none of the attitudes expressed by the narrator which the commentators have tried very hard to reconcile are the views held by Chaucer is impossible to determine in any definitive way. And what one reads into the tone or attitude is after all dependent upon *a priori* notions of what is wisdom. An orthodox Christian might assume that the conclusion offers the ultimate wisdom. But many Catholics today might find the extremism of the epilogue quite unacceptable. There is a strong possibility that Catholics in Chaucer's day and Chaucer himself would have felt the same way. Could the Chaucer who saw life "whole" have viewed the Troilus and Criseyde relationship as a paradigm? He must have known as we do that not all women are faithless and that men do not necessarily die because they have lost the love of a faithless woman. He must have been as aware as we are that many men and women do have good and lasting love relationships. Why then would he have been naive enough to interpret the love story of Troilus and Criseyde as the archetypical pattern for all love affairs? Even as a Catholic he would have recognized the reductionist fallacy inherent in the view that the only true happiness for man is to be sought in divine love.

It is, therefore, tempting to believe with Reiss, Nagarajan and Markland that Chaucer is not to be identified with the narrator of the poem. But I do not believe that such a view is any less hypothetical than the one which asserts positively that the narrator and Chaucer have identical beliefs. As long as we pursue the ephemeral Chaucer in all of his poems, we will end up with a ghostly quarry who eludes the historical hunt. The narrator may or may not be expressing the views of the "real" Chaucer. Also we should be wary of the hyperbolic effusions of those who write about the narrator as if he were the most important character in the poem. When Sister Ann Barbara Gill writes that "the narrator bears the same fundamentally fixed yet seemingly varying attitude to his fictive world as that of the divine Maker to the cosmos,"[47] we have a clear example of this kind of distortion.

The narrator performs a valuable but not indispensable function for *Troilus*. His point of view enhances the telling of the tale, but the tale could be told without him, whereas the absence of Troilus and Criseyde and even Pandarus would not give us Chaucer's poem. Perhaps the sanest comment on the narrator comes from Stephen Knight: "In each of his five formal appearances, the four prohemia and his final speech, the narrator has prompted in the reader an attitude towards the poem at the relevant stage. The five formal appearances do not link up into a coherent characterization of the narrator; rather, they are carefully organised commentaries on the material of the books to which they belong, and on the poem as far as it has gone at the time."[48] But if Knight is correct, then we would have to discard the discussions of many critics who have expended so much effort in explaining the character of the "narrator," and we would have to agree with Bertrand H. Bronson that "nine-tenths of this talk [about the narrator] is misguided and palpably mistaken."[49]

Several interesting attempts have been made to identify what R. S. Crane calls the "shaping principle" of the poem. Robert O. Payne believes that *Troilus* is a success precisely because it utilizes conventional and "more academically orthodox poetics." He claims that the kind of criticism practiced in the rhetorical manuals will yield a more satisfactory analysis of *Troilus* than of any other major Chaucerian pieces, "and there is something to be learned from the observation that, generically speaking, the conventionality of *Troilus and Criseyde* lies principally in its conformity to one type of stylistically elaborate, morally tendentious, and emotionally moving narrative defined theoretically in the textbooks." The poem is not a romance, a love vision, an allegory, a legend, or complaint or any one of the structural types associated with the French tradition, but "Dante's words can be made into as accurate a historical definition as we are likely to have of *Troilus and Criseyde*; it is an exercise of the eloquent and courtly vulgar tongue (though not entirely in the high style); it is a piece of rhetoric set to music, to move the hearts of men." Thus the shaping principle of the poem seems to be *rhetorical*, and Payne specifies the exact sense in which the poem may be viewed as "rhetoric set to music."

> All of these things—consciousness of a situation in which speaker confronts audience, awareness of an element of pretense as necessary to communication in the situation, agreement to tolerate specified artifices to keep the pretense working, identification of similarities and differences in speaker's and audience's reactions to a subject, the search for a larger ground of agreement between them (i.e., persuasion) —all of these things constitute a large part of what we mean by the term "rhetorical," even when it is used in a limited historical sense.[50]

Payne devotes considerable attention to the specified artifices which are the figures most often employed by the poem, and they turn out to be *digressio, sententia, comparatio, exclamatio, translatio, frequentio, repetitio*, and *traductio*. The most fundamental aim of poetry in the rhetorical tradition is the "double validation of truth by finding it in the past and making it live in the present." Chaucer achieves the double validation by utilizing the techniques of selection, amplification, and abbreviation, the means by which an old style can be reconstituted. Four agencies of effect are utilized: action, characterization, lyric interpolation, and authorial commentary.

Payne disposes of action by pointing out that Chaucer and the rhetoricians believed that action was merely the potential which style develops. The rhetorician rarely discusses the plotting of an action, and Chaucer hardly ever bothers to invent one. The characterization is also viewed as being in strict accord with the rhetorician's notion of a static personality. "Fixity and fitness—character established and unchanging, given typical significance through the selection of attributes consistent with the status of the character in the action; these are the controlling ideas in the presentation of character for the rhetoricians, as they evidently were for many medieval poets as well."[51] For example, the so-called reality of Criseyde is merely the illusion created by set blocks of exposition by the narrator and some kind of non-representational monologue. Each character is a means by which the author can develop his theme of courtly love. "Each character is given a set of constant characteristics with respect to that love, and in no case are we given any information—especially concerning motivation—that does not contribute to the elucidation of the nature of that love. What we have in the three characters is a series of types, superbly realized and vitalized, which, taken together as an element in the structure of the poem, give Chaucer an area in which to develop an effectively complex presentation of courtly love, and prepare for a commentary upon it."[52]

The lyric interpolations or *amplificatio* are important for conveying the meanings implicit in the structure. There are in the *Troilus* a series of lyrics and apostrophes set into the structure of the narrative which offer Chaucer the opportunity to move into an evaluation of the action. The examples appear in the first *canticus Troili* (I, 400-434); Antigone's song (II, 827-875); Criseyde's *aubade* (III, 1422-1442); Troilus' answering *aubade* (III, 1450-1470); Troilus' second *aubade* (III, 1702-1708); Troilus' hymn to Love (III, 1744-1771); Troilus' predestination soliloquy (IV, 958-1082); Troilus' "Wher is myn owene lady" (V, 218-245); Troilus' plaint to the empty palace (V, 540-553); second *canticus Troili* (V, 638-658). These ten lyrics, according to Payne, constitute a kind of "distillation of the emotional progress of the poem" with their thematic imagery functioning like that of the imagery of a sonnet sequence. "They lead away from the action for its own sake to the final level of commentary containing Chaucer's digressions as author-interpreter."[53]

Although Payne ends by noting that *Troilus* is more than a rhetorical poem because its endless concentric ironies constitute Chaucer's way of reconciling human wisdom with human limitation, Payne's emphasis on rhetoric results in the kind of discussion which gives more emphasis to the ten lyrics than to the characters who offer no more than nonrepresentational monologues. Nor do I see how the ten lyrics can be said to supply the thematic progress of a poem that has 8239 lines. Few readers would miss the ten lyrics if they were omitted, but surely they would miss Troilus, Criseyde and Pandarus. The limitation of such rhetorical analysis is obvious. Too much is made of the lyrics and the narrative commentary at the expense of the characterization. To know that Chaucer used *descriptio*, and *amplificatio* and *contentio* is interesting, but many mediocre medieval writers used rhetorical devices and to concentrate on them is to pass up the "kernel" for the "chaf."

As for the narrative structure of *Troilus*, there are those who praise its marvelous symmetry and those who extol its asymmetry. Patch refers to the "logical precision" of its symmetry.[54] Kemp Malone believes it is possible to diagram the structure of *Troilus* as a W, with the three high points representing (1) the scenes before Troilus falls in love; (2) the major love scene between Troilus and Criseyde, and (3) Troilus' appearance in the eighth sphere while the two low points designate the scenes in which Troilus admits his love to Pandarus and sees his brooch on Diomede's coat-armor.[55] Meech uses the inverted V to describe the rising and falling action of *Troilus* as medieval tragedy.[56] Gill claims the action of the poem is a circular structure based on the metaphor of the wheel of Fortune.[57] T. R. Price believes that *Troilus* reveals "consummate skill in dramatic construction," and he identifies fifty scenes in the "drama."[58] Francis Utley objects to calling the poem a drama, and he identifies 83 episodes in dialogue or monologue form with 35 digressions or transitions.[59] But Rudolf Fischer and Meech find only 72 dramatic scenes in *Troilus*.[60]

Gerry Brenner distinguishes two kinds of structure: "one type of narrative structure, the surface harmony, that narrative repetition creates, lends itself easily to a metaphor of harmony." The other type of structure, "the underlying chaos that inverted parallels, ironic foreshadowing, and multiple points of view wreak upon the surface harmony, lends itself to a metaphor of cacaphony and disorder." The second type of structure is "merely a negative way of bolstering a harmonic view of the poem." For the symmetry of the narrative structure can be seen as another ally for the Christian, otherworldly, deterministic, and tragic view of the poem's ultimate meaning.[61]

William Provost offers what he describes as the first "rigorous," "objective," "professional," "non-interpretive," structural analysis of *Troilus*. He lists the following units: the five books; 37 objective and 23 subjective time units; 122 narrative units consisting of direct narrative, summary narrative, narrator's comment, description, invocation, and 33 structural devices consisting of proems, lyrics, temporal references, dreams, letters, and epilogues.[62]

To muddy the waters even more, Robert M. Jordan judges the structure of *Troilus* to be like the structure of a Gothic cathedral. Defending Chaucer against Sydney's and Dryden's views that the irregularities in Chaucer's style are signs of a primitive genius, Jordan finds aesthetic justification for the form of *Troilus* in the medieval principle of inorganic art. He attempts to show that the structure of the poem is by analogy "of the Gothic fashion, toward direct participation in the total harmony of Creation."[63] Like the Gothic cathedral, the poem is built of inert materials put together in an organic quantitative mode. The love story is offered as a finite preconceived whole. The reader is placed outside the action as the narrator summarizes the entire tale in the opening stanzas. The narrator has to dispose of the elements of a known totality, and he helps to distinguish those which characterize non-organic narrative. This narrator contributes to the effect of the poem as being on the one hand a finished, sophisticated, complex work and this complexity, on the other hand, gives the illusion that it is a conversational, naive, simple work of non-art. The narrator's commentary imparts verticality or elevation of perspective—two distinct levels of action, one serious, and one humorous, providing the illusion of the story, and also proving the reality which breaks the illusion. This compound quality is illustrated by the scene in which Troilus is described as falling in love. The narrator also presents the sequential or horizontal progress of the tale through his comments at the beginning of each book to the complex epilogue to indicate the stages in the movement of the action. Jordan is aware that "the characters and episodes of a poem—especially a Chaucerian poem—lack the fixity of stone and glass and therefore cannot be reduced into the mathematical regularity of a Gothic interior." But he maintains that *Troilus* "exhibits the same impulse to clarify structure by delineating individual parts of the whole. The function of line in the Gothic interior, dividing the whole into parts and parts of parts, is approximated in *Troilus* by the voice of the narrator."[64]

Jordan analyzes the passage in which Troilus falls in love to show how it uses the "additive or aggregative mode." The narrative voice divides the poem into discrete parts through repetition and dilation. The governing principle is the Pythagorean and Platonic one which conceives of the whole serving as a macrocosmic model for its inner portions:

> The wholeness of the poem, as delineated by particularly elaborate framing statements—the proem to Book One and the peroration that concludes the poem—is reflected in the whole of the component parts. The same relationship is analogous to that between the wholeness of Plato's cosmic exemplar and the wholeness of its constituent parts. The same relationship is evident in a Gothic wall section, the whole arch being the model for the constituent arches deduced from it. In all cases the structural integrity of the part precludes a continuous, organic relationship among the parts and between part and whole. The principle of creation is not growth but aggregation.[65]

The inorganic unity is not the kind the organicist speaks of but is achieved through a type of "forced accommodation." The parts do not "grow"; they are "made." Each book of the *Troilus* is analyzed in terms of the narrator's role. His apparent gaucherie and overstatement increase our awareness of how closely the poem follows the Gothic penchant for clarification. Thus *Troilus* reveals an architectural and poetic preconception of truth. The cosmic structure is revealed at the end where the truths of divine perception appear. The incongruous comic relief of the narrator, his clownishness, and naiveté can be compared to the "diversity of subjects depicted in the cathedral statuary. . . ."

There is no real psychological motivation in the poem; Criseyde's role is to demonstrate the universal truth of love. In his "Go little Book" Chaucer drops the mask of the persona and acknowledges himself as a man of letters and serious poet who is aware of the problems of linguistic morphology, and who is concerned with the integrity of the text. This is the *real* Chaucer. His tone changes at the end—serious, free of ironic humor—in the concluding one hundred lines of lyric grandeur. Chaucer abandons the artifices of his narrator, not to divorce himself from the fiction "but in order to place himself along the way to salvation, the actual way, through the illusion and delusions of this world." In the palinode (V, 1842-1848) Chaucer transcends his poem as Chaucer himself is transcended by the Creator. Troilus in the eighth sphere achieves a vision which comprehends morality—from temporal life to eternal life. In its explicit Gothic fashion it has made clear the separation between fiction and reality. The narration alone recalls present reality. But the final stanza offers the Christian perspective, the revelation, the Dantesque prayer. The final stanza is the pinnacle upon which the structural forces of the poem converge. The ultimate shift of perspective brings the poem, the poet, and ourselves into communion with the divine order of creation. This is the ultimate upward thrust of the poem where the vertical structure reaches completion. What Dante said of the *Commedia* is true of the *Troilus and Criseyde*: "The work ends in God himself."[66]

The entire reading experience has to be reevaluated in the light of one stanza. Backward and downward, it is complete in temporal and spatial dimensions. When the horizontal and vertical dimensions are brought together, they offer magnificent testimony to the glory of God and the continuity of all his works. "Recalling the envoi, we recognize that God has indeed sent the poet the powers to transform his tragedy into comedy. For in the vision of God there can be no tragedy since there is no change. The distinctions between past and present, life and death, man's fictions and his truths, dissolve in the eternal simultaneity of divine vision."[67] Thus we see that Chaucer's poem and the Gothic cathedral are analogous. They use "fundamental relationships of the universe to create structures which are in touch with Truth: the mathematical ratios which order the cathedral order creation and have their source in the perfection of the Creator, and the stages of perception which order the poem order man's ascent through illusion and lead upward to total perception, which is God. Throughout its course *Troilus* emphasizes the processes of construction as does the Gothic cathedral, and the culmination of the continuing restless movement among its articulated parts and perspectives is the arrival in eternal stillness."[68]

The analogy used by Jordan to explain the structure of the poem is based on the principle of transposition. This tendency to talk about poetry in terms of music, or painting, or architecture has been a characteristic of some types of critical discourse, particularly at the end of the last century, but transposition is not in very good repute today. To compare the effects of different art forms is to run afoul of misused analogy. Jordan is aware that his analogy is questionable, because, as he notes, stone and glass are not words. But he tries to overcome this difficulty by insisting that stone and glass and words have the same "impulse" to clarify structure by delineating parts of the whole. But he does not explain how either a word or a stone can have an "impulse," and he compounds the difficulty by anthropomorphizing the concept. Furthermore, Jordan's description of the process of delineating parts of a whole is a description that might apply equally well to the process of making a cake. To make anything we usually have to relate parts to a whole.

Just as Payne finds the thematic distillation of the whole poem in ten lyrics, so Jordan allots a disproportionate emphasis to the concluding stanza of the *Troilus*: "The work ends in God himself." An interpretation which makes God the manufacturer of the cathedral and the poem and which extinguishes the distinction between divinity and poetry is both mystical and mystifying.

Some commentators still talk about Chaucer's stylistic clarity. But E. Talbot Donaldson uses the expression "elusion of clarity" to describe Chaucer's penchant for utilizing "diaphanously clear statements utterly destructive of one another's meaning."[69] With wit and humor Donaldson describes some of the "substantial" examples of "elusion" in *Troilus*. For example, while Criseyde is described as a widow and "allone/Of any frend to whom she dorste hir mone," (I, 97-98), inventory reveals that she is not alone, living in an "unfashionable part of town," in a "one-room walk-up." Donaldson's inventory includes:

> Item, folk, an unknown number but still enough to be called folk, who were her servants and met Pandarus at the door; Item, two other ladies in the paved parlour besides "she". . . . Item, one book with one literate maiden reading it aloud. . . . Whoever her husband was, he had left her well off, and that *meinee* she kept was a large one; later, three of the ladies who formed part of her household are given names . . . and include at least two nieces, while the total number of women-in-waiting is said to form . . . a large crowd. And then, of course, there was uncle Pandarus, . . . a man eminent enough in Troy so that . . . he sometimes has

to spend the whole day with King Priam . . . and is the best
friend of Hector's younger brother Troilus.[70]

Donaldson offers an amusing description of the ambiguities
in the famous "overcrowded" bedroom scene, and he reminds
us of the "elusion of clarity" in the characterizations of Troilus
and Criseyde. He concludes that "for Chaucer truth was never
simple, always so qualified that the only way to express it
satisfactorily was to mix statements of fact with many
contradictory truths. In a way, the image of his poetry is that of
the false report and the true one which unite inseparably to get
out of the House of Rumor into history. To try to analyse the
'truth' in poetry of this kind is at best humiliating, and one can
only confess that, compared with the poetry, the best in this
critical kind are but shadows, and neither learning nor
imagination much amends them."[71]

But the desire to explicate the concept of ambiguity in art is
insatiable. The most famous attempt is William Empson's
definition: ambiguity is "any verbal nuance, however slight,
which gives room for alternative reactions to the same piece of
language."[72] Yet Schlomith Rimmon, who has scrutinized the
modern analyses of ambiguity in the work of Copi, Wheel-
wright, Kaplan, Kris, Perry, and Nowottny, to name only a
few, rejects Empson's definition. In Rimmon's view, it is too
broad, and actually describes double or multiple meaning or
plurisignation. Rimmon also denies that irony, paradox,
allegory, and symbolic complexity are forms of ambiguity. She
upsets common usage by arguing that the only real type of
ambiguity is disjunctive where the separate meanings function
in the interpretation of a work as alternatives, "excluding and
inhibiting each other."[73] As I interpret her definition, she would
maintain that *Troilus* is truly ambiguous if, like James' *The
Turn of the Screw*, it elicits two or more contradictory
hypotheses that cannot under any circumstances be reconciled
and in effect exclude each other.

Since William Empson is the only New Critic with a special
interest in the subject of ambiguity in *Troilus*, I will examine
his analysis first before I turn to the Chaucerian specialists
who, unlike Donaldson, feel that they can dissipate the
"elusion of clarity" in Chaucer's poem. By analyzing some
lines from *Troilus*, Empson hopes to demonstrate that ambiguity was already in full swing during the medieval period and

was *native* to the English language. According to Empson, *Troilus* is "one of the most leisurely, simplest as to imagery" poems, and employs a second type of ambiguity "in which two or more alternative meanings are fully resolved into one."[74] (Rimmon would, of course, deny that this is ambiguity.) However, Empson finds a passage in Book II which he judges to have lines of concentrated imagery that remind him of Shakespeare's mature style. In this passage Criseyde guesses Pandarus' meaning in relation to Troilus' unhappiness, and seems to be outraged:

> "What! is this al the joye and al the feste?
> Is this youre reed? Is this my blisful cas?
> Is this the verray mede of your byheeste?
> Is all this paynted proces seyd, allas!
> Right for this fyn?"   (II, 421-425)

Empson tells us that at first he thought that the meaning of this passage might have been clear in Chaucer's day, and that it acquired a patina of subtlety in the course of time. But he claims that the *NED* shows that time has faded rather than enriched the original ambiguity. Then he reminds us of the medieval meanings of the following words: *mede*—"a bribe," "merit," "a meadow," "drink with honey"; *byheste*—"a vow," "a promise," "a command"; *proces*—"series of actions," "the course of a narrative," "proceedings in an action at law," "a procession"; *fyn*—"end," "object of an action," "death," "a contract," "money offered in the hope of exemption."

Empson then refers to lines spoken by Pandarus to clarify the meaning of *byheste*:

> "Now understonde, that I yow nought requere
> To bynde yow to him thorugh no byheste,
> But only that ye make hym bettre chiere
> Than ye han don er this, and moore feste,
> So that his lif be saved atte leeste." (II, 358-364)

In this context *byheste* may mean, "I do not ask it, as a *command* from your guardian, that you should bind yourself to him (permanently or sinfully)," or it may mean, "I do not ask you to bind yourself to him with anything so definite as a *vow*." Empson calls attention to the last two lines of Pandarus' speech in the following passage:

> "Thenk ek, how elde wasteth every houre
> In ech of yow a partie of beautee;
> And therfore, er that age the devoure,
> Go love; for old, ther wol no wight of the.
> Lat this proverbe a loore unto yow be;
> 'To late ywar, quod beaute, whan it paste';
> And elde daunteth daunger at the laste."
>
> (II, 393-399)

Here *ywar* may mean "prudent" or "experienced"; *to late* has the sense of "then first when too late"; or "going on until too late."

So Empson derives the following possible meanings:

(1) *First prudent when too late*, "I have found that one should be careful to avoid risks, perhaps such as that of never getting a lover, but, more strongly, such as are involved in unlawful satisfactions."

(2) *First conscious when too late*, "I have found too late that one should be determined to obtain satisfaction."

(3) *Having been prudent until too late*, "I have found that one can wait too long for the safest moment for one's pleasures."

(4) *Having been conscious till too late*, "I have found that one can seek one's pleasure once too often."

Pandarus means only the second and third meanings. Chaucer, not using irony here, but merely reflecting a melancholy view, means all four meanings. This particular example represents the fourth type of ambiguity distinguished by Empson in which alternative readings combine to make clear a complicated state of mind in the author. As for *elde daunteth daunger at the last*, since *daunteth* means "subdue" or "frighten" and *daunger* can mean "disdain," "imperiousness," "liability," "miserliness," and "power," Empson derives the following meaning from the line, when *elde* is interpreted as "old age":

> 'Old age will break your pride, will make you afraid of the independence you are now prizing; the coming of old age is stronger than the greatness of kings, stronger than all the brutal powers that you are now afraid of, stronger even than the stubborn passion of misers that defeat it for so long; you must act now because when you are old you will be afraid to take risks, and you may take heart because, however badly

> you are caught, it will be all the same after another century;
> even in your own lifetime, by the time you are an old woman
> you will have lived down scandal.'

But if *elde* is taken to mean "old woman" rather than "age,"

> the phrase interacts with the passing of beauty, whether after
> a life of sin or of seclusion . . . in the preceding line, and the
> old hag is finally so ugly that all the powers in *daunger* shrink
> away from the gloom of her grandeur, are either lost to her or
> subdued to her, and the amorous risks and adventures will be
> at last afraid to come near.

This line is a "straightforward ambiguity of the second type."
Now Empson is ready to return to the original lines:

> "Is this the verray mede of your byheeste?
> Is this youre reed? Is this my blisful cas?"

Criseyde's reply to Pandarus is then interpreted in the
following ways:
1. "Is this the wage that is offered to me in return for
obeying your commands?"
2. "Is this my inducement to be a good ward, that I must
continually have the trouble, and pain to think you so wicked,
of repelling solicitations?"
3. "Is this what your advice is worth? Is this what your
promise to look after me is worth?"
The "honest" meaning (wage) signifies contempt; the "dis-
honest" meaning contains an accusation. 1. "Is this why the
prince has been so friendly with you?" 2. "Is this what you
stand to make out of being my guardian?"
4. "Is this the meadow, or the beer you had promised me or
proposed for yourself?" "Is this my blissful case you have
described?" The two meanings of *byheeste* give Creseyde a
powerful weapon against Pandarus as guardian and go-
between.
    The puns in *fyn* and *proces* in "Is al this peynted proces seyd,
allas,/ Right for this fyn?" make the lines more complex. They
make us think of a "brightly coloured procession." *Peynted*
suggests frescoes in churches moving on, leading Criseyde "to
dusty death and the everlasting bonfire"; *proces* "hints at a
parallel with legal proceedings, ending where none of the

parties wanted, when at last the lawyers, like Pandarus, stop talking and demand to be paid," and also containing "a threat that she may expose him," and *peyn*-ted and *fyn* suggest "legal pains and penalties."

To whom do they suggest these things, the reader may ask, and there is no obvious reply. Admitting this, Empson contends that it all depends upon how carefully the passage is read. Whereas many passages in a long poem are clearly not read as carefully as parts of a short poem, the effect of imagery in a longer poem can be cumulative, and this particular section, an original addition, needs to have the meaning concentrated. Empson also admits that it may be unfair to use Chaucer to illustrate ambiguity because of the unfamiliar stress and the unfamiliar use of words. This latter point seems to me to be crucial. For aside from the fact that words had many meanings in Chaucer's day which they do not have today, there is also the mechanism of usage in a context which enables the reader to understand the idiom involved. Thus there is always the danger that where we see ambiguity, the particular meaning might have been transparently clear to Chaucer's contemporaries. The historicist might well argue that the most famous expression in Chaucerian biography *de meo raptu* is an ambiguity only because we do not really know the context in which the word was used, and the word's meaning would be clear once we knew what kind of rape was involved. Readers in Chaucer's age would pick out the meaning of *byheeste* just as the modern reader picks the meaning of *daunger* that suits the sense rather than trying to fit all the possible meanings of *daunger* into the context to make it ambiguous. Empson points out that such words as *lusty, leese* at first seemed complexly ambiguous to him, but he admits that there is no warrant for reading more than a second level ambiguity into these expressions:

> "Right yong, and stonde unteyd in lusty leese,
> Withouten jalousie or swich debat." (II, 752-753)

Leese has a variety of meanings: 'lies," "a snare for rabbits," "a quantity of thread," "a net," "a whip lash," and the "thong holding hunting dogs," "a contract giving land or tenements for life," "a term of years or at will," "open pasture land, picking fruit," "the act of coursing," and "a set of three, the symbol of companionship as opposed to passion." *Lusty* can mean "hearty," "delightful," or have sexual connotations of desire. But the only meanings Empson feels sure of are "I am not entangled in the net of desire," and "I am disentangled like a colt in a meadow." Why is he sure of these meanings and not of the others? The context gives it to him. In the end he doesn't like the passage, he finds it "clotted," and he advises writers not to imitate the ambiguity of such lines.

I do not know why these lines are clotted. They have always seemed to me to have a very obvious meaning once the proper meaning for the context is selected. It might well be argued that it is Empson who is doing the clotting by excising multiple meanings where none exist. This is Raymond Preston's view of Empson's interpretation of *paynted proces*: " . . . [E]very reader must judge for himself, from the many occasions when Chaucer uses the word *proces*, how near Criseyde is to saying: 'Good heavens, is *that* what all your plausible rigmarole was leading up to?' "[75]

Still Derek Brewer is probably correct when he judges Empson's unique *explication de texte* to be "one of the most brilliantly original and perceptive pieces of incidental criticism of Chaucer ever written."[76] But except for Preston's brief comment in his *Chaucer* and Ida Gordon's reference to Empson's definition of ambiguity in her *The Double Sorrow of Troilus*, I have not discovered any real concern with Empson's analysis in *Troilus* criticism. In fact, those who have made the term *irony* fashionable in Chaucer studies seem to be unaware that what they are describing is Empson's seventh type of ambiguity, the most complex kind. This is hardly the simple kind that Empson finds in *Troilus*.

The term *irony* has been used so often to characterize Chaucer's style that Alan T. Gaylord has warned against its overuse.[77] But not only is it *au courant* to write about Chaucer's irony; it is also necessary to offer special definitions of the word. Take, for example, the discussions of Anthony E. Farnham, Peter Elbow, and Charles Muscatine. In their analyses Chaucer is never viewed as a simple ironist. According to Farnham, Chaucer's special kind of irony involves the dialectical presentation of alternatives which, despite their categorical opposition to each other, share equally in the truth of experience. This is irony of a higher order. The central example of irony is to be found in the line, "What nedeth feynede loves for to seke?" (V, 1848). From one point of view this question implies a moral answer which the whole story is supposed to exemplify, namely, that the love of Troilus and Criseyde is feigned, that both practice a kind of deception and violate the requirement of absolute honesty. Since the only love free of corruption is heavenly love, we obtain the ironic implication of *Troilus'* theme: while man should try to live in an ideal fashion, he really cannot do so, and he will therefore not be perfect and he will suffer because he has practiced deception. So the irony is "the supreme defeated irony of all human existence."[78] Chaucer remains impartial because he also sees that the characters are not to blame. He is an ironist because he sees both sides of the question.

Peter Elbow goes one step further. He claims that Chaucer sees three sides of the question![79] We agree with one view, then disagree with it, and then end up accepting the validity of both views. Our ironic reaction involves a yes, no, and a yes. Therefore both positions are affirmed. Chaucer means what he says both ways and thus there is no joke as there would be if simple irony were involved or if meaning the opposite of what one says always involves a joke. The etiological confusion in *Troilus* reveals the nature of the irony. Troilus' speech on the question of free will and determinism seems to say that all is predetermined and the references throughout the poem to fortune and destiny reinforce this view. But at other times the characters make us think their actions are free. For example, Criseyde decides what she is going to do most of the time and seems to have free will, but then if we look more closely, she is not free. She does what she does because of her character. She is free and not free. Thus the following views are affirmed: all is determined and sad, there is freedom and happiness, and each one of these is affirmed through the denial of its contrary. These three responses affirm both positions and deny nothing. So Chaucer in this poem is not merely accepting two alternatives, but he also accepts the denial of these alternatives. He affirms nothing and denies nothing.

Charles Muscatine speaks also of the pervasive literary structural irony of the poem which reveals Chaucer's ironic view of life. This ironic view is what he calls "multi-consciousness," an awareness of different and opposite planes of reality. As a result we always get from Chaucer a double view of every situation which turns out to be neither the

romantic convention nor the naturalistic tradition but a
mixture of both. "If between Troilus and Pandarus the mixed
style produces an irony turning on human incapacity to see,
within Criseyde it produces an ambiguity turning on human
inability to be." Troilus is both weak and strong, both ideal and
quixotic. Too perfect a courtly lover, his antics make for humor
by means of which Chaucer shows understanding of the
insufficiency of courtly vision. Troilus is an archaic figure of the
past. The narrator deliberately produces a controlled ambiguity in relation to Criseyde in the following ways. He doesn't
know whether she had children or how long it was before she
became involved with Diomede; he doesn't know her age; he
doesn't know how afraid she really was of her first meeting
with Troilus, or whether she really believed that Troilus had
gone out of town when Pandarus invited her to his home, or
whether she loved Troilus at first sight. She is both calculating
and innocent, and we hold moral condemnation of her in
suspense because her ambiguity is her meaning. "Her betrayal
is symbolic rather than psychological. Criseyde's ambiguity is
the world's."[80] In the palinode, Chaucer reveals himself to be a
critical conservative who has mastered the characteristic
experiences of his age and offers the implied moral of the poem,
a criticism as well as a celebration of secular life.

What we have here is the thorny problem of definition. It is
one thing to speak of ambiguity in a general way, but it is still
another matter to narrow it down to the principle of irony. We
know that there are all kinds of irony, that the textbooks
distinguish Socratic, paradoxical, verbal, dramatic, Sopho-
clean, tragic or romantic irony. And to see how confusing
a discussion of this subject can be, we can read William
Empson's review of Wayne C. Booth's *A Rhetoric of Irony*, in
which Booth offers the concept of "stable or fixed irony."
Empson himself says, "I warmly agree with Professor Booth
that the term *irony* is applied much too loosely, so that it
becomes almost useless." Empson offers an interesting
definition of irony: "The basic situation for the trope of irony,
without which it would not have been invented, involves three
people. There is a speaker, 'A,' an understanding hearer, 'B,'
and a censor who can be outwitted, a stupid tyrant, 'C.' A
successful use of the pure form is not very frequent, because
people in the position of 'C' aren't such fools as you
think. . . . Or the ironist may be taking a balanced view,

trying to be friends with both sides, 'B' and 'C'; but even so one of them can be picked out as holding the more official position or straight-faced belief, and the literal meaning will support that one."[81]

Ida L. Gordon in her study *The Double Sorrow of Troilus: A Study of Ambiguities in Troilus and Criseyde* seems to be using the pure form of the trope of irony as Empson describes it. The understanding hearer "B" is trying to outwit "C" the censor. "C" in her view is the stupid reader who thinks that *Troilus* is a poem about the glory and tragedy of love, whereas "B," "the understanding hearer," knows that the poem is really describing the perversion of divine love into a love of a false "good" illustrated by the use of the *Consolation of Philosophy*. This meaning is evident in the way Chaucer uses the *Consolation* as a pervasive influence in phraseology, figures of speech, longer passages, close paraphrases, topics and motifs. There is nothing new about this view except that unlike others who examine the Boethian influence, Gordon insists that Chaucer uses the language of Boethius for ironic effects of a very complex kind. Chaucer uses Boethian arguments as if he were unaware of the conclusions of arguments in the *Consolation* and this is what makes for the ambiguity of the poem. Although Gordon uses the word *irony* throughout her book, she does not stop to define it in any way and assumes all the way through her analysis that what she means at a given time by ironic effect is what is usually meant by the term. She begins and ends her study by quoting Empson on ambiguity, but she takes an even stricter view than he does of what constitutes ambiguity. Whereas Empson uses the word in a loose sense to take in any verbal nuance which is capable of providing alternative reactions to the same words, she limits the meaning to "witty or deceitful verbal nuances."[82] But then she proceeds to equate ambiguity with irony, and in the end with allegory. This makes for confusion since her notion of irony seems to change at different times. However, it is important to note that while her study emphasizes ambiguity and irony and seems to promise a very unusual approach to the poem, the entire discussion depends upon her acceptance of what is after all a very orthodox position in Chaucerian criticism, namely, the Christian view that only divine love can lead to true happiness and that sexual passion is suspect. She believes that all the characters are utilized to illustrate this view. When Chaucer gives to Criseyde the statement that there is no worldly happiness (III, 813-816), she does not have the real understanding of what this argument is in Boethius and gives only part of it. The resultant irony consists in the fact that the proof of the falsity of worldly happiness is given to a character who is herself the instrument of the proof in action. Similarly, Troilus is made so blind by his physical passion that he says and does things which make for ironic effect; that is, his Christian allusions do not mean to him what they mean to us.

His speech on free will is ironic because although Troilus insists on predetermination, he arrives at a conclusion which is reached in the *Consolation* by false reasoning. Troilus is parodying Boethius in the speech. Boethius teaches that man's will is free and he may lose his freedom, as Troilus does, by choice. His own actions negate the point of his speech. There are several other passages which show us that Troilus does not love Criseyde for her goodness but for her physical body and as a result he is punished by Fortune. In the "Benign love, thow holy bond of thynges" (III, 1261), we see that Troilus is unable to distinguish between cupidinous and charitable love. This is a parodic passage which reminds the audience of the existence of a higher love. It is a travesty of the *Paradiso* and reminds us of the absurdity of elevating sexual passion into a religion. The convention which allows the blending of secular and Christian terms, the convention which describes the lovers' bed as "so heigh a place that thilke boundes may no blisse pace" (III, 1272), shows the *reductio ad absurdum* of the commonplaces which identify sexual passion with beatific vision. Since the poem has moral significance, the ironic effect of these lines cannot be overlooked. Gordon also offers an analysis of Pandarus which shows that his so-called practical wisdom is inadequate. In relation to Boethius all his comments on Fortune indicate that he doesn't really understand what Boethius means by Fortune which is controlled by Providence. Pandarus doesn't know that even bad Fortune is a good part of the providential order. Thus most of his warnings are ironic in that as a mentor he has incomplete wisdom.[83]

To illustrate her generalizations, Gordon deals with the language employed in certain ambiguous passages in the poem. For example, she discusses the use of the word *queynte* in Book V:

". . . O paleys desolate,
O hous of houses whilom best ihight,
O paleys empty and disconsolat,
O thow lanterne of which queynt is the light,
O paleys, whilom day, that now art nyght,
Wel oughtestow to falle, and I to dye,
Syn she is went that wont was us to gye!

O paleis, whilom crowne of houses alle,
Enlumyned with sonne of alle blisse!
O ryng, fro which the ruby is out falle,
O cause of wo, that cause hast ben of lisse!
Yet, syn I may no bet, fayn wolde I kisse
Thy colde dores, dorste I for this route;
And farwel shryne, of which the seynt is oute!"
(540-553)

J. F. Adams and D. W. Robertson have taken the position that Troilus' apostrophe to the vacant house is a means by which Chaucer condemns the idolatrous worship of love and lust. They both agree that the sexual pun on *queynt* in "O thow lanterne of which queynt is the light" is an "ironic pun" which is a "bitter comment on what it is that Troilus actually misses."[84] Gordon agrees with them and elaborates further on the idea that Troilus' deficient reasoning, and his valuation of sexual passion prevent him from recognizing the dirty joke in the sexual pun that we and Chaucer recognize. Troilus doesn't know the double meaning of *queynt* since it is the same blindness which prevents him from realizing that what he is missing is Criseyde's physical body rather than her spiritual nature. The pun on *queynte* takes on added significance when it is related to the light metaphor which is a figure for Christian charity. Gordon also identifies the sexual pun on *ruby* as do the other critics, but she does not believe that the puns involve self-betrayal or Freudian slips. Troilus is simply unaware of how defective his concept of profane love is.

Morton Bloomfield contends that the point of the paraclausithyron is simply the age-old theme of human mutability with the sexual overtones revealing that Troilus "wants to make love to Criseyde, but he also really loves her. She is not merely a sex object to him. If it were so, he could easily find other sexual entertainment when she departs. He

would not be so decent as he obviously is. Nor would he have
given her up as he did." So Bloomfield rejects what he calls the
"unChristian-Christian attitude" that condemns Troilus for
deifying his loved one and for enjoying sexual intercourse
outside of marriage. "Even if the love of the Christian God is
not available for such pagans, they must still be pursued by, if
they deviated one iota from His stern commandments, the
relentless puritanical Chaucer, who hated the Flesh, loved
nothing but the Trinity Itself and ignored God's creation and
handiwork. That they had no opportunity to know Him would
make no difference."[85] We cannot have a clearer indication of
how a commitment to a particular hypothesis leads to the
interpretation of puns in Chaucer in two diametrically opposed
ways.

For Gordon, however, the problem is simple; all ambiguities
can be explained in terms of Boethian language. She even finds
Boethian ideas in stanzas which do not specifically refer to
Boethius:

> Now sith it may nat goodly ben withstonde,
> And is a thing so vertuous in kynde,
> Refuseth nat to Love for to ben bonde;
> Syn, as hymselven liste, he may yow bynde.
> The yerde is bet that bowen wole and wynde
> Than that that brest; and therfore I yow rede
> To folowen hym that so wel kan yow lede.
> (I, 253-259)

According to Gordon, all that is necessary to show the
ambiguity of this summarizing stanza is to put capital letters to
love, he and *hym*. What she, of course, wants the reader to see is
that Chaucer is not only talking about the virtuous effects of
sexual love but of a higher love. The point is, however, that he
and hym are not capitalized while Love is, and that Gordon
herself provides the ambiguity by adding capitals.[86]

She finds an example of vague meaning in *The Invocation to
Venus* in the proem to the third book. This seems at first glance
to be pagan, but if in accordance with Christian symbolism
"heighe Jove" is identified with God "who commits to Fortune
by purveyance and disposicioun the permutation of thynges,"
then "Joves doughter deere" is ambiguous. Venus is not clearly
representative of sexual desire. If in the third stanza the "holy
spirit of Jove" is read as providence, then a claim can be made

for Venus to represent Divine Love as well as sexual desire.
Note how all this ambiguity depends upon Gordon's quite
arbitrary assumption that Jove in this passage is to be
identified with Christian providence.[87]

Still another example of Gordon's tendency to intrude
Boethian philosophy where the passages do not readily conjure
up such associations is her discussion of the following passage
where Criseyde reveals the fears she has about beginning a
love affair with Troilus:

> But right as when the sonne shyneth brighte,
> In March, that chaungeth ofte tyme his face,
> And that a cloude is put with wynd to flighte,
> Which oversprat the sonne as for a space,
> A cloudy thought gan throrugh hire soule pace,
> That overspradde hire brighte thoughtes alle,
> So that for feere almost she gan to falle.
>
> That thoughte was this: "Allas! syn I am free,
> Sholde I now love, and put in jupartie
> My sikernesse, and thrallen libertee? . . .
> For love is yet the mooste stormy lyf,
> Right of hymself, that evere was bigonne;
> For evere som mystrust or nice strif
> Ther is in love, som cloude is over that sonne."
>   (II, 764-781)

As Gordon observes correctly, the analogy employed here is
rather odd. For while the sun is made to shine again after the
clouds have been chased away by the sun, Criseyde's cloudy
thoughts are not, as they logically should be if they follow the
analogy, "chased away from her soul," but instead the cloudy
thought "oversprat hire brighte thoughtes alle," and "som
cloude is over that sonne." Gordon calls this a paradoxical
expression. She finds the explanation for the analogy in
Antigone's song where Antigone tries to reassure Criseyde and
to defend love:

> "And whoso seith that for to love is vice
> Or thraldom, though he feele in it destresse,
> He outher is envyous, or right nyce,
> Or is unmyghty, for his shrewednesse,
> To loven for swich manere folk, I gesse,
> Defamen Love, as nothing of him knowe;
> Thei speken, but thei benten nevere his bowe!

> What is the sonne wers, of kynde right,
> Though that a man, for feeblesse of his yen,
> May nought endure on it to see for bright?
> Or love the wers, though wrecches on it crien?
> No wele is worth, that may no sorwe dryen.
> And, forthi, who that hath an hed of verre,
> Fro cast of stones war hym in the werre!"
>
> (II, 855-868)

What this passage says is that "the cloud is really the feeble sight of those who cannot look upon love's sun. . . ." And the passage contains an oblique allusion to the ideas expressed in the *Consolation*, which uses the whole complex of the imagery of sun, cloud, and feeble sight where the "wrecches" are those who "have their eien so wont to the derknesse of erthly thynges that thei ne may nat lyften hem up to the light cler sothfast-nesse."[88] It is only by the "light of his ynwarde sighte," if he will use it, that man can see what the "blake cloude of errour" covers, namely, that what love is really seeking is the "sover-ayne good" which is the "sun" of love. This, according to Gordon, explains the sun-cloud analogy: "Momentarily 'a cloude is put with wynd to flight' when a 'cloudy thought' passes through her 'soule,' overspreading all her 'brighte thoughtes'; for this 'cloudy thought' is really a glimpse of the truth. But it is only a passing glimpse, for she [Criseyde] fails to see the ambiguity of Antigone's song."[89] We might well be tempted to ask at this point, if Criseyde fails to see the ambiguity, why do *we* see it? The reasoning which equates a "cloudy thought" with a glimpse of the truth, Boethian fashion, is to say the least much too labored a distinction. There is always the possibility that Chaucer simply erred in writing this passage and we got a poor analogy from him. Modern Shakespearean critics are no longer afraid to say that Shakespeare was responsible for some of the bad poetry in the *Two Noble Kinsmen*. I do not see why we cannot assume there is a flaw in the text, nor can we eliminate the possibility of the use of Chaucer's tongue-in-cheek technique here; perhaps he was poking fun at Criseyde's so-called "fear" by using a ridiculous analogy.

Finally, Ida Gordon confuses the issue when she ends by labelling the ambiguity an allegory: "The 'allegory' is not simply saying one thing to mean another; it is allegory that works by providing a kind of living experience of what is allegorized, by involving the reader at all levels. At the most obvious level there are the many evocations of our pity for the lover's suffering. . . . But the irony ensures that our pity is not just the ready pity that suffering evokes; by opening our eyes to the nature of their love, it helps us to see the suffering as a consequence of the lovers' blindness, or 'sickness' of soul, and as such to be pitied in all charity."[90] First, the poem is viewed as an allegory, but then the usual definition of allegory is modified to mean a realistic poem that allegorizes. Secondly, the moral allegory uses irony to make us see what is wrong with the lovers; they refuse to follow Boethius' advice. So in the end, despite all the talk about ambiguity, there really is no ambiguity in *Troilus* because once we understand the medieval Boethian doctrine of love which "serves throughout as the touchstone for the irony," then the moral or meaning of the poem is quite clear. Ambiguity, irony, and allegory are terms used by the author to characterize what she considers to be Chaucer's very sophisticated use of language. But his so-called sophistication seems to consist essentially in his ability to emphasize one idea, namely, that suspect sexual passion is clearly inferior to the cosmic principle of divine love.

Gordon admits that in her analysis of the Boethian influence,

> there has been, inevitably, a distortion, a too narrow view of the poem. A poet does not write like a philosopher: what philosophy his poem is expressing becomes a part of a homogeneous whole that is the poem; and though we may look for its message in its philosophical or social relevance, we would be unwise to assume that this is the *raison d'être* of the poem. In *Troilus* the emotional effect of the poetry, the comedy, and the wit are important factors in the total effect; and while it is true that these are inseparable from its moralist relevance, who could say whether Chaucer wrote the poem in the way he did because he saw in the story an opportunity to illustrate ironically the Boethian topics, or whether he saw in the Boethian topics an opportunity to tell his story in these witty terms.[91]

There is, of course, a third alternative, namely that the Boethian material is not as important as Gordon would have us believe.

However, what seems to be undeniable is the fact that critics tend to interpret the ambiguities in *Troilus* in terms of *a priori* assumptions about the true nature of the poem. In Gordon's view, Chaucer clearly uses language to reveal a moral and religious theme. But if someone believes that Chaucer manipulates language to dramatize a comic vision of life, then he would write a book like Thomas Ross' *Chaucer's Bawdy*. In this work Ross offers a glossary of Chaucer's use of words which is based on the premise that he had an inordinate fondness for sexual innuuendo.

Ross reminds us that many changes have occurred since the Reverend Skeat could only bring himself to use the famous euphemism for *queynt, pudendum*, literally meaning in Latin, "the shameful thing" instead of glossing the word literally as vagina. (Both Robinson and Baugh and others still gloss the word in the same way as Skeat). Although critics of the past knew that Chaucer's poetry was complex because he was saying more than one thing at a time, they didn't realize the extent to which Chaucer's use of paronomasia pervaded his entire writings. It is hard to believe that in 1892 Lounsbury found only 2 puns in Chaucer.[92] F. N. Robinson found 9 in his 1933 edition and stated that puns were unusual. In 1957 he said puns were "relatively unusual." But such writers as Helge Kökeritz and Haldeen Braddy and Ross have helped us to become aware of what the older critics ignored.[93] No one today can read Ross' *Chaucer's Bawdy* without a heightened awareness of Chaucer's use of language any more than he can read Partridge's *Shakespeare's Bawdy* without the same effect. The significance of this kind of linguistic analysis is that it takes into account the paronomasia which former critics generally ignored. Ross is aware that others such as the patristic exegetes found *double entendres* in Chaucer's poetry, but for them the jests were always, as for Gordon, ultimately anti-erotic in their significance. But Ross claims that Chaucer "uses risqué words for one major purpose: to delineate comic characters and thus to make us laugh."[94] He admits that the equivoque cannot be identified with the scientific precision of lexicographical study, and that he often has to use words like possible, likely, and probable when identifying *double entendres*. In relation to *Troilus*, he identifies the comic obscenity in terms of such words as *bier, rise, die, ruby, ring, hol, sterve, serve, daunce, jape, spendeth, joly, grace*, and, of course, *queynt*.

We know how Gordon deals with the sexual pun on *queynt*, but Ross shows how it is "perhaps the most interesting of all the sexual double-meaning locutions in the poet's work." It is used in the tales told by the Miller, the Wife of Bath, the Merchant, the Knight, the Shipman, and in *Troilus*. Besides meaning "strange," "curious," "curiously contrived," "elaborate," "ornamented," "neat," "disdainful," "artful," "sly," "graceful," "make it," "difficult," "show pleasure," or "satisfaction," *queynt* was used as the forerunner of the modern word *cunt* and as a vulgarism for *vagina*. Abandoned, Troilus "can no longer behold his lover. She must leave Troy, and the metaphor for her absence 'Syn she is *queynt*, that wont was yow to lighte' (IV, 313) is an extinguished light." *Queynt* means "quenched," and "vagina," and *light* means "give you illumination" and "morally loose." Thus Ross gives the paraclausithyron an unequivocally sexual interpretation.

Although the myth of the puritanical Chaucer was dispelled long ago, some critics are repelled by the search for obscene puns in Chaucer. For example, Derek Brewer complains about the attribution of sexual meaning to the aforementioned line (IV, 313):

> Why should this peculiarly pointless crudity be attributed to Chaucer? What would the passage gain, compared with the vastness of the loss, if it were accepted? Any study of the occurrences of the word [*queynte*] in Chaucer shows that it was normal to use it without any obscene sense, and that on the over forty occasions on which Chaucer used the word, only three have the obscene sense, and that direct, without a quibble. Chaucer does indeed make more puns than I for one used to realise, and is on very rare occasions obscene, but this kind of quibble only reflects the normal obscenity of modern literature.[95]

It is, of course, possible to argue that *queynte* has a lewd meaning in Chaucer on more than three occasions. Even in the "refined" tale told by the Knight, Chaucer plays with the word *queynte* (2331-2337) and uses the *double entendre* in line 1042. Moreover, to state that Chaucer is "obscene on very rare occasions" is very odd indeed in view of the pervasive scatological element in his brand of humor. Thomas D. Cooke reminds us that the fabliau is the most "frequently represented" genre in the *Canterbury Tales*, and since, in his words, it contains "sexual activity and excremental action. . . ," it would quite appropriately use the obscenity when necessary.[96]

What conclusion can be drawn from this survey of the

various views which constitute the formalistic approach to *Troilus*? Obviously critics do not agree about the point of view, structure, language, or style of the poem. Some of them, like Jordan and Gordon, rely heavily on the historical reading, while others, like Empson and Ross, offer interpretations which are strongly influenced by modern conceptions of ambiguity and sexuality. But the exclusive concern with formal elements often leads critics to treat characters in the *Troilus* in a peripheral fashion to reinforce a rhetorical, structural or stylistic principle. Clearly Henry James was right; nothing is as important in art as the depiction of character. I turn now to a discussion of what interests us most in *Troilus*—its people.

"What is character but the determination of incident? What is incident but the illustration of character. What is either a picture or a novel that is *not* of *character?*"

"There are few things more exciting to me than a psychological reason. . . ."

Henry James,
The Art of Fiction

"ACTION IS CHARACTER"

F. Scott Fitzgerald
Notes for *The Last Tycoon*

THE PSYCHOLOGICAL APPROACH TO *TROILUS*

Chapter Five

 The influence of psychology upon literature and literary study has been so pervasive in this century that the most popular kind of of criticism is probably the psychological analysis. Literary critics have adopted the terminology of psychology. The widespread use of terms (often undefined) such as *collective, neurosis, psychosis, oedipus complex, projection, displacement, splitting,* as well as the famous *ego, id,* and *libido,* makes us forget that these words originated in a scientific rather than a literary context. Sigmund Freud is, of course, the most significant influence, and Frederick J. Hoffman has documented for us the role of Freudianism in literary study.[1] But critics have been influenced by other psychologists; I. A. Richards, Edmund Wilson, Kenneth Burke, Leslie Fiedler, and Herbert Read have borrowed the jargon and the insights of various psychological theories.

Such writers can choose to concentrate on the psychology of the author to explicate the meaning of his art, or they can explore the motivations of the characters in the work. The former type is illustrated by Saul Rosenzweig's analysis of Henry James. Rosenzweig probes the psyche of Henry James and then explains the characters in his novels as reflections of James' personal traumas.[2] This kind of literary psychoanalysis is justifiably suspect, particularly when it is practiced on a dead subject. Chaucer has not escaped this kind of psychoanalytic probing. Writers like Edward Wagenknecht and George Williams have treated Chaucer as if he were a live patient, and as if his poetry definitely revealed his feelings, his beliefs, and his experiences. Fortunately, however, most of the discussion of the characters of *Troilus* is concerned with the psychology of Troilus, Criseyde, and Pandarus.

Again the analyses of the psychology of the characters in *Troilus* have been both historical and nonhistorical in orientation. The historicist tries to understand what kind of people Chaucer intended to create in the poem. For many years the psychology of courtly love was widely recognized as the favorite hypothesis but recently, since some writers claim that Troilus and Criseyde were married, the psychology of married lovers has been offered as a basis for understanding the characters. The nonhistorical reading views the lovers as real people whose behavior and motivation would be intelligible to anyone in any age.

I have already noted that some writers, like Kelly and Robertson, do not believe in the existence of the courtly love code. But the belief in the reality of this code persists, and the characters in *Troilus* are often analyzed as if they were motivated essentially by courtly love doctrines. Thus such writers usually begin with a brief summary of the main tenets of courtly love or else they assume such knowledge on the part of the reader and move immediately into an interpretation of the psychology of motivation in terms of the code in *Troilus*. I list below the courtly love doctrines which many still think comprise the gospel of love in the Middle Ages.

1. Love is a religion, which means it is a sacred and valuable force in life.

2. Such love is ennobling and purifying; however, it is not merely platonic, but involves the gratification of physical desire.

3. Love is incompatible with marriage and is illicit and adulterous.

4. Since it is illicit, it also must be secret.

5. The lover must be humble and courteous and obey his lady's wishes.

6. The lover must submit to the will of his lady and devote himself absolutely to her service.

7. His lady must not be easily won, but once she is, she must be constant.

8. The process of falling in love and the symptoms of love

make him behave in a very strange way, for he faints, becomes pale, raves, has insomnia, loses his speech and all in all seems to suffer from a real illness. So strong is the power of love! And so contradictory is its effect, for on the one hand, it makes a strong, valorous hero out of the lover, and yet at the same time, it makes him act like a raving maniac with a very weak will. The valiant Lancelot whose prowess is proverbial is reduced to idiocy by the displeasure of Guinevere and wanders for a year without regaining his senses merely because his loved one is displeased with him. Such are the excesses of behavior required by this peculiar code. And most contradictory of all is the position of the woman in this society, for while legally and theologically she is the inferior to the male, in the view of the code she is his superior, and her every whim and desire is to be fulfilled by her "vassal in love."[3]

C. S. Lewis, G. L. Kittredge, J. L. Lowes, Karl Young, W. G. Dodd, and T. A. Kirby have all analyzed the characters of the *Troilus* as if they were participants in a courtly love drama.[4] While differences of opinion appear in relation to certain details of characterization, their general orientation is so similar that it is possible to summarize what they all say about the main characters as if they were speaking with one voice. William G. Dodd speaks for those who believe that courtly love was a historical phenomenon that Chaucer depicted in a serious fashion:

> . . . [L]ove was a very vital question in all the higher circles at the time at which Chaucer wrote. From the early feudal days, love was the ruling spirit in courtly society. . . . And love-making was considered as the great business of social life. That these ideas persisted to the later times in France is shown by the works of such writers as Machaut, Deschamps, and Froissart, in which no suspicion of burlesque may be found. In England, at the court of Richard II, one form of entertainment was the division into the orders of the Flower and the Leaf, and the discussion of the qualities for which these emblems stood. All the members of this courtly group were supposed to be lovers, and were designated as "servants of love." The fact that Chaucer was poet to this courtly society makes it seem highly improbable that he would deliberately set out to satirize the thing in which his patrons were highly interested—especially in a work with which he would be particularly anxious to please them.[5]

I do not think the logic of this passage is irrefutable, for the premise that a society cannot satirize its values and conventions is questionable. Shakespeare wrote plays for royalty, but the irreverence of Falstaff pleased Queen Elizabeth. Nor did Shakespeare hesitate to portray the mean and dark side of kings. There were religious people in the Court of Richard II, and Henry IV, yet Chaucer did not hesitate to satirize the deficiencies of churchmen. If courtly lovers existed in Chaucer's age, his comic genius could have propelled him into writing satires of the foolish extravagances of the courtly code of behavior.

Another theory is that Chaucer explored the psychology of love in his age by reading writers who had been influenced by courtly love doctrines. Thus Karl Young maintains that the tradition of the romances with its chivalric code pervades the *Troilus* and is responsible for the major changes Chaucer made in the adaptation of the *Filostrato*. What may seem to be remarkably innovative psychologizing to the reader unfamiliar with medieval romances is present in such stories as *Cligèes, Enéas, Ipomedon, Amadas et Ydoine, Méraugis, Li Hystere de Julius César, Eric et Enide, Lancelot, Châtelain de Coucy,* and *Roman de Troie.*[6] C. S. Lewis describes the role of the *Roman de la Rose* in allegorizing the erotic experience of these romances.[7]

While the view of Troilus and Criseyde as courtly lovers has been widely accepted for many years, their relationship has been interpreted in a new way by Henry A. Kelly and John B. Maguire who have come to the conclusion that Troilus and Criseyde were not courtly lovers. Instead they insist that Troilus and Criseyde were secretly married, that is, they had a clandestine marriage. Kelly defines a clandestine marriage in the medieval period as one "made by the consent of the bride and groom. No other permission, authorization, witness, minister, ceremony, or action was required for the marriage to take effect."[8] After 1215 the Lateran Council decreed that a marriage was clandestine when no banns were published. The *Tametsi* decree of the Council of Trent mandated that future clandestine marriages would no longer be recognized as valid by the church. But as Kelly notes, "In Chaucer's time, of course, there was no question about the law: secret marriage, though valid, was prohibited; the prohibition was well known and freely violated, and at least certain categories of clandestine spouses were frequently punished."⁹ For example, while such spouses in the diocese of Ely were not punished but were required to have a public wedding, in the Rochester diocese they were usually subjected to a public whipping after confessing to fornication before or after the matrimonial contract. Kelly describes the case of a man who did not consummate his first clandestine marriage with a woman, and then bigamously contracted and consummated marriage with another woman. The judge ordered him to marry the first woman and all three were publicly whipped, even the first woman, for entering into a secret contract.

Kelly offers an extensive discussion of the Canon Law on clandestine marriage in the Canons of Gratian of Bologna, the Decretals of Gregory I and other canonical writings, and in the literature of the period. He shows how clandestine marriage was a problem to the church, and how various authorities tried to deal with this complicated issue. The civil law was quite clear about marriage since a man was supposed to state explicitly that he was taking a woman as his legitimate wife. Thus Troilus and Criseyde were not married either *in facie ecclesia* or in a civil ceremony. That they were married clandestinely is the contention of Maguire and Kelly who use the consummation scene, as we shall see, to demonstrate that Troilus and Criseyde had an honorable although secret love affair. Much of Maguire's and Kelly's evidence depends upon the way in which they interpret Chaucer's modification of Boccaccio's consummation scene. Both Maguire and Kelly, however, admit that Chaucer does not specify that such a marriage took place, and both admit that Chaucer is not only ambiguous but at times seems to imply that the love affair is dishonorable, as for example when Pandarus says to Troilus:

> "For wel thow woost, the name as yet of here
> Among the people, as who seyth, halwed is;
> For that man is unbore, I dar wel swere,
> That evere wiste that she dide amys."
> (III, 167-270)

The original lines translated from Boccaccio state clearly that Criseyde is committing a wrong act. Kelly believes that the reason we have the "false impression" here that the affair is dishonorable is the result of Chaucer's "imperfect modification of his source." Chaucer was simply negligent and unconcerned

about consistency like many medieval story tellers: "I realize
that this conclusion might seem an easy way out to most critics,
who would generally be reluctant to admit a lack of full
authorial control in Chaucer's masterpiece. One could, of
course, appeal to his well-established gifts of irony and humor
and find a positive motive in his failure to adapt Boccaccio at
this point. Pandarus's suggestiveness here would be in keeping
with the vague air of prurience that we notice in him elsewhere
as he busies himself about his niece's affair, and it would
confirm the obvious truth that Pandarus's canons of morality
are not as rigorous as those of Troilus. I admit the possibility of
such a reading but still find it rather more likely that Chaucer
has simply slipped."[10] But Kelly doesn't explain why he finds it
"more likely" except that it fits his basic premise. In another
context, he is willing to give Chaucer the benefit of the doubt in
adapting consciously as a careful artist, but here where it would
tellingly cast doubt on his hypothesis, he simply chooses not to
believe.

Even weaker is his explanation for the ambiguity. "There
was no incompatibility between love and marriage; lovers
usually did get married if they could, and they could do so very
easily. It is clear that Troilus and his lady strove to practice the
'love that makes couples dwell in virtue,' and that this, in
Chaucer's book, meant marriage. But since an overt marriage
would betray a weakness in the plot, he decided to make it
clandestine in a double sense; it was hidden not only from the
world of Troy, but also, to a certain degree, from the eyes of his
own audience." Chaucer wanted to exploit the ambiguity and
he "could reasonably rely on his readers from their own
experience to be aware of the uncertainty that existed in all
secret alliances. He could treat his characters either as married
or as not married, depending on the immediate needs of the
story."[11]

Maguire notes that whereas Boccacio clearly dramatizes the
love affair as an illicit one between lovers who have different
social status, Chaucer views the love affair as a noble
relationship involving "love of kynde." His changes in the
account of the consummation scene remind us of medieval
marriage customs: "The exchange of oaths and rings, the
repeated and almost ritualistic echoes of the words of the
marriage ceremony, 'I plight thee my trouthe.' " Also Troilus
addresses Criseyde as "wommanliche wif" (III, 106, 1296), and

Troilus' "song of joy" mentions Hymen, the God of marriage (III, 1258). (Note, however, that Criseyde tells Diomede she is *not* married in V, 975-978.) Why is there no mention of the clandestine marriage? "First, he was dealing with a traditional story, perhaps known in some detail to many of his audience, and in the earlier versions the love story was always certainly immoral in Christian terms. At the same time, I think he intended to be materially faithful to his sources on this point and yet give sufficient hint that in fact he was departing from them in a way that his audience could easily grasp."[12] But this means that Chaucer had a special understanding with his audience which we no longer fathom. Furthermore, if we grant Maguire's premise that Chaucer committed himself *to being* and *not being* faithful to his sources *at the same time*, a rather remarkable feat for an artist, we are forced to accept a paradoxical statement which logically proves nothing. Neither Maguire nor Kelly succeed in demonstrating anything more than a very questionable hypothesis. But we shall see how this hypothesis makes them reinterpret the characters of Troilus and Criseyde.

Still another approach praises Chaucer for making the first genuine attempt to reveal character with the kind of psychological insight that is characteristic of the modern novelist. The following remarks by T. R. Price exemplify this view. In the *Troilus*, Price says,

> all complete delineation of dramatic character, and all full display of dramatic passion, are concentrated on the study of only four persons. In this again there is the same anticipation by Chaucer of the method of our most modern school of dramatists and romancers. The poet's interest is less in the external action, in the romantic adventures, in the stir and movement of his characters, than in their motives, in the evolution of their emotions, in the careful study of their minds and hearts. And so, as he diminishes the number of his characters, he is able to give to each one a more subtle interpretation; and by this powerful concentration of psychological method, he reaches in the fourteenth century that full and remorseless discovery of the secrets of character and of the springs of human action which we are prone to regard as the special achievement of our nineteenth century literature.[13]

Now if a reader were unfamiliar with *Troilus* he would expect to find the kind of characterization present in the dramas of Shakespeare or the novels of Proust. According to Price, in Chaucer as in the great modern writers, "There is the same conscious and deliberate subordination of action to emotion. There is the same minute and realistic delineation both of the environment of human action and of the characters involved. There is the same psychological study of human character as revealed in the supreme moments of emotional excitement. There is the same scornful rejection of the supernatural element, and the same inevitable deduction of human action from purely human motives."[14] In this view, *Troilus* is not only a great psychological work, but it is also a realistic work which excludes supernatural elements. This represents the extreme form of the modern reading that judges it to be a poem far ahead of its time in relation to the psychological nature of its approach. Various writers have expressed the view that Chaucer's characters are realistic creations. Remembering that Jordan and Payne consider Troilus and Criseyde to be static personalities, we can see that Chaucer confuses the critics.

Price speaks of four characters, but it seems quite farfetched to speak of the *development* of Diomede. In actuality Troilus, Criseyde and Pandarus absorb the interest of critics with the discussion of Diomede thrown in as an afterthought. Diomede will be discussed, along with the minor characters, Calkas, Antigone, Hector, Cassandra and Helen, at the end of this chapter. But the primary concern in the following pages is with the three major characters.

C. S. Lewis describes Troilus as an ideal figure about whom "there still hangs something of the anonymity of the Dreamer, the mere 'I' of the allegories." Troilus seems to be so much an "embodiment of the medieval ideal of the lover and warrior [that] he stands second only to Malory's Lancelot. . . . We never doubt . . . [Troilus'] valour, his constancy, or the 'daily beauty' of his life. His humility, his easy tears, and his unabashed self-pity in adversity will not be admired in our own age. They must however, be confessed to be true (intolerably true in places) to nature. . . ."[15] Because he is so readily made happy and suffers so much and takes it all, Troilus cannot be called a tragic hero. He is not, like Criseyde, an Aristotelian type of character. Of Troilus' despair in waiting for Criseyde's return Lewis writes: "Chaucer spares us no detail of the prolonged and sickening process to despair; every fluctuation of gnawing hope, every pitiful subterfuge of the flattering imagination, is held up to our eyes without mercy. The thing is so painful that perhaps no one without reluctance reads it twice. In our cowardice we are tempted to call it sentimental. We turn, for relief, to the titanic passions and heroic deaths of tragedy because they are sublime and remote, and hence endurable."[16] Troilus is a serious, admirable hero whose portrayal produces pathos.

Dodd and Kirby discuss Troilus' actions and beliefs solely in terms of the psychology of courtly love. Like Lewis, Dodd is aware that to the modern age, the sighing, swooning, and weeping of the lover seem to be effeminate and unmanly. But all is explained and warranted as far as he is concerned by the conventions of courtly love literature. Medieval lovers, explains Dodd, "if we are to believe the literature, were an extraordinarily lachrymose lot. Lament was the principal article of their conduct, at least up to the point when they gained the favor of their ladies and swoons were certain to occur under any unusual stress of emotion."[17] Dodd evidently believes that the literature does reflect actual practice. Troilus may overdo the weeping and the wailing, and his love may make him more of a sentimentalist than other lovers. But such sentimentality is not a sign of weakness and is not inconsistent with his physical courage and strength of character. Although we may regard his actions with Criseyde as signs of weakness, his refusal to run away with her shows him to be a true courtly lover who refuses to make his will more important than that of his lady and who knows that his honor demands that he keep her secret at all costs.

In fact, the character of Troilus is so completely molded by the courtly love convention that he has to be represented as a fatalist. Kirby's explanation for the inclusion of many references to fate in the poem and for the predestination passage is that courtly love denies the existence of free will. The lover is forced to love; he has no choice at all. "The classical ideal of a god whose arrows cause love to spring up, together with the troubadour conceit of love originating through the eyes, implies that men must love 'by necessitee'; for no one is able to protect himself against a god who may at any time attack without warning nor can a man be held responsible if he sees a lady and then suddenly finds himself in love with her. So likewise is the lover's conduct entirely foreign to the idea of free will; as the slave of his lady, he is absolutely powerless and is able to do nothing of his own choice."[18] Small wonder then that Troilus as an out and out fatalist should become melancholy. It is not merely the absence of the physical pleasure which he derives from his beloved but the knowledge that he is serving a very exacting deity, the God of Love, who requires the utmost from the devotees of his severe cult, a cult which makes Troilus an "ascetic of love."

Quite a number of critics have classified him as a flat character. However, in criticism the pendulum invariably swings from one extreme to another. If the courtly love interpretation has seemed to make him too much of an ideal hero, then the other extreme approach has tried to make him too tragic a figure. Thus trying to counter the interpretations which make Troilus too conventional a symbol of chivalric romance, critics give him depth, complexity, intelligence, and development to provide him with the qualities the hero of a tragedy should have. So, for example, Alfred David, agreeing with B. H. Bronson, insists that in Troilus is to be found the essential meaning of the poem, since the "depth" of the tragic experience depends upon the "depth" of the hero.[19] I do not know whether the French critic Camille Looten has been read by many English or American critics or whether they found his comment quoted in Kirby, but what Looten has to say about Troilus exemplifies this humanizing process which transforms Troilus into a very remarkable man.

> Troilo est tout expansion, tout exubérance de paroles. Troilus est un âme méditative, telle que sera Hamlet. Il a le tempérament des hommes du Nord: moins en dehors que ceux du Midi, moins à la merci des élans primesautiers de l'instinct, subissant moins la tyrannie du sentiment, ils cherchent obstinément la cause de leurs états d'âme. Tels sont les héros shakespeariens, "The cause"! C'est l'idée fixe d'Othello, il la poursuit même lorsqu'il est au paroxysme de la jalousie, et quand il la découverte, aussitôt, il se rue dans le crime et la mort.[20]

The element of introspection which Looten uses as the basis for comparing Troilus to Hamlet is at the root of several attempts to analyze Troilus as an intellectual. For example, to read David's and Wenzel's descriptions of the character of Troilus is to feel that we are in the presence of a Shakespearean hero, a courtly love Hamlet who engages in profound reflection.

David notes that Chaucer did not merely adapt the established courtly love convention; he offered an original interpretation of this code. Courtly love no more explains the *Troilus* than it explains the *Vita Nuova*, and presumably because Troilus is a very intelligent lover. Besides being brave and constant, he must be credited "with a quality rarely if ever attributed to the chivalric lover—intelligence. Troilus' passion for introspection has often been noted, but his lengthy soliloquies and speeches on love and fate are usually written off as the conventional outpourings of the lover or as evidence of Troilus' morbid preoccupation with his own feelings. But if their content is examined closely, they can also be read as the dramatic statements of a man searching out the universal meaning of his personal experience."[21] In a very real sense we have come back here to the notion of Troilus as a Boethius on a philosophical quest, only this time he is clearly identified as a courtly lover Boethius. For in this view while Troilus is the least vital, dramatically speaking, his is the most ambitious portrait of all, for, "he alone among all the characters in Chaucer's works (with the possible exception of the Chaucerian narrator) exhibits symptoms of growth and change and becomes by the end of the poem different from what he was at the beginning."[22] In the first half of the poem he is shown suffering minor indignities which are the usual techniques employed in romantic comedy, but in the last two books his deeper emotions and maturity are revealed to us so that the psychological realism of the portrait gets our complete sympathy. In the beginning Troilus is ignorant of the true nature and source of love but at the end he is wise. In no other romantic work are the concepts of the lover's guilt in laughing at love and the lady's mercy taken in such a literal sense. "Almost from the moment of his conversion, Troilus displays a marked Calvinistic streak. He lives in horror of his original sin of mocking the god of love, and he feels no merit in himself that could contribute to his redemption."[23] But his union with Criseyde brings him both "moral and intellectual fulfillment," and there is a "metaphysical quality" about his happiness as he is transformed from being the victim of an angry God to servant in an ordered universe run by a mighty force.

David claims that it is patently unjust to claim that Troilus is weak when he does nothing to stop Criseyde from leaving Troy. Troilus refuses to act, and this is after all very different from the inability to act. In Troilus' case the refusal to act is a nobler and

more difficult decision, for what is of paramount importance in
his consideration is the oath he has taken to yield absolute
sovereignty to his lady and his need to protect her reputation.
He wants to fight for Criseyde, but "his desire is controlled by
his reason." His predestination monologue is perfectly in
character for it is the philosophical exposition of his personal
dilemma. "Chaucer makes Troilus consistently see his individual experience as part of a universal pattern, and his
understanding grows as he searches for the ultimate meaning
both in his joy and in his despair. The discovery of Criseyde's
grace has led him to the radiant vision of a universe ordered by
love, and now the imminent loss of Criseyde brings him to the
concept of a universe ruled by an iron destiny. Only through
achieving the height of human happiness could Troilus come to
realize the depth of human misery. What is the meaning of it
all? Troilus confronts, even though he does not solve, the
fundamental mystery of the human condition and the central
question of Chaucer's poem."[24] Mistakenly in this passage
Troilus comes to the conclusion that there is no free will. All
through the poem Troilus exercises his free will to act nobly.
"He chooses to let Criseyde go, not because he is too weak to
hold her, but because he cannot keep her except on his own high
terms." One might then expect in an analysis of this kind, that
Troilus' tragic error would be that while he was intelligent, he
"in the darkness of his human reason," lacked the enlightenment of a Boethius and therefore lived with the wrong
philosophy. But this is not what is seen as his *tragic* error. His
tragic error is to have tried to love a human being as if she were
a divinity. His "uncompromising constancy to an ideal"
prevents him from revoking his promise to Criseyde and
prevents him from seeing her for what she really is. All that is
left to him in Book V after he has exhausted all rational hope is
to love irrationally, and Book V offers us "a convincing and
deeply moving psychological study of the painful and
relentless disintegration of hope."[25] The Christian moral at the
end should be read as signifying that Troilus has found the
ideals of love by which he tried to live on earth in an eternal
state of being.

S. Wenzel, who agrees with the efforts to rehabilitate the
character of Troilus, develops some of the ideas mentioned by
David. Troilus is an ideal heroic figure, whose adherence to
reason instead of desire, leads to the destruction of his

happiness. What Wenzel does is to try to resolve the dilemma of a Troilus who is intelligent but who does not understand that he has free will. Troilus is to be understood not as a contradictory but as a complex character, who " 'is reasonable' *in reference to his world of chivalry*, of courtly ethics, where he appears noble and ideal. But he is irrational *in relation to the world of philosophy*, where he appears blind and weak (or simply, he lacks the Boethian 'intelligence'). The positive and the negative sides of his rational behavior do not logically exclude each other, because they refer to different levels of rationality."[26] But although Troilus lacks the Boethian intelligence, and even though the medieval reader can anticipate his fall, Troilus' ideals emanating from the chivalric ethos are not devaluated, for his reason and his *courtoisie* remain positive qualities. His ascent is somewhat of a poetic reward for his heroic loyalty to the values of his world. Of the three levels of value structured in the poem, sensuality, noble courtly love, and divine speculation, Troilus is primarily in the middle world of *courtoisie* "where reason controls low appetites, where love of a noble ' woman raises the lover's character to the heights of refinement, of social graces, and of moral virtues, where such love is based on service and total submission to the lady's desires."[27]

Also Wenzel seems to be one of those who believes that the ethos of courtly love was a reflection of a wider chivalric ethos which actually existed outside the literature. At least that is what he implies when he writes: "Chivalry and courtesy, as an ideal of life, rested on rationality, on the subordination of personal desires to universal norms embodied in a particular social structure. Courtly love, as only one aspect of that ideal, was commonly thought to be the great social and psychological power to educate the knight in the perfect behaviour of his class."[28]

These writers offer what is unquestionably the most flattering view of Troilus' character. In none of these analyses is much attention paid to the humorous scenes and lines in the poem. David is so intent on revealing the intellectual nature of Troilus and strains so hard that even the obviously funny parts of the poem are reinterpreted by him to be indications of Troilus' profound struggles with philosophical problems. For example, the scene in which Troilus faints as he stands listening to Pandarus lie to Criseyde becomes not only the source of his greatest humiliation, but also, according to David, the moment of his deepest humility. Throwing himself completely upon his lady's mercy, he receives his absolution from her, and her words, "Of gilt misericorde" (III, 1177), "are words that any man might hope to hear someday, and we should recognize the words of grace, even in what to some might appear a sinful context. Pardon and free submission—more than this no man can ask of love, except permanence." Also we are asked to take more seriously than Pandarus does the scene in which Troilus prays to the six planetary deities in Book II. The scene is funny but is also to be understood as one which reveals the dramatic statement of a man searching out the universal meaning of his personal experiences.[29]

Those who believe that Troilus is a married man also treat him as an admirable character. Both Kelly and Maguire describe him as a noble, faithful human being who commits no sin except to love a woman who betrays their "trouthe." However, Troilus fares better as a courtly than as a married lover since his penchant for secrecy is explained by the courtly code, but it is not explained by the clandestine marriage principle. Neither Kelly nor Maguire succeeds in explaining why Troilus as a clandestine husband doesn't make clear to his father that Criseyde is his wife. If he is secretly married to her, and he loves her so desperately, and he knows she is going to leave him, why doesn't he admit publicly that he is her husband? What shame would be involved in that? Both Kelly and Maguire admit that Chaucer omits what Boccaccio makes explicit; the Italian heroine is too low in social status to be a Prince's wife. Chaucer does everything he can to make us believe that Criseyde is *not* inferior to Troilus, so why would Priam have objected to the marriage as a *fait accompli*? Priam certainly accepts Helen and Paris; and Criseyde is after all a widow, not an adulteress. If Priam had objected to the marriage, the explicit avowal of the marriage would have made their relationship even more binding in the eyes of the law, and if Criseyde had to be exchanged for Antenor, at the very least Troilus could have told Diomede "Take care of my *wommanliche wif*" (III, 106, 1296). The logic of the material conditional *if-then*, is applicable as I have used it above since the basic premise utilized by Maguire and Kelly is also nothing more than a material conditional.

If Troilus *is* married, then he would act in the way that he does, refusing to acknowledge his bride. As we have noted,

Kelly claims that the ambiguity about the marriage is deliberately employed by Chaucer because he could rely on his readers to be cognizant of the "uncertainty that existed in all secret alliances." He could treat them as married or not, depending upon the needs of his story. While in one context he talks about their holy love, when he has Troilus think about whether he should ask Priam for her (IV, 554-560), he does not speak specifically in terms of marriage whereas Boccaccio's hero does. In the *Filocolo* and the *Decameron*, a son can marry without the father's permission. But since the original plot required that Criseyde leave Troy, Chaucer "could not present marriage as a viable alternative. . . . But if Chaucer's audience would naturally assume they were really married, then all the more caution would be required."[30] Criseyde seems less guilty since she is never described as being married, and Pandarus seems less immoral when he suggests that Troilus find another love. "And Troilus seems all the more noble when he remains faithful till the end, not because he is bound to her in wedlock, but because he loves her." But it is equally possible to argue that such a Troilus is a weak, cowardly man, afraid of his father, afraid of what society thinks, unable to form a plan of action to be with his wife.

Nor is Maguire's view any more convincing. Troilus realizes he cannot prevent the exchange of Criseyde and Antenor since the whole war was caused by Paris' rape of Helen, and Criseyde's exchange is for the good of the town. Maguire comments: "Since no one knows of the marriage, Troilus cannot simply run off with Criseyde without staining her honor, a point on which she later backs him up by saying that she would suffer shame 'If *in this forme* I sholde with yow wende' " (IV, 1579).[31] Now if they were courtly lovers and they were not married, then she could speak of shame. But if "this forme" is clandestine marriage, what shame is involved? Furthermore, if the night of love shared by Troilus and Criseyde was also a night of marriage, would not Pandarus have been aware of their vows? His very presence in the bedroom and his zealous attempts to bring them together might have constituted the actions of a witness who is legitimizing the clandestine relationship. In any event Kelly and Maguire do not deal with this matter.

They both have difficulty with Troilus because their basic premise turns him into a very unsatisfactory hero and husband. Nor does the notion of a clandestine marriage explain why Criseyde, who is usually so resourceful, doesn't ask her noble friend Hector to help her husband. As long as Kelly and Maguire feel that they can entertain the hypothesis of the clandestine marriage on such slim evidence, other equally interesting conjectures can also be submitted. For example, it is possible to argue on the basis of certain lines and scenes in the poem that Criseyde is tired of Troilus and anxious to begin a new life with a new lover.

But Troilus hasn't fared too well from another perspective. Instead of the courtly love reading we have the modern interpretation which views Troilus as a type of amiable but foolish lover, or worse, as a psychologically disturbed person. To such critics he does not seem to be a very satisfactory hero. His passive and pusillanimous nature lacks the depth a hero— particularly a tragic hero—is supposed to have. He is not a complex or interesting personality and his reactions are too predictable, if not mechanical or schematic.

It is hard to understand why McAlpine says: "Admittedly, only one critic [Gordon H. Gerould] has challenged the consensus to the extent of questioning Troilus' tragic stature. . . ." There are quite a number of writers who do more than question his "tragic stature"; they deny its existence. While C. S. Rutherford contends that Troilus' "silliness," "absurdity," and "immaturity" are apparent only in the first two books, other critics maintain that he is just as passive and weak in the later books. Patch contends that Troilus deserves his suffering because he is such an unresourceful lover. B. J. Whiting describes how Troilus could have disguised himself as an Asian pilgrim to visit Criseyde among the Greeks: "If his assumed character were accepted, he could expect a decent welcome, entertainment and a friendly exchange of information and gossip, in the course of which he might easily hope to see Criseyde."[32] But Troilus is incapable of initiating action unless someone leads him "by the lappe."

> . . . [He] may not contrefete
> To ben unknowen of folk that weren wise,
> Ne fynde excuse aright that may suffise,
> If he among the Grekis knowen were;
> For which he wep ful ofte and many a tere.
> (V, 1578-1582)

Van Doren describes Troilus as being infantile with a childlike simplicity. He acts so foolishly when he is lovesick that Pandarus is forced to ask, "Who ever saw a grown man acting so?" Chaucer shows us that Troilus is not mature because "he has no sense of humor. Once he smiles weakly at Pandarus' joke; yet by and large he has lost his wits—a calamity which Chaucer understands and pities, but is careful not to praise."[33] Unlike Criseyde who does not share Troilus' wild delusion about love, Troilus' monomaniacal obsession with love makes him soft. Pandarus knows this, and "can soften his word to Criseyde because he knows she is hard. To Troilus he must be harder than he feels: if he is not, the shapeless youth will melt away. His words to the lover are like the slaps we administer as medicine for hysteria. Troilus, paralyzed by his infatuation, must be taught how to walk again like a natural man. Pandar's favorite criticism of him is that he cries . . . before it is clear that nothing can be done to cure him."[34] Troilus seems to enjoy his grief, "but fools alone do that. Pandar does not spare his friend the name of fool, infant, or whatever else occurs to his rough tongue. He must run through a long list, for the trouble in Troilus is chronic. The lover never learns to be up and doing. . . ."[35] Pandarus' aim is to shock Troilus out of playing love's fool, and to help him, no matter how much nonsense he utters. And the truth is, says Van Doren, much of what Troilus says *is* nonsense. I think this may well be the best explanation for Troilus' nasty apostrophe to Fortune:

> "Why ne haddestow my fader, kyng of Troye,
> Byraft the lif, or don my bretheren dye,
> Or slayn myself, that thus compleyne and
>   crye. . . ?
> If that Criseyde allone were me laft,
> Nought roughte I whider thow woldest me
>   steere. . . ."
>
> (IV, 276-282)

Van Doren does not mention these lines, but he would surely regard them as the utterance of an "infantile Troilus whose lovesickness runs so true to medieval form. . . . [He] is Chaucer's hero only in that sense that it is he to whom love happens—love, whose true terrors Chaucer knows better than any love-calf could."[36]

But at least Van Doren merely describes Troilus as "love's fool." Another interpretation makes him a "psychologically disturbed person." Utilizing Aristotelian psychology, Michael Masi "psychoanalyzes Troilus in terms that Chaucer would have understood." Troilus' illness was the result of frustrated love which led him to hallucinate. According to Aristotle, the process of knowing has three stages: simple knowing or sensation, imagination, and rational thought. The central sense organ is the heart, not the brain, to which flow the images of the eye, the most important organ for life. Masi shows how Troilus' malady develops through (1) receiving Criseyde's image through his eye; that is, falling in love (2) remembering her image fondly when he is absent, brooding about her love, and (3) mistaking her image for other images because of the stress of physical and mental exhaustion. "The final result of this psychological process is a confusion of truth and illusion, loss of contact between mind and reality, and eventual disappearance of Troilus' desire to live. . . . Such an interpretation puts much of the responsibility for his eventual death and disillusionment on the love melancholy which fed itself and, partially through his own fault, became increasingly intense until it led Troilus into a world of unrealities, a world of phantasms which governed him both sleeping and waking, beyond which he could not see."[37] Since Masi does not mention the epilogue, it is left up to us to decide whether in the eighth sphere Troilus has finally recovered his sanity.

So criticism gives us a flat, uninteresting knight, a sinner, a noble, courtly or married lover, a courtly Boethius, a tragic intellectual Hamlet-like figure, a comic fool, and a psychologically disturbed hero. Troilus has also been described as an early existentialist; he has been compared to Oedipus; he has been judged to be a "great man" and an exemplar of Pauline charity.[38] Such criticism runs the gamut of trying to fathom what Chaucer thought of him and what we think of him today.

Like Troilus, Pandarus has been discussed in terms of the courtly love doctrine. Thomas Kirby and C. S. Lewis maintain that Pandarus' role as *internuntius* is sanctioned by the courtly love code. The *internuntius* has a definite function in courtly love literature, the most obvious example being Galehot in *Lancelot du Lac*. Pandarus is not a procurer; his function in

Troilus is conventional and understandable. What he does for Troilus is what any good friend of a courtly lover would do. It is, therefore, irrelevant to fret about his morality. J. L. Lowes insists that Pandarus' task is not to ask Criseyde to give up her chastity, but to convince her to give up her scruples about scandal.[39]

C. S. Lewis finds no irony in Pandarus' attitude and claims that he is a "lover and a doctor in Love's law. . . . The 'ironic' Pandarus is not to be found in the pages of Chaucer . . . I do not say that he did not in some way enjoy his frequent tears; but he enjoyed them not as a vulgar scoffer but as a convinced servant of the god of Love, in whose considered opinion the bliss and pathos of a gravely conducted amour are the finest flower of human life."[40] Admitting that there is a comic side to Pandarus' role, Lewis maintains that Chaucer wanted to teach as well as to paint the mystery of courtly love, and Pandarus seriously explicates the commandments of the general philosophy of love to Troilus. In fact, he is actually given the doctrine which Love himself, or Frend, or the Vekke, would have spoken in an allegory. Lewis warns us not to think of Pandarus as a satiric abstraction, contending instead that he is a very complex, concrete human being. On the other hand, De Sélincourt, who admits that Pandarus has a sympathetic attitude toward *amour courtois* contends that his attitude is also ironical. Pandarus "is realist enough to pierce through the subterfuges and illusions of lovers who, because they are conscious of the idealistic element in their passion, persuade themselves that it is wholly Platonic, and either refuse to recognize its physical basis, or think that they will be content, or indeed have the self-control, to stop short of its full satisfaction. But, above all, his irony exposes the lover's preposterous absorption in his own woes, as though nothing in the world existed outside them."[41]

Van Doren believes that Pandarus is used to satirize the courtly love code. Pandarus knows what love is and sympathizes with Troilus' feelings; Pandarus has experienced "loves shotes keene." But Troilus revels in being love's fool while "Pandar has no use for any kind of fool." And so he administers the slaps which serve as "medicine for hysteria"; he "brings figures from the world of fact, and the more absurd they are the better for his purpose, which is to shock Troilus out of his conventional stupor . . . employing the therapy of tartness and suppressing, or seeming to suppress, the subtlety of which his mind is capable. Just as his figures are Philistine, so his imagination sounds like that of a literal brute." But he has a more subtle mind than his crude figures would sometimes lead us to believe. Pandarus' proverbs provide "the envelope of sun"

> that dries the tears from metaphor, that substitutes the speech of men for poetry's vapors. "My old hat," "a hill of beans," "not worth a pin,"—such motes of the vernacular are always dancing in its beam, as proverbs get up and stretch in the dry light of noon. . . . Sleeping dogs, the stable door locked too late, the fire that time will cool, the nine days' wonder, the grave too deep for medicine—[Troilus] . . . thinks them irrelevant to his epoch-making case. But they have their effect upon him as the poem ages, so do they upon us. They remind us that love is long, though the life of one lover may be perilous.[42]

Chaucer's Pandarus is more imaginative and more ironic than Boccaccio's, and he provides the medium through which the helpless love of Troilus can be viewed as being both unique and typical.

But other critics of Pandarus censure him for his misdeeds. Thus he has been called a naive pimp, a tricky parasite, a cunning immoral, outwardly charming, inwardly corrupt, with the wisdom of the base villain. Robertson calls Pandarus a "Priest of Satan," and states: "His 'devel,' as Troilus once calls him (I, 623), is convincingly decked out in sheep's clothing."[43] Robertson quotes the relevant lines from Root's edition, which is the only one that sets off *devel* with commas as a vocative form:

> "Thow koudest nevere in love thiselven wisse;
> How, devel, maistow brynge me to blisse?"
> (I, 622-623)

Charlotte D'Evelyn has clearly demonstrated that most modern editors and translators read the line as "How the devil" or "How, you devil." Denying that Pandarus ever acts with "evil intention," she rejects Robertson's reading. "On the literal level, Robertson's interpretation of this single line is out-of-character and dogmatic. It may prove to be a straw in the wind pointing out the misdirection of his reading of the whole poem on the tropological level."[44]

Critical opinion is clearly divided on the question of whether Pandarus is, or is not, a "devil" in a human sense, that is, whether he is a good or a bad friend. Gaylord doesn't think Pandarus is a good friend. In Book I his behaviour can be viewed as a parody of Boethian counsel, for he turns "up-so-doun" Boethian passages by describing the love of Criseyde as the symbol of true happiness, and by valuing the role of Fortune. "Pandarus acts the part of Lady Philosophy, but in reality is much more like the muses of false eloquence she had dismissed, in offering a friendly aid and counsel which (according to Boethius) 'destroyen the corn plentyvous of fruytes of resoun.' "[45] In other words, in Pandarus' hands "the fruits of reason wither," and he gives the wrong kind of advice as a friend cultivating the garden of Narcissus instead of the one planted by Lady Philosophy.

Robert G. Cook claims that Pandarus is a more devious and disreputable character than Boccaccio's Pandaro. Why? Because he tells the following four lies: he lies to Deiphebus about the danger to Criseyde (II, 1416 ff); Pandarus lies to Criseyde about the "false Poliphete" (II, 1464-1469); he later lies to Criseyde when he invites her to his house; he swears that Troilus is out of town; at his house he lies when he tells her Troilus has come to see her because of jealousy of Horaste (III, 785-798). "I suggest," says Cook, "that Chaucer, fully aware that such dishonorable means have no place in true friendship, deliberately made the alterations in Pandarus' behavior in order to undercut the notion that Pandarus is a true friend."[46] Cook also reminds us of what Muscatine noted, that Pandarus' scheme at the house of Deiphebus parallels the Biblical story of Amnon, Thamar, and Jonadab. The strategy of Troilus' feigned illness devised by Pandarus is like the strategy utilized by Jonadab who told his friend Amnon to feign illness so that Thamar, his brother's sister whom he loved, would visit him. Thamar visited Amnon, and he raped Thamar. Small wonder then that medieval treatises on friendship use this story as an example of what friends should not do for one another. However, in all fairness to Pandarus, the striking difference is that Troilus never overpowers Criseyde.[47]

No one has written less sympathetically of Pandarus than Émile Legouis, who states:

. . . [É]tant donnée cette chaste Crisède, le rôle de Pandarus devenait nécessairement plus répugnant. Il ne s'agissait plus de se faire le complice d'une coquetterie prudente, mais de corrompre la vertu. Le personnage eût même été intolérable si Chaucer n'avait masqué la vilenie derrière les ridicules. . . . Chaucer s'est complu à donner tout au long ses dissertations, ses anecdotes, ses sentences enfilées, ses précautions oratoires, les sinuosités de son hypocrisie. . . . Son Pandarus est intermédiaire entre le jeune chevalier de l'amitié présenté par Boccace, parfait de zèle et de sagacité dans un rôle spécial, et le Pandare shakespearien, oncle dévoyé . . . celui-ci agit moins par affection pour Troilus que par amour du métier. . . . On n'arrive pas à le juger, ni à le voir. Ou plutôt on voit double; une silhouette de jeune homme caustique comme dans Boccace, une figure âgée et grimaçante, comme dans Shakespeare. Le Pandare de Chaucer fait loucher.[48]

And Pandarus does indeed make the critics see double. There are those who not only judge Pandarus to be a good friend, but who also believe that he reflects Chaucer's views more than any other character in the poem. Sherman B. Neff says of Pandarus: "It is unfortunate that such a character as this, so unobjectionable, so worthy of our respect and admiration, so altogether delightful, should suffer the opprobrium that later and less skilful hands have heaped upon him."[49] To Neff Pandarus is a true friend; furthermore, he is "more like Chaucer than any other character the poet has drawn." Then Neff offers a description of Pandarus that is diametrically opposed to the ones offered by Gaylord and Cook: ". . . [Pandarus] has Chaucer's wit and kindly spirit, and Chaucer's sanity. He appears at times a little disillusioned, partly, perhaps, because of his unhappy love affair, but he is never bitter. There is nothing vulgar about him, or mean, or little. He is generous to a fault. He gives himself unstintingly. He is everything to Troilus that a friend could be. He comes to him, he stays with him, he comforts him, he counsels with him, he weeps with him, . . . and with no thought of reward other than the benefit to Troilus that his services may bring."[50]

But while the comic elements in the characterization of Troilus and Criseyde have been ignored, even the most serious commentators have had to say something about the humorous side of Pandarus' nature. De Sélincourt describes Pandarus as the first "great triumph of English humour, to whom, in all the great gallery of our comic characters, Falstaff alone is comparable for brilliance of conception and execution."[51] And indeed, while Pandarus' role as a go-between may offend those with more fastidious notions of behaviour, the ethical issues, as in the case of Falstaff, are dwarfed in the light of the impact of personality which delights and intrigues us. Thus in the course of discussions Pandarus has been compared to the comic Sancho Panza, to Juliet's nurse, and to Polonius. Even Speirs, who contends that Pandarus deteriorates somewhat in the manner of Falstaff in *Henry IV, Part II*, believes that Pandarus is the focal point of meaning in the poem as a thoroughly comic figure. He represents goliardism, for he is on the side of the profane, not the sacred, "a protagonist of 'jolytee,' and 'lustiness' and disrespectful of 'holinesse'. . . . [He is] the protagonist of the worldly life and the joy of the natural heart as opposed to book-learning, the widow's seclusion and religion."[52] He seems to represent both the superior and inferior possibilities of human life. His main desire is to help Troilus, and he stands out in contrast to Troilus whose capacity as a devotee of the courtly love tradition for self-delusion and self-pity is so exaggerated that it verges on self caricature. Pandarus' role is that of the rationalist as he tries to convince Troilus that nothing has really happened to him after Criseyde's absence of a few days to justify his absurd, excessive posturing of grief. His "melancholy heroics" are merely melodramatic. And Pandarus tells him

> "That it is folye for to sorwen thus
> And causeles. . . .
> I kan not sen in him no remedie
> But lat hym worthen with his fantasie."
> (V, 325-329)

In the passage in which he urges Troilus not to fear his dreams, we see Pandarus as a "wise as well as confident doctor of the mind." In his lines on dreams is displayed a "triumph of the rationalizing intelligence—a clarifying of ignorance and dispersing of superstitious fears—and identical with a clear and rational self-knowledge. . . . [E]ven if Pandarus' particular conception of life and enjoyment is a crude one, [it] is at least preferable . . . to the dreams and self-pitying fantasies

on which Troilus feeds his heart. The wisdom that is identified
with Pandarus here is thus not a purely negative scepticism but
carries with it a positive acceptance of life and a confident
promise of possible ultimate self-mastery."[53] "Rys, lat us speke
of lusty life in Troy," says Pandarus, and we must approve his
invocation to "live and enjoy."

That is, we can approve if, like Speirs, we value "living and
enjoying." Other critics with less hedonistic and more
moralistic and ascetic leanings tend to evaluate Pandarus in
rather derogatory terms. Pandarus is a great comic jester, a
buffoon, a hypocrite, a liar, a bad friend, a pimp, a voyeur, a
pervert, a treacherous Tantalus, a Devil. But as we have seen,
he has also been described as a realistic pragmatist, a good
friend, and he has even been equated with Chaucer himself!

Criseyde is, of course, the most fascinating enigma in the
poem. What Chaucer really thought about her has puzzled
readers for many years. Later writers such as Robert Henryson
and William Shakespeare depicted her clearly enough as a
dissolute woman. Ulysses in Shakespeare's *Troilus and
Cressida* tells us that Criseyde's "wanton spirits look out at
every joint and motive of her body" (IV. v. 65-66). But Chaucer
left his readers with the dilemma of fathoming Criseyde's
character. According to one critic, those who attempt to resolve
the dilemma, "stagger from the task like troops from a
Napoleonic defeat; their pride may be intact and showing, but
they are clearly losers all."[54] Still another writer states that the
final word on Criseyde will never be pronounced.[55] Undaunted,
explicators who do motivational research on Criseyde continue
to search for the "final word."

By far the largest and most orthodox group of critics attempt
to analyze Criseyde by utilizing a historical approach. Those
who employ religious exegesis in analyzing medieval literature
find it very easy to understand her. She is no complicated
phenomenon to them. In light of the sexology of the medieval
church she is simply bad. For a religious exegete like D. W.
Robertson, Criseyde is the fallen Eve, manipulated by the
"diabolical" Pandarus. She is the feminine Everyman "faithful
only to her own selfish desires of the moment. . . . Her
conception of honor is pitifully inadequate, as is her understanding of virtue and truth."[56]

However, those who are not impervious to Criseyde's charm,
and who find the religious view to be too simplistic use the

doctrine of courtly love to explain Criseyde's character. The most well known explanation in this connection is offered by C. S. Lewis in his *Allegory of Love*. He maintains that the first three books of the poem contain a

> touching and beautiful picture of a woman by nature both virtuous and amorous, but above all affectionate; a woman who in a chaste society would certainly have lived a chaste widow. But she lives, nominally, in Troy, really in fourteenth-century England, where love is the greatest of earthly goods and love has nothing to do with marriage. She lives in it alone. . . . [H]er only natural protector [Pandarus] . . . is on her lover's side, and working upon her by appeals to her curiosity, her pity and her natural passions, as well as by direct lying and trickery. . . . If, in such circumstances, she yields, she commits no sin against the social code of her age and country: she commits no unpardonable sin against any code I know of—unless, perhaps, against that of the Hindus. By Christian standards, forgivable; by the rules of courtly love, needing no forgiveness: this is all that need be said of Cryseide's act in granting the Rose to Troilus.[57]

Those who, like Lewis, accept the doctrine of courtly love agree that Criseyde's relationship with Troilus involves no sin. Courtly love ladies were primarily and properly concerned, as Andreas Capellanus tells us, with the art of love; indeed it amounted to what psychologists today might well describe as obsessive behavior. Women in the courts of Eleanor of Aquitaine and Marie de Champagne were more interested in love than any other activity. One doesn't ever think of them as teachers or mothers. They have one basic interest which romantic expression may camouflage, but which ultimately involves obtaining and holding on to an extra-marital lover. Now Criseyde seems to fulfill that role since everything we know about her concerns her reaction to Troilus as a potential and then actual lover. We never know what she thinks about the Trojan war or the role of women in Trojan society, etc. We only see her amorous nature.

But Lewis explains her "betrayal" of Troilus by making her more than a courtly mistress. In the end she is an Aristotelian heroine with a tragic flaw. According to Lewis, Chaucer reconciles her sincerity and unselfishness in the earlier portions of the poem with her treachery in the last section. Lewis notes that Chaucer "has so emphasized the ruling passion of his heroine, that we cannot mistake it. It is Fear—fear of loneliness, of old age, of death, of love, and of hostility; of everything, indeed, that can be feared. And from this Fear springs the only positive passion which can be permanent in such a nature; the pitiable longing, more childlike than womanly, for protection, for some strong and stable thing that will hide her away and take the burden from her shoulders."[58] Under ordinary circumstances if fate had not tested her character, and thrown her into extraordinary circumstances she might have been a happy and faithful woman. But fate converted this weakness in her nature into a tragic flaw. She is a "tragic figure in the strictest Aristotelian sense, for she is neither very good nor execrably wicked. . . . But there is a flaw in her, and Chaucer has told us what it is; 'she was the ferfulleste wight that mighte be.' "[59]

Those who feel that Chaucer satirized the courtly love convention have a different view of Criseyde. She is not an Aristotelian heroine who acts out of fear. Van Doren sees "some hardness in her that makes us wonder what on earth she means when she tells Troilus she loves him for his 'moral virtue.' " She is not as innocent as Troilus; Pandarus knows this, but he pretends that she is. She never accepts the madness of the courtly love code or Troilus' "wild" delusion that she is the only woman who can exist for him, "for in the sanity she keeps she knows that this is not true." We are never really sure we know why she loves Troilus or whether she does indeed love him. The gift of herself is somehow incomplete:

> She saves something out, as if she knew that another man than Troilus exists—and Diomede in the sequel does. It is not that she anticipates her treachery, or that treachery is the word for what so naturally she does. It is simply that she never belongs to Troilus in the same way that Troilus belongs to her. Nor does Chaucer appear to suggest that she should. He no sooner indicts her for desertion than he softens the charge to unkindness. He does not know her secret well enough to be sure that he can decide her fate with us. He counts on her to seduce us, as she must, but he does not insist that we be angry when she turns away and listens to a Greek. . . . He does not denounce Criseyde any more than he would denounce the sting that comes with honey.[60]

Love is, Chaucer tells us in her characterization, a mystery and puzzling so that even when in the dialogues with Diomede she almost becomes Shakespeare's trollop, we think "it is still possible that she does only what she must."

Then there is the newest view of Criseyde as a secretly married woman who commits the "heinous crime" of adultery. But these interpretations of Criseyde as courtly lover, Aristotelian heroine, sinner Eve, and adulteress have in common a basic tendency to minimize the effect of her sexuality. It is almost as if there is some tacit agreement among the orthodox Chaucerian critics to transform Criseyde into an a-sexual being. Writing about the most important sexual scene in the poem, the consummation love scene in Book III, these critics treat Criseyde as if she were praying to God instead of having sexual intercourse with Troilus!

Critics have praised the way in which Chaucer rewrites this portion of Boccaccio's poem by blending romantic and erotic elements. Thus Donald R. Howard, who has examined the sexuality of this love episode, concludes that the "frank erotic rendezvous" in Boccaccio's poem is transformed by Chaucer into a scene in which "the innocence, timidity and discretion [of the lovers] make their desire seem greater, more unbearable. Hence, the reader imagines its fulfillment the more ecstatic."[61] By avoiding sexual detail and employing erotic suggestiveness, Chaucer shows us "love as a game of the spirit," an ideal kind of love. According to Robert P. apRoberts, Chaucer has modified the sensuality of the Italian version so that Criseyde "admits Troilus to her bedside because of love and pity and not merely because of sensual desire. Even the admission of Troilus to her bed is made with an emphasis upon motives other than desire."[62] These motives have to do with the spiritual qualities of courtly love: devotion, merit, *gentilesse* and other values. Kelly states that "incredible as it may seem during all the time, and the many times, that Troilus and Criseyde are in bed together there is only the slightest hint of carnal intercourse between them."[63] Like apRoberts, he claims that Chaucer tones down Boccaccio's sexual descriptions in this scene.

Chaucer himself is so overcome with feeling when Troilus and Criseyde finally sleep together that he says:

> This is no litel thyng of for to seye;
> This passeth every wit for to devyse;

> For ech of hem gan otheres lust obeye.
> Felicite, which that thise clerkes wise
> Comenden so, ne may nought here suffise;
> This joie may nought writen be with inke;
> This passeth al that herte may bythynke.
>
> (III, 1688-1694)

Now it would seem to be perfectly clear to any reader that what Chaucer is describing here is not a midnight conversation but, to use Kelly's Victorian terminology, a "carnal" relationship. That Chaucer chooses to use *occupatio* at this moment in the story comes, he tells us, from his inability to write "with inke" the "joie" that came to Troilus and Criseyde when "ech of hem gan otheres lust obeye." That Chaucer speaks in such glowing terms of the "lust" they fulfill doesn't detract from the erotic effect. Indeed it might well be argued that what Chaucer leaves to the imagination makes the love scene more erotic than what Boccaccio makes explicit.

In his zeal to demonstrate that Chaucer has spiritualized the Troilus and Criseyde love scene, Kelly deals with the word *pleye* in the following passages:

> But juggeth ye that han ben at the feste
> Of swich gladnesse, if that hem liste
>   *pleye.*
>
> (III, 1312-1313)

> Soone after this they spake of sondry
>   thynges,
> As fel to purpose of this aventure,
> And *pleyinge* entrechaungeden hire rynges,
> Of which I kan nought tellen no scripture;
> But wel I woot, a broche, gold and asure,
> In which a ruby set was lik an herte,
> Criseyde hym yaf, and stak it on his
>   sherte.
>
> (III, 1366-1372)

> Thise ilke two, of whom that I yow seye,
> Whan that hire hertes wel assured were,
> Tho gonne they to speken and to *pleye*,
> And ek rehercen how, and whan, and where
> Thei knewe hem first, and every wo and
>   feere

> That passed was; but al swich heveynesse,
> I thank it God, was torned to gladnesse.
> > (III, 1394-1400)

Kelly interprets the word *pleye* here not to mean sexual intercourse, which he admits it often means in Chaucer, but to mean "lightheartedness rather than ardent erotic passion. . . ."[64] But other critics would not accept his reading of the word *pleye*. For them the word clearly has a sexual meaning, and some of them even go so far as to suggest that Criseyde not only "pleyes" with Troilus but that some peculiar "pleyinge" goes on the morning after the night of love. That morning Pandarus approaches Criseyde as she lies in bed after Troilus has left her, and the following three stanzas which do not appear in Boccaccio describe what happens:

> And ner he come, and seyde, "How stant it now,
> This mury morwe? Nece, how kan ye fare?"
> Criseyde answerde, "Nevere the bet for yow,
> Fox that ye ben! God yeve youre herte kare!
> God help me so, ye caused al this fare,
> Trowe I," quod she; "for al youre wordes white,
> O! whoso seeth yow, knoweth yow ful lite."
>
> With that she gan hire face for to wrye
> With the shete, and wax for shame al reed;
> And Pandarus gan under for to prie,
> And seyde, "Nece, if that I shal be ded,
> Have here a swerd and smyteth of myn hed!"
> With that his arm al sodeynly he thriste
> Under hire nekke, and at the laste hire kyste.
>
> I passe al that which chargeth nought to seye,
> What! God foryaf his deth, and she al so
> Foryaf, and with here uncle gan to pleye,
> For other cause was there noon than so.
> But of this thing right to the effect to go,
> Whan tyme was, hom to here hous she wente,
> And Pandarus hath fully his entente.
> > (III, 1562-1582)

None of the important editors, such as Skeat, Robinson, Root, or Baugh, comments on the word play in these stanzas. But some English and American critics seem to have arrived independently at the opinion that this scene contains a *double-entendre* which puts Pandarus in the position of enjoying Criseyde the morning after her first night of love with Troilus. Haldeen Braddy claims to have first noted that "a type of incest becomes the basis of uncle Pandarus's relationship with his niece Criseyde. Chaucer unmistakably communicates the idea of their unwholesome alliance, but he does so, not by coarse vulgarisms that match their unnatural 'dede,' but by inoffensive verses that conform to both the social status of his characters and the tastes of his courtly audience."[65] Braddy contends that in "God foryaf Pandarus his deth," Chaucer employs the word *death* to mean Pandarus' coition with Criseyde. Braddy points out that Donne, Shakespeare, and other writers have used *death* to mean sexual intercourse.

Beryl Rowland agrees with Braddy that when Chaucer refuses to talk about what transpired between uncle and niece,

> I passe al that which chargeth nought to seye,
> What! God foryaf his deth, and she al so
> Foryaf. . . ,

Chaucer is not referring to Christ's death, but to Pandarus' death, that is, to his sexual relationship with Criseyde. Rowland believes that Pandarus' behavior in the consummation scene is not normal. Pandarus loves both Troilus and Criseyde; Pandarus is a bi-sexual pimp and voyeur who "employs extraordinary eloquence, cunning, physical strategy to bring them together. Then, having achieved her seduction, he apparently makes love to his niece himself, at the same time using an image which confirms his sexual interest in her."[66] This image is the figure of the knife which symbolizes the act of sexual intercourse not only in *Troilus* in

> . . . Pandarus gan under for to prie,
> And seyde, "Nece, if that I shal be ded,
> Have here a swerd and smyteth of myn hed!"

and in

> "But if ye late hym deyen, I wold sterve. . . .
> Al sholde I with this knyf my throte kerve."
> (II, 323-325)

but also in the "Wife of Bath's Tale" (577-582), the "Merchant's Tale" (1839-1840), and the "Parson's Tale" (859).

T. W. Ross also discusses the main love scene in *Troilus* under the heading of *incest* and suggests that the word *pleye* has the meaning of sexual intercourse.[67] He thinks that this scene strikes an "ugly little note." David Sims tells us that his friend Cecil Morgan first suggested that "hath fully his entente" is an obscene *double entendre* suggesting that Pandarus has his sexual desires fulfilled by Criseyde. Sims reminds us that moral Gower used the word *entente* in *Confessio Amantis* with a sexual connotation.[68]

Ian Robinson also finds it possible to accept the view that Pandarus would "pleye" with Criseyde. Voyeur as well as pandar, Pandarus is interested in love as a sexual game, and his participation in the bedroom farce shows how sexually interested he is in both Troilus and Criseyde.[69] His "pleye" with Criseyde in the following passages is hardly avuncular:

> "Refuse it naught," quod he, and hente hire
> faste,
> And in hire bosom the lettre down he
> thraste.   (II, 1154-1155)

> And Pandare wep as he to water wolde,
> And poked evere his nece newe and
> newe.
>   (III, 115-116)

Pandarus does seem to enjoy kissing, poking, nudging, and stroking his niece.

I should also like to call attention to another possible pun which has not been mentioned, possibly because most writers use Robinson's rather than Root's edition of *Troilus*. It is interesting to note that in Robinson and Baugh we find the expression "hath fully his entente," but the Root edition has "hath hoolly his entente" because the most authoritative manuscripts have that reading. Punster that he was, Chaucer did not overlook the possibilities offered by the homophones *hol* and *whole* and he sometimes used the word *holy* in a very irreverent fashion. The MED lists *hol* as meaning, among other things, external body organs or the female pudendum. Remember Alisoun's rectum in the "Miller's Tale" when "at

the wyndow out she putte hir hole." At the end of *Troilus* where
the reader is asked to love Christ and "herte al holly on hym
leye," *holly* is obviously not an equivoque. But Ross points to
several passages where Chaucer may be punning on either *hol*
or *holly*.

The most interesting one is the following conversation
between Pandarus and Criseyde:

> "And, be ye wis, as ye be fair to see,
> Wel in the rynge than is the ruby set.
> Ther were nevere two so wel ymet,
> Whan ye ben his al hool, as he is youre:
> Ther myghty God yet graunte us see that
>   houre!"
>
> "Nay, therof spak I nought, ha ha!"   quod
>   she;
> "As helpe me God, ye shenden every deel!"
> "O! mercy, dere nece," anon quod he,
> "What so I spak, I mente naught but wel."
> (II, 584-592)

According to Ross, the *ruby* is the penis, the *ring* is the vulva,
and the *hool* is the pudendum. He comments:

> The cluster of "ruby," "ring," and "hole" is too much for
> Criseyde, who is not so innocent as she sometimes likes to
> pretend (she is a widow, after all, though we are likely to forget
> it). She breaks out into uncontrollable giggles. Then Pandarus
> realizes what he has said, or implied, and tries to make
> amends.[70]

Thus it is possible to believe that Chaucer uses *hoolly* as well
as *deth, entente,* and *pleye* in Pandarus' and Criseyde's bed
scene to obtain double meanings. If the critics who maintain
that this coition does take place are correct, then this
"infamous" scene has the effect of emasculating the mood of
the preceding love scene and of making Criseyde seem like an
incestuous whore. It may well be that these passages represent
no more than a lapse of taste, a little horseplay that Chaucer
did not intend us to take seriously. He often intrudes seemingly
inappropriate bits of humor in serious portions of his poems.
Even D. R. Howard is puzzled by some lines in the beautiful love
scene in Book III because they seem to suggest a vulgar

bawdiness which is not in harmony with the ecstatic effect of the love episode: "The heroine, in an effort to revive Troilus, 'did al hire peyne' (1118); on reviving, his first words are 'O mercy, God, what thyng is this?' (1124). One assumes they are talking about his having fainted, but her next line is puzzling: 'Why do ye with youreselven thus amys? . . . Is this a mannes game?/ What, Troilus, wol ye do thus for shame?' We are left to imagine 'what thing' this is. . . ." Howard also asks, "When Pandarus, delivering the hero into the lady's bed, asks her if she will 'pullen out the thorn/ That stiketh in his herte' (1104-1105), what on earth does it mean? Is it an outrageous bit of phallic bawdry? Or is it the thorn in the flesh which St. Paul described?"[71] Note also the odd fact that Chaucer uses the word *stewe* to indicate the place where Troilus is hidden (III, 601, 698). While Skeat, Robinson and Baugh interpret *stewe* to mean "room," Ross reminds us that *stewe* clearly means "brothel" in several passages in the *Canterbury Tales*. "Surely," says Ross, ". . . Chaucer did not *have* to hide his hero in a nook the name for which will recall the brothel!"[72]

But even as horseplay, the bed scene involving Criseyde and Pandarus is disquieting, and we wonder why Criseyde is having fun with her uncle so soon after her night of love with Troilus. Sims explains her behavior in the following way: "Left alone in bed, she is in as excited a state as Troilus returned to his [sic] in his royal palace. . . . If it is Criseyde's desire that enables Pandarus to have 'fully his entente,' it is not mere desire that does it but her love's desire for Troilus and his noble qualities."[73] In other words, she sleeps with Pandarus because she loves Troilus! We have moved very far indeed from fourteenth-century England with this explanation, and I'm afraid that it is even too modern a view for twentieth-century readers.

Perhaps there is aesthetic justification for Chaucer's inclusion of this scene. Chaucer may have wished to provide us with a clearer view of her character by revealing her sexual nature. Despite the efforts of apRoberts and others to convince us that Boccaccio's poem is more erotic than Chaucer's, close scrutiny of Criseyde's behavior makes Boccaccio's heroine seem like an innocent sensualist. Criseyde's sexual responses are more complicated, more illicit, and more puzzling.

The well known linguistic crux in the fifth book of the poem may help to shed enlightenment on the nature of her sexuality.

In this section Chaucer offers us the only specific description of her character. After he describes her physical beauty, he says:

> She sobre was, ek symple, and wys withal,
> The best ynorisshed ek that myght be,
> And goodly of hire speche in general
> Charitable, estatlich, lusty, and fre;
> Ne nevere mo ne lakkede hire pite;
> Tendre-herted, slydynge of corage;
> But, trewely, I kan nat telle hire age.
>
> (V, 820-826)

Since the expression *slydynge of corage* appears nowhere else in Chaucer, and since it is a crucial one, critics have attempted to define it. W. W. Skeat, R. K. Root, F. N. Robinson, J. L. Lowes, and A. C. Cawley interpret it to mean "unstable of heart."[74] G. Krapp, M. Smith, and P.D.V. Shelly believe it means a "tender heart that moves in sympathy."[75] In fact, Smith even goes so far as to equate *tendre-hearted* with the conscience of the Prioress. He excuses Criseyde's lack of fidelity to Troilus on the grounds that she is too good a woman; she is too tender-hearted to refuse Diomede (the obverse being, I suppose, that the loyal woman is hardhearted). R. Preston has an interesting reading for *slydynge* which he translates as "slippery" (Chaucer's translation of the Latin *lubrica* of Boethius). For him Criseyde is a prime example of the inconsistently probable in characterization.[76] She "trembles at will" and is never deceived but permits herself the luxury of deceiving herself. Clearly *slydynge* means something like our modern "sliding" or it may mean "slippery." *Corage* has several meanings in Middle English—"valor," "heart," "virility," and "sexual desire." Ross points to several instances in which *corage* clearly means "sexual desire" or "lust." Ross and John Fisher note that *corage* can mean "penis," "sexual desire," and "lust."[77] Thus I suggest that the phrase not only refers to Criseyde's fickle heart, but also to her fickle sexuality. This may be what her morning "pleye" with Pandarus and her response to Diomede convey. While *lusty* usually means "lively," it can also have the modern sense of sexual desire. Pairing *lusty* with *fre* might reinforce the theme of Criseyde's capricious nature, generous to a fault in bestowing heart and body.

Those critics who believe that Criseyde's sexuality must be emphasized to explain her behavior would not consider the *double entendre* for "slydynge of corage" to be any more farfetched than the view which depicts her as a sacerdotal symbol of original sin. Wherever there is sex, there is bound to be Freudian theory. The most extreme analyses of Criseyde's character have been offered by Freudian critics like John Hagopian and Helen S. Corsa who maintain that Chaucer transformed the *Filostrato* into a "story that has unmistakable oedipal vibrations."[78] According to Hagopian, Troilus probably has an oedipal tie to his mother. Corsa thinks that Troilus' swoon in the love scene reveals an oedipal triangle with Pandarus as father and Criseyde as mother. "Troilus," she explains, "*had* to faint not only because he felt guilty for his participation in Pandarus' machinations, not only because he could not bear Criseyde's reproaches for believing rumors about her, but also because of interpsychic conflicts far more powerful than the apparent demands of the moment. The swoon reveals a deep anxiety, an anxiety generated by Troilus' having been brought almost to the point of achieving his infantile punishment, of primary loss. And the incredible wish, that the father will approve, is fulfilled when friendly 'uncle' Pandarus places him in Criseyde's bed."[79]

Furthermore, if there are dreams in the *Troilus*, and there are, and these dreams concern animals, and they do, then Freudians would expect them to be sexual symbols. While some of the critics who have explicated the eagle dream in Book II have not discussed its erotic elements, other critics like Joseph E. Gallagher and Helen Corsa provide an explicit sexual interpretation of Criseyde's encounter with the eagle:

> And, as she slep, anonright tho hire mette,
> How that an egle, fethered whit as bon,
> Under hire brest his longe clawes sette,
> And out hire herte he rente, and that anon,
> And dide his herte into hire brest to gon,
> Of which she nought agroos, ne no thyng smerte;
> And forth he fleigh, with herte left for herte.
>
> (II, 925-931).

Gallagher believes that the dream signifies that Criseyde is having sexual intercourse with Troilus, the eagle. Corsa contends that this is an oedipal dream in which the dreamer "deeply desires ravishment but at no cost of pain or disturbance. One need not be so literal minded as to see in this dream any 'reference' to Criseyde's relation to her father, Calkas. However, it does seem to me to be an oedipal dream that reveals a sexual fantasy of 'an extraordinarily passive and masochistic character.' "[80] According to Corsa, women like Criseyde are aggressively masculine in their struggle for survival and extremely passive in their sexual life. The eagle dream offers us an insight into Criseyde's real nature and explains why she forsakes Troilus. She refuses to suffer the pain of deep involvement, and accepting passively the fate that returns her to her father, she yields to the "brutality" of Diomede.[81]

The other important dream, which occurs in Book Five, is originally a simple one in Boccaccio's poem; the hero identifies the boar simply as Diomede and then interprets the dream to reveal Criseyde's betrayal. In the Italian poem Criseyde is attacked by the boar and derives pleasure from the attack. The lines in Chaucer's version tell us that Troilus dreams

> That in a forest faste he welk to wepe
> For love of here that hym these peynes
>   wroughte;
> And up and duun as he the forest soughte,
> He mette he saugh a bor with tuskes grete,
> That slepte ayeyn the bryghte sonnes hete;
>
> And by this bor, faste in his armes
>   folde,
> Lay, kissynge ay, his lady bryght,
>   Criseyde.
> For sorwe of which, whan he it gan
>   byholde,
> And for despit, out of his slep he
>   breyde,
> And loude he cride on Pandarus, and
>   seyde;
> "O Pandarus, now know I crop and roote.
> I n'am but ded; ther nys non other bote.
>
> "My lady bright, Cryseyde, hath me
>   bytrayed,
> In whom I trusted most of any wight;
> She elliswhere hath now here herte
>   apayed.

> The blysful goddes, thorugh here grete
>   myght,
> Han in my dream yshewed it ful right.
> Thus in my dream Criseyde have I by-
>   holde"—
> And al this thing to Pandarus he tolde.
>   (1235-1253)

Pandarus' interpretation of the dream is "most astonishing." Pandarus suggests that the boar symbolizes Criseyde's father who is old and at the point of dying, and in sorrow she kisses him on the ground and begins to weep. (Later Cassandra identifies Diomede as the boar.) Corsa quotes Ernest Jones again to the effect that animals in a dream usually signify the sexual theme of incest. Troilus' dream is a primal scene nightmare involving mental conflict over incestuous desire.[82] "The pastoral peacefulness of Troilus' dream, so sharply contrasting with the brutality of Troilo's, has all the suggestions of the primal scene; the sorrowful vision of Criseyde's passive contentment in the boar's embrace conveys movingly the agony of a child's sense of exclusion, of loss, of inevitable separation. Surely it is a scene that is one of the first moments a child is forced to recognize that he has 'lost,' that he has been betrayed, that all his one-time joy is a thing of the past."[83] Not only does the dream signify a form of the oedipal fantasy, but also Chaucer's falling in love with his heroine seems to have something of the oedipal nature about it. "I am not suggesting," concludes Corsa "that we read this poem autobiographically—how Chaucer felt about his mother, Agnes Chaucer, or about her substitute is not relevant. What is relevant is that he seems to have intuited the deeply important human fantasy at the very core of Boccaccio's story and responded to it in small as well as large ways. . . ."[84]

Thus modern rhetorical and psychological analysis has Criseyde sleeping with her uncle, involved in some curious way with her father, at least in the dreams of Troilus, and finally she symbolizes Troilus' mother. Poor Criseyde! What a mess modern criticism makes of her. But while we may justifiably deplore the excesses of Freudian analysis, what we cannot do if we are explaining Criseyde from a twentieth-century vantage point is to ignore the problem posed by her sexual behavior.

If we try to interpret Criseyde as we view her in this decade, we would have to reconsider the concept of sexual betrayal which has been used so often by the historicists. And such reconsideration might well lead us to argue that the term *betrayal* is no longer as meaningful to us today as it was in the past. D. and L. Brewer suggest that we may already be entering a period described by Huxley in *Brave New World*: "If, as seems possible, sex becomes a promiscuous, pleasant sporting activity, played between pairs, rather like tennis, and about as public, it will have no significant relation to personality, and will become completely trivial. It will give far less pain than it did, and by the inexorable law that action equals reaction, will give far less joy. The feeling of a Troilus or a Romeo, incomprehensible now to the complete extrovert or boor, will then have become as remote even to the imaginative as the scientific [concepts of that age]. . . ."[85] Moreover, all the brouhaha about Criseyde's defection will also become incomprehensible. For what was clearly understood to be sexual betrayal in the last century is less clearly understood today, and it is entirely possible that these words will vanish from the vocabulary of 2500. Meanwhile, we may well feel that Criseyde did not betray Troilus because she took another lover when she was separated from him by the exigencies of war. The pledge of eternal loyalty that he demanded of her would be viewed by us as being somewhat unrealistic. She was not bound to remain like the figures on Keats' Urn "forever panting" and "forever loving."

In this age with its permissive notions of love and sex, the obsessive love of a Heathcliff or a Romeo seems to be a fictional delusion. No real man would spend his life yearning after a dead woman to the exclusion of every other feeling, and no man kills himself over a woman unless he is mentally ill. This Troilus with his crying and swooning might strike us as rather effeminate and lacking in virility. We would expect a normal Troilus, after a certain amount of time, to follow Pandarus' advice, forget Criseyde, and find another beautiful woman. And as we have noted, someone *has* argued that Troilus is not normal, that he is psychologically maladjusted, and that Criseyde falls in love with Diomede because he behaves like a man. He doesn't faint and require a Pandarus to get him into bed. In other words, Criseyde loves Diomede because she recognizes that he is the better man. After all, even Troilus himself admits that the "bold, strong knights of Greece are superior to the foolish Trojans in wit and heart and might" (IV,

1485-1491). It is usually assumed that Criseyde is not married to Troilus, but even if, as Kelly and Maguire claim, she and Troilus have a clandestine marriage, she can still take a lover without being castigated as evil. The modern world accepts as a fact of life the transitory nature of human relationships. It is a lovely ideal for a woman to love one and only one man. But Chaucer's Wife of Bath reminds us that even in his time that ideal was not taken seriously. The concept of undying love seems to many of us in this century to be a romantic illusion. We can, therefore, more readily understand why Criseyde who supposedly "loves" Troilus would, in view of the special nature of her sexuality, become Diomede's mistress. Whether her sexual relationships involve real love in the romantic or ideal sense is a fact which the poem does not make clear to us.

What Chaucer does convey very clearly is the sense in which her sexuality becomes a symbol for endurance. She is no tragic heroine acting out of fear or loneliness. She likes men and reacts with pleasure to their desires. That is why the Henryson sequel *The Testament of Cresseid* strikes us as unreal. Criseyde, no more than her famous counterpart Helen, would be reduced to beggary. That is the myth of poetic justice fostered by Christian moralists. Chaucer knew better, and this is why he never tells us what happened to her. He knew that she would survive just as her famous counterpart survived. In this connection we can use our knowledge of the past, our knowledge of a myth, to confirm the meaning we presently find in the poem; that is, the historical reading can reinforce a modern reading.

There is a scene at the end of Book II at Deiphebus' house where Troilus and Criseyde meet. Deiphebus is Helen's brother-in-law and Paris' rival for the affections of Helen. She comes alone to Deiphebus' house

> . . . an houre after the prime,
> With Deiphebus to whom she nolde
> feyne;
> But as his suster, homly, soth to
> seyne,
> She com to dyner in hire pleyne entente.
> But God and Pandare wist al what
> this mente.

(1557-1561)

Edward H. Kelly notes:

> On the surface these lines protest that Queen Helen has come
> to dinner merely because her brother-in-law Deiphebus has
> invited her; but at the same time they specify she "nolde
> feyne" him, and that God and Pandarus know the full
> meaning of their meeting. In this verse paragraph Chaucer
> loads his diction with subtle levels of meaning that leave little
> doubt of Helen's real reasons for attending the meeting
> without her husband. *Homly* at first glance means "to be at
> home with," "as a member of the family." But when one
> knows the mythic relationship between the brother and sister-
> in-law its second sense becomes primary: "sexually intimate
> with," "of parts of the body: closely associated." "Pleyne," of
> course, yields "clear," "obvious," but the more appropriate
> meaning in this case is "amorous (wanton) dalliance,"
> "playful self-amusement." In any case, the punning sense of
> both words is evident.[86]

Deiphebus' constant attention to Helen in this scene reminds
us that after Paris dies, Deiphebus takes over as Helen's
spouse, and it is from the bed of Deiphebus that Menelaus
rescues Helen. Menelaus kills Deiphebus.

Gaylord has pointed to an interesting inconsistency in the
treatment of the Trojan nobility.[87] He reminds us that when
Pandarus seeks help from Deiphebus for the dinner party for
Criseyde, Deiphebus expresses personal enthusiasm and
friendship for Criseyde.

> " . . . O, is nat this,
> That thow spekest of to me thus
>   straungely,
> Criseÿda, my frend?" . . .
> "Then nedeth . . . hardyly,
> Namore to speke, for trusteth wel that I
> Wol be hire champioun with spore and
>   yerde;
> I rought nought though alle hire foos
>   it herde."
>
> (II, 1421-1428)

He assures Pandarus that he will also involve Helen because
"she may leden Paris as hire leste." As for Hector, says
Deiphebus, he can be counted on because

> "It nedeth naught to preye hym frend
>   to be;
> For I have herd hym, o tyme and ek
>   oother,
> Speke of Cryseyde swich honour, that
>   he
> May seyn no bet, swich hap to hym
>   hath she.
> It nedeth naught his helpes for to
>   crave;
> He shal be swich, right as we wol hym
>   have."
>
>   (II, 1451-1456)

Why then, asks Gaylord, if these three powerful nobles, Paris, Deiphebus, and Hector are personal friends and admirers of Criseyde, do they not *do* something to keep her in Troy? Hector merely tries with the weak "we usen here no wommen for to selle" in the debate in Parliament, and Troilus keeps quiet "lest men sholde his affeccioun espye." (Once again, we might well ask how his "affeccioun" could compromise her reputation, expecially if they are married.) Gaylord thinks the Trojan lords are "insincere friends, their graciousness not supplemented with the strength of deeds." He believes that Chaucer is deliberately criticizing the Trojan aristocracy, for the noble life is full of superficial "politesse" and fainthearted courtliness.

Furthermore, we should remember that when Pandarus expresses guilt about the role he has played, Troilus tries to reassure his pander by offering him any one of his fair sisters, including Helen. Surely this is a very generous offer and clearly reveals the sexual standards of Trojan royalty. Just as Helen goes from Menelaus to Paris to Deiphebus back to Menelaus, we suspect that Criseyde, who goes from Troilus, perhaps incidentally to Pandarus, and then to Diomede, will go on to find someone else. When she tells Troilus before yielding to him,

> "Ne hadde I er now, my swete herte
>   deere,
> Ben yold, ywis, I were now nought
>   heere!"
>
>   (III, 1210-1211),

we know that she means exactly what she says. No one ever

really makes Criseyde do what she doesn't want to do, although she is adept at furthering the illusion that she is being manipulated.

Now this modern view of Criseyde is based on the premise that Criseyde is like a real woman. Admittedly, some critics have insisted that Criseyde is not real. A. Mizener, J. Bayley, and a few other writers, consider her to be static and flat; L. Durham even goes so far as to describe her as an archetypal love goddess symbolizing the principle of life.[88] But by and large there is a consensus that praises Chaucer lavishly for creating the first real study of a woman in the first "psychological novel" in English literature. In a widely disseminated tape discussion of this poem, D. Pearsall and E. Salter refer to the realistic characters in the poem without defining the sense in which they use the troublesome term *realistic.*[89] Corrigan berates Chaucer for creating a woman who would seem real only to fourteenth-century readers with mistaken notions of what constitutes the "female principle." Also Corrigan writes that with Criseyde Chaucer "does nothing particularly profound to illuminate an understanding of the psychic, social or biological needs of woman, and in this he reflects the *Zeitgeist* of an age which would not allow an understanding of woman as different from rather than inferior to man."[90] In other words, Chaucer fails with Criseyde because he doesn't have the modern world's superior understanding of the nature of woman! I suspect that Corrigan tends to overemphasize the polarity of the male-female principle. Furthermore, his progressivist notion that the modern world knows more about women than the fourteenth-century world did is at best a highly dubious contention.

But what we can speak of with assurance is that Criseyde is not represented as being inferior to Troilus. In every scene in which she appears she clearly reveals herself to be the "stronger sex." We know she will survive, not because, like Faulkner's Delsey, she has spiritual tenaciousness but because of a flexible nature which will enable her to adjust to any and all situations. And Chaucer has provided us with signposts that she will use her sexuality to guarantee not only her pleasure but her security. Unlike Troilus she has learned to disassociate sex and love. We may or may not approve of this, depending upon our view of how a woman should behave. But pragmatic Criseyde doesn't stand for the female principle any more than the excessively romantic Troilus stands for the male principle. She doesn't symbolize or personify WOMAN. We believe in her because we recognize that she resembles certain kinds of Criseydes alive and well and living in Paris. Note that other kinds of women are also alive and well, but these Nanas and Bovaries do not have as high a survival rate. Thus the result of this modern reading of Criseyde's character is that she is not viewed as a Christian example of the sinfulness of love. For the real Criseyde who stands up for me today, a sensual woman with a strong will to survive, is a composite of my view of human sexuality as I see it dramatized in *Troilus*.

Such an "unhistorical" Criseyde would be an unacceptable reconstruction for the orthodox medievalist. For example, Peter M. Vermeer objects strongly to Ian Robinson's suggestion that Pandarus "hath fully his entente" means that he has had sexual intercourse with Criseyde: "Evidence for all this is provided, but it is historically unsound, and out of character with the poem as an organic whole, especially in view of the overall characterization of Criseyde and Pandarus. The distortion results again from a lack of historical insight, from a reading of (parts of) a Middle English text as if it belonged (in language and in spirit) to our own age."[91] But again we see how premises are treated as if they were true statements. Not all critics believe that *Troilus* belongs in "spirit and language" *only* to the Middle Ages; indeed through translation and explication they try to interest the modern reader in its universality. Not all critics believe that *Troilus* is an "organic whole." For example, Elizabeth Salter writes that *Troilus* "is, above all, a striking example of a medieval poem which forbids the easy use of terms such as 'unity,' 'consistency'. . . . In short, Chaucer could never have intended his poem to be seen as a unified whole, except in the crudest narrative sense."[92] And not all critics believe that Criseyde is a moral character who would *never* misbehave with Pandarus. When we place alongside William Godwin's judgment in 1804 that Criseyde is a "false, inconstant whore," Constance Saintonge's description of the bewitching and admirable Criseyde who even when she betrays Troilus, "embodies the traits which men have traditionally desired in women; she is soft, amorous, sweet, timorous, and mysterious," we have a clear idea of the polarity which has characterized the criticism of Criseyde for hundreds of years.[93]

It is very easy to imagine what a conservative medievalist would think about the intrusion of the women's liberation movement into the world of Chaucer. But Arlyn Diamond has written a spirited defense of the examination of Chaucer which is inspired by feminist concerns. Such concern, she claims,

> is not an historical perversity to be equated with wondering what he thought about the Copernican system, but a very natural way of approaching him, given the lively, even obsessive interest the later Middle Ages took in the problem of female nature. Christine de Pisan, "the first of her sex to protest in writing against the scurrilous attacks that had been made upon it," set a neglected precedent for modern critics when in 1399 she wrote an "Epistle to the God of Love," objecting to the treatment of women in . . . *Roman de la Rose.* It would be easy to cite dozens of medieval poems, sermons, plays, educational treatises, etc. whose discussion of how women ought to be regarded, justify sharing Christine's concern with images of her sex in literature, if not her methods.[94]

In other words, a modern reading can be supported by the facts of history.

From a feminist viewpoint, Laila Gross' reference to the "enormity of [Criseyde's] crime"[95] would be an example of the way in which male critics have influenced the gullible to accept a false view of Chaucer's heroine. The following lines which are spoken by Criseyde are taken to be crucial evidence for the view that Criseyde is an early feminist. They underscore her desire to be a free and independent woman:

> "I am myn owene womman, wel at ese,
> I thank it God, as after myn estat,
> Right yong, and stonde unteyd in lusty
>   leese,
> Withouten jalousie or swich debat:
> Shal noon housbonde seyn to me 'chek
>   mat!'
> For either they ben ful of jalousie,
> Or maisterfull, or loven novelrie."
>
> (II, 750-756)

Ann Haskell calls it her "speech on liberation."[96] Maureen Fries contends that it reveals "feminism of the *word* rather than feminism of the deed." Criseyde is a "would-be feminist . . . betrayed by the sexist nature of her nurture as she attempts to cope with circumstances for which that nurture had not provided."[97] Only the Wife of Bath is a "truly practicing feminist." Criseyde tries to extricate herself from male dominance at the same time that she submits to "widespread male victimization." She is controlled by Hector, Pandarus, Troilus, Calkas, Diomede and the people of Troy *en masse*. She is "betrayed by the tenderness and lack of fortitude [slydynge of corage] which was the almost inevitable result of a culture which, both in the experience of its daily life and in the 'auctoritee' of its books and laws, continually emphasized the physical and mental weakness of women."[98]

Pat T. Overbeck notes that Criseyde, unlike the good women in the *Legend of Good Women*, does not die; "she *survives*."[99] I have offered my own interpretation of how she, as a realist, survives in an imperfect world. But the feminist interpretation views her primarily as *victim*. She is a woman who truly deserves Chaucer's judgment: "I wolde excuse hire yet for routhe." We should also take note of the fact that men who sympathize with woman's "search for liberation" defend Criseyde's behavior. H. R. Hays in his fascinating study of the myths of feminine evil writes:

> Unlike the compulsive and unbalanced shaman and cleric, Chaucer contributes a more civilized outlook towards woman. He makes it clear that he feels no primitive compulsion to discriminate against women. . . . Criseyde is the pawn of male authority in both camps. . . . By his minute analysis of Criseyde's actions he shows clearly that she conforms to a submissive pattern. Criseyde, a creature of her time, is simply all too human.[100]

It would be very satisfying to believe that Chaucer was one of the early champions of women's rights. But we do not know what he really thought about the subject. The feminist interpretation of Criseyde is an essentially modern reading of her role which reflects the shift in attitude towards women.

For very good reason the minor characters have not aroused as much interest as the three main figures. But every now and then someone tries to assign major significance to the roles played by Diomede, Calkas, Antigone, Cassandra and Hector. Diomede is, of course, the most interesting of the minor characters in the poem because he is the reason why Criseyde "betrays" Troilus. Stephen Knight claims that Diomede is the "most openly malevolent influence" on Criseyde; he is always "ful redy" for action in contrast to Troilus whose inaction stems from his honorable concern about Criseyde's safety. How different he is from the "ful redy" Diomede who is perceptive, brusque, crafty with a callously cheerful self-concern. In Book V Chaucer gives him lines which reveal his deceit. He is a "fine moulder of phrases," and a "great insinuator." First, he uses simple, forceful language interspersed with proverbs. Then, in lines 102-105, he turns to a "roundabout approach" as he tries to "trap" Criseyde. His cunning is revealed when he employs the subtle and powerful language of the courtly lover—*disese, encresse, ese, commende.* He reassures Criseyde of his friendship by playing on the word *frend,* meaning both brother and lover, and he finally declares his undying love in the "saccharine conclusion" of lines 174-175. In his next appearance Diomede is less gentle, less straightforward, and Chaucer uses the fishing metaphor in his "crude and trite wooing," replete with trite proverbs. These maxims reveal the "poverty-stricken nature" of his mind just as Criseyde's proverbs reveal her "shallow conceptual powers and plasticity." There is, therefore, this contrast between what Diomede thinks and says to Criseyde which intensifies our sense of his dishonesty. The more carefully we examine his style, the less moral a being he seems to be. The diction, rhythm, syntax, and rhyming patterns of the stanza form combine to tell us this. In essence Knight uses an examination of Chaucer's poetic form to reinforce what others before him, such as Speirs, Donaldson, French, and Tatlock, have said about Diomede.[101]

The portrait of Diomede in lines 801-805 shows him to be a powerful, forbidding figure. The "chivalrous" reference is not significant because Diomede is merely chivalric in relation to "dedes." Then Knight points to Diomede's words in lines 844-847 and 855-861 which are full of dishonesty, for in the guise of a lover, he "savagely" tells Criseyde to forget Troilus. He makes her afraid because he tells her Troy is doomed, and then he gently offers her his love. In view of the "malign skill" of his assault, we expect Criseyde to fall victim to this "sodeyn" Diomede.

As we would expect, there is a dissenting voice. Paul Edmunds argues that Diomede is a "verray gentil parfit knyght." Knight dismisses Edmunds' view by jeering at his misquotation, and by invoking the appeal to authority that critics generally agree that Diomede is a bad fellow. Edmunds' premise is highly dubious. He states: "Were Diomede less noble than Troilus, were he deprived of any of his excellent traits, physical or intellectual, Criseyde's choice would be absurd and the entire tale would be worthless as an artistic creation."[102] I do not see why we have to accept this argument, for Criseyde's choice of a less noble man than Troilus would not seem absurd but realistic, and such a choice would hardly make the tale "worthless." Even if we agreed with Edmunds, we would still have to consider the hyperbole of his description of Diomede. Edmunds wishes us to believe that when Criseyde was nursing Diomede she recognized "his many assets: his eloquence, courage, nobility, valor, and something even more commendable which Chaucer indicated without pointing directly at it—Diomede's manliness."[103] His pursuit of Criseyde was conducted with "vitality, vigor, enthusiasm and a dazzling gallantry" which enhances the contrast with Troilus' effeminate behavior. There is no reason to assume that Diomede was unfaithful to Criseyde, and no reason for believing that Diomede's hasty courtship of Criseyde was Chaucer's way of condemning Diomede. To speak of Diomede's *sleighte* is to refer to his skill, not to his trickery; Diomede is not the villain of the poem.

It is possible to argue that Knight strains too hard to make Diomede a bad character. If we start with the premise that there is nothing inherently evil about trying to "make it" with an unmarried woman, it is easy to take a more affirmative position on Diomede. Edmunds speaks in ridiculously glowing terms of Diomede. But he is neither as bad nor as good as these critics make him out to be. He appears briefly as a certain kind of man with recognizably real desires, and if his method of wooing is different from Troilus' method, he desires what Troilus wants; despite all the spiritual and philosophical rhetoric Troilus employs, he "lusts" after Criseyde in as physical a fashion as the "sodeyn" Diomede. The preference for a slow or fast lover is, after all, a matter of taste, and some modern women might well prefer Diomede; perhaps medieval women did as well. All of this is, of course, highly conjectural, but what is not disputable is the fact that Diomede is minimally developed as a character.

Knight, following Greenfield's example, also tries to make a good deal more of Calkas' appearance than he should. Both Knight and Greenfield speak of Calkas' "2 major appearances in the poem." Greenfield attempts to show that while he is present for a total of only 130 lines in the poem, he is "thematically   and   structurally . . . the   antithesis   to Troilus."[104] He represents blind lust, the desire for security in a material world which his knowledge of Destiny as an astrologer-prophet gives him. However, Troilus knows what Calkas does not know, namely, that truth or happiness is attained outside Destiny. It may well be that Calkas represents the falseness-blindness theme of the prophet, but that Chaucer invested him with more than a prophetic mantle is hardly borne out by the dramatic depiction of the character. Knight tries to show that Chaucer uses a "biting" tone and jingles to create an "abject" traitor with "slippery intellectualism" who uses "double wordes slye." But whereas Greenfield thinks he is contrasted with Troilus, Knight believes Calkas is contrasted with Hector. But to claim that what Chaucer achieves in 130 lines is a "remarkably thorough and successful piece of characterization by style" is still another example of the hyperbole into which Knight's enthusiasm leads him.[105]

Nor does he succeed in making us believe that Hector and Antigone are "thoroughly" developed characters. Knight tells us that Hector speaks in a noble, blunt fashion, and his limited power as a speaker in pleading for Criseyde perhaps sounds the minor theme in the poem, namely, "the inarticulacy of true honour and the articulacy of those whose manipulations lead to disaster."[106] This is an interesting point but nowhere in the brief passages spoken by Hector can there be said to be more than a minimal development of the usual stereotyped noble Hector of antiquity.

As for Antigone, Knight's discussion centers on the song she sings and how it affects Criseyde. Antigone is the means by which we learn more about Criseyde. Antigone functions as a dramatic device; she personifies the concept of love as a beautiful and reassuring force. Knight's discussion of the song Antigone sings and of the nature of the poetic style in the scene in which she appears reinforces the view that Antigone is a symbol rather than a realistic characterization.[107]

Henry H. Peyton III, who also analyzes the minor characters, believes that the sensual, passionate Helen by her presence in Deiphebus' house "encourages Troilus in his complete surrender to his own sensual nature, the result of which will be the destruction of his perfect universe." As for Chaucer's handling of Cassandra, it is "nothing short of brilliant." Not only does she serve as a "painfully accurate" and "crudely blunt" prophetess of evil, but she also physically resembles the Goddess Fortuna when she smiles as she predicts disaster: "Cassandra's divination is delivered with the diabolic intensity of a harpy."[108]

But Nicholas Russell believes that there is a "conscious lack of characterization" of these minor figures. They lack personality and are "significantly under-emphasized" so that Troilus and Criseyde "exist virtually *in vacuo*."[109] This is perhaps too extreme a judgment, but it is true that Diomede, Hector, Calkas, Helen, Antigone, and Cassandra are, after all, minor reverberations in the three major chords of the story, Troilus, Criseyde and Pandarus. As we have seen, these three characters inspire such disparate interpretations that it may well be impossible to harmonize the dissonance of opinion. Generally the explanations used to explicate their behavior are based wholly or partially on a historical reading so that nonhistorical analyses stand out in sharp contrast as maverick, unorthodox views.

"To see the contemporary in the timeless, to be able to hold up immortal plays as mirrors for his own time—that is surely the noblest function of a critic, the best justification for his work."

Martin Esslin, Introduction to Jan Kott, *Shakespeare Our Contemporary*

"By discovering in Shakespeare's plays problems that are relevant to our own time, modern audiences, often, unexpectedly, find themselves near to the Elizabethans; or at least are in the position to understand them well."

Jan Kott, *Shakespeare Our Contemporary*

"Sir Frank: I hear that another poor innocent is about to write a book on Chaucer. What would you advise him to do?
Maker: Write a *critical study*, and not be afraid to distinguish. I will give him a rough stratification. 1. The richest humane narrative verse, which is not always separate from 2. The best work of the *grant translateur*, or from 3. Inferior stuff, shoddy adaptation, over-literal versions, worthless catalogues. It is the critic's business to make such distinctions firmly and delicately, and so to help the reader. Chaucer can stand it. We have more information and speculation about facts than anyone can digest; we could do with further criticism."

Raymond Preston, *Chaucer*

CONCLUSION

Chapter Six

 Bloomfield reminds us that Chaucer's sense of history is revealed at the end of *Troilus* (1793 ff.) "where Chaucer argues from the contemporary diversity of the English language and from the sound changes going on in his time to the conclusion that English may change so drastically in the future that some may miswrite, mismeter or misunderstand him."[1] The extant manuscripts reveal that he has been "miswriten." As for "mismetering" his poetry, it has certainly been read in odd ways through the years. What F. N. Robinson, Baugh, and Baum tell us about Chaucer's use of iambic pentameter, and the pronunciation of the final *e* is not what Stephen Knight, James G. Southworth, and Ian Robinson tell us about Chaucer's prosody.[2] Alan T. Gaylord in his "Scanning the Prosodists: An Essay in Metacriticism" asks: "What would happen to a beginner who put down Knight and picked up Southworth, or Ian Robinson? He would have to think either he or the author had gone mad."[3]

My "scanning the critics" in this "essay in metacriticism" has revealed such a diversity of opinion and so many contrary interpretations that the reader might well wonder whether he or the critics "had gone mad." However, it is to the credit of those who write about *Troilus* that they usually disagree with a *gentilesse* spirit. This is why Edmund Reiss" comment that Ian Robinson's *Chaucer and the English Tradition* is a "foolish book" stands out as being unusually vituperative, and John Gardner's judgment that "there's a great deal of plain stupidity in Chaucer criticism" seems to be excessively brusque.[4] It is almost as if there is a gentleman's agreement to disagree about every important aspect of the poem from its time scheme[5] to its ending. Writers tell us that *Troilus* is a religious poem, a love poem, a Boethian poem or a muddled poem. It is a novel, a tragedy, a comedy, an epic, a romance, a rhetorical exercise. The imagery is aggregative; it is circular. The ending is beautiful; the ending is irrelevant. Chaucer creates real, flat, or archetypal people. Troilus is good, noble, heroic, tragic, foolish and sick. Criseyde is good, bad, aggressive, frightened, bright, specious, amoral, and oversexed. Pandarus is comic, obscene, delightful, friendly, and villainous.

Are we then left with a "wise eclecticism"? Do we accept all judgments because in the end they contribute to the total vision of truth about *Troilus*. This is Donaldson's view; *Troilus*, he says,

> possesses to the highest degree that quality, which characterizes most great poetry, of being always open to reinterpretation, of yielding different meanings to different generations and kinds of readers, who, no matter how they may disagree with one another on even its most important points, nevertheless agree in sharing the profoundly moving experience the poem offers them. Its highly elusive quality, which not only permits but encourages a multiplicity of interpretations, is in no way the result of incompetence on the part of the poet, but something carefully sought after as the best way of expressing a complex situation.[6]

Such relativism seems to offer a simple, sensible solution to the critical problem resulting from a "multiplicity of inter-pretations."

To the question, "Which one of the critical statements about *Troilus* is true or false?" we would have to answer *none*. For this survey of *Troilus* criticism has reaffirmed what Weitz's study of *Hamlet* revealed: namely, that criticism does not supply us with true or false conclusions, but with more or less reliable hypotheses. These range in the discussion of *Troilus* from the privileged ones which the orthodox, scholarly establishment favors to subsidiary, less favored ones related in some way to the main hypotheses and to unorthodox hypotheses frowned upon by the establishment. For example, to illustrate the range, we have the "historical Boethian hypothesis," which, as I have shown, is the most widely used and respected approach to *Troilus*. Then there is the "defense of Criseyde theory" defended by Joseph Graydon who claims that Criseyde is justified in rejecting Troilus because his jealousy leads him to break the courtly code of secrecy by informing Cassandra of his dream. I have not even bothered to discuss this theory because it is so patently ludicrous. J. M. French clearly demonstrates that Graydon's view is based on a distortion of the "raw data" of the poem.[7] What is amazing is that the prestigious journal *PMLA* should have printed Graydon's glaringly deficient essay, but again this illustrates how any novel discussion can be published regardless of the level of substantiation in the analysis.

But while hypothesizing is the primary means by which *Troilus* is criticized in the historical, philosophical, formalistic, and psychological approaches to criticism, and in the more specific theories deduced from these general approaches, it is also true that we can distinguish between more or less reliable hypotheses. Unfortunately, in relation to *Troilus* the degree of reliability a hypothesis has for each individual reader depends upon his ideological preferences. It should be clear to any reader that I agree with John Ellis that logical analysis "must be uniquely at the center of literary theory" and that I disagree with Erich Heller that criticism of literature "cannot be taught, but only 'caught,' like a passion."[8] *Troilus* criticism, it seems to me, has been least effective and convincing when it has been most "passionate." But my commitment to logical inquiry has not provided me with a foolproof kind of literary scientism, and like any analyst I have been influenced by preconceptions. Just as there is no such phenomenon as "pure induction" for the scientist, there is no such phenomenon as "pure objectivity" in criticism. Perhaps it is safest to speak of logical biases which predispose us to accept one hypothesis over another.

Most medievalists seem to favor the historical hypothesis, and this is why the preponderance of *Troilus* criticism is historically oriented. Now if it could be shown that historicism gives us the means by which we can attain a consensus as to what the poem is and means, we would be justified in accepting all of its hypotheses as privileged. But as we have seen, the conclusions of the historicists are at variance with each other, not only in relation to interpretation, but even in regard to the so-called facts of the poem. When Donaldson tried to practice what he preached in his edition of Chaucer's poetry, *An Anthology for the Modern Reader* (1958), he wrote in his Preface: "I have . . . eschewed the historical approach used both by the great Chaucerians of the earlier part of this century and by those scholars who have recently been reading Chaucer primarily as an exponent of medieval Christianity. The fact that the difference between what these two historical approaches have attained is absolute—if Chaucer means what the older Chaucerians thought he meant he cannot possibly mean what these newer Chaucerians think he means—has encouraged me to rely on the poems as the principal source of their meaning."[9]

Donaldson and other writers have criticized Robertson's type of historical analysis. In 1973 Robert O. Payne and Martin Stevens broadened the attack against the historicists to include more than the Robertsonians. Payne objects to the historical criticism employed by Baugh, Bronson, Manly, as well as Robertson. Payne does not reject the historical approach; instead he suggests that ". . . we must create—the best whole literary past we can. We need not only a cultural history, but a *musée imaginaire*, a refined and informed sense of what we need most and love best in the past. We need to stock our literary *musée imaginaire* with things both this side and the other side of Chaucer. Once we have read Spenser, Yeats, and Stevens, there is no way that Chaucer can look the same to us as he looked to his contemporaries. If we are to have a literary past which doesn't end with Chaucer's death and which is still alive in our active sense of values, then it is aesthetic suicide to commit ourselves to the aesthetic charade we have been offered recently as 'historical criticism.' "[10]

While Payne asks us to substitute a diachronic for an archaeological view of history, Martin Stevens takes the plunge and calls for a modern interpretation of Chaucer:

> We have tried for too long now to approach Chaucer's artistry over the highways, and even more often the byways, of the past. True, the *De Doctrina Christiana*, the Gothic cathedral, the cumulative French tradition, icons and allusions of Christianity, the topoi and structures of medieval rhetoric, the study of the Bible and the Saints, the intimate acquaintance of Ricardian life and times—all these and more subjects are of vital concern to students who seek to know fully Chaucer the man, his times, and his works. But they will suffice only to

bring knowledge, not understanding at the deepest level of all those qualities that we finally recognize as the artistry of Chaucer. I propose, therefore, that Chaucerians abandon the common practice of deploring and eschewing the modern, that instead they make every effort to know its impulses and substance, for I believe that, properly defined and understood, it will help us to reenter the realm of Chaucer's art more meaningfully and profoundly than we can expect from any other avenue of approach.[11]

However, Stevens relies almost exclusively on Jose Ortega y Gasset's "The Dehumanization of Art" for his definition of modernism. By claiming that the modern world has abandoned romantic, realistic, and organic views of art, and shares with the medieval world a belief in the principal of disunity, Stevens may be as guilty as the historicist of making broad generalizations about the nature of an age.

Another argument for the modern reading of Chaucer has been offered by Harriett Hawkins who also supplies us with a modern analysis of the "Clerk's Tale." In her view, Robertson's interpretation of the tale cannot be reconciled with the primary responses it elicits from modern readers with modern standards concerning women. She comments:

Ideally, a full interpretation of a work written hundreds of years ago will reconcile historical, critical, and subjective interpretations of it in some fruitful and illuminating way, so that the work can be read on its own terms as well as (though not instead of) our own. For instance, a modern interpretation of *The Knight's Tale* might be based upon the critic's personal response to it, be influenced by twentieth-century ideas about some of the absurdities inherent in the ways of the world, and also be enhanced, supplemented, or corrected by pertinent information concerning the philosophy of Boethius, the conventions of medieval poetry, and the code of courtly love. It would thus be possible to interpret *The Knight's Tale* in terms of the literary, historical, and philosophical context in which it was written, and still read it, in Professor Leavis's words, "as we read the living."[12]

This would indeed constitute a *full* interpretation. But then Hawkins asks the same question that I ask about *Troilus* criticism: "But what happens if historical or theological interpretations of a comparable work do not complement but, rather, conflict with subjective responses to it? And should various levels of scholarly interpretation contradict each other, which should finally take precedence over the others?"[13] We know how Donaldson replied to this question. We simply live with the contradictions. But contemporary critics like John Reichert, E.D. Hirsch, and Walter A. Davis believe that we should be able to distinguish first order and second order hypotheses in literary criticism; ultimately we should use first order hypotheses to construct reliable or objective or correct interpretations. This is what, as R. B. Braithwaite notes, happens in scientific inquiry.[14] But in literary inquiry the reality falls far short of the ideal.

Hawkins suggests that after we have tried to discover all that we can about the literary, philosophical, and historical "facts" concerning a literary work, we should then "ask whether the work itself upholds or challenges contemporary assumptions; and, finally, to decide for ourselves how we, personally, think and feel about it."[15] She is unconcerned about the affective fallacy inherent in such an approach; she claims that criticism is overly concerned with objectivity. I would hardly want to argue for an endless proliferation of subjective responses to *Troilus*. The reading of poetry involves personal or subjective reactions, but the *critical* act demands objective validation in terms of the data of the poem. But I agree with Hawkins that we should ask whether a work "upholds or challenges contemporary assumptions."

Jennifer Strauss believes that in order to teach *Troilus* we must recognize that it has a "unique verbal structure, of its time but not bounded by that time. To this we are obliged to give twentieth-century minds, for it seems to me to be a very dangerous delusion to imagine that it is within our grasp to read as a mediaeval reader (too much must be mentally deleted as well as acquired)."[16] Similarly, Jane Adamson comments:

> . . . [T]hose critics who have tried to discuss the poem as deeply moving, intelligent and very much alive, and who don't think that the best way to praise Chaucer is to bury him under Boethius or Boccaccio for instance, seem generally to labour under the dark suspicion of the "experts" that they are reading modern preoccupations into it. Depressingly enough, it still seems one has to repeat what ought to be perfectly obvious: that although Chaucer's poem *is* profoundly

mediaeval . . . it is not a historical relic fit only for the
specialists' private museum; and that while trying (as always)
to avoid the trap of reading anything into it, one can—and
should—try to grasp just what makes it so alive for us today.[17]

Sister Gill maintains that it is difficult for a modern reader to
understand and sympathize with the medieval view of love: "A
twentieth-century reader who does not relate sexual love to any
ultimate end beyond satisfaction of mutual desires of male and
female may have difficulty in discerning the cosmic explanation of love incorporated into the *Troilus* text."[18] If we admit the
dissimilarity in medieval and modern notions of love, it
becomes imperative in criticism to be concerned with the
modern reader's view of love. For it is the modern, not the
medieval, reader who is trying to understand *Troilus*. Sister
Gill's statement implies that modern love is deficient because it
lacks the cosmic view. But it is possible to argue that the theory
of love in this century is superior precisely because it lacks the
cosmic view. It was, after all, the "cosmic explanation of love"
in the Middle Ages that led to the public whipping of people who
committed sexual or marital indiscretions and to the cutting of
the nipples of adulterous women. As William Empson has
observed, we do not have to apologize for progress.[19] Furthermore, modern readers are quite capable of appreciating the
human and humane elements in the love story of Troilus and
Criseyde.

Trilling states that if "we try to make Shakespeare literally
contemporaneous, we make him monstrous. He is contemporaneous only if we know how much of a man of his own age
he was; he is relevant to us only if we see his distance to us."[20]
The reverse seems to me to be true. Shakespeare is meaningful
insofar as we see his nearness to us. Several years ago I
watched a witless performance of *The Merchant of Venice*
which dismayed the audience precisely because it attempted to
reconstruct the production that Shakespeare's audience saw.
Shylock was played as an odious, evil Jew, and the subtle,
magnificent speeches in the play were all subverted for comic
effect. The point is that Shylock has not been viewed as
"literally" contemporaneous, but that he has been interpreted
in different ways through the ages because his distance from us
has not been found to be relevant. For the same reason, readers
have re-examined the supposed "anti-semitism" of the

"Prioress' Tale." Scholars have used their knowledge of the Middle Ages to reconstruct the reactions of Chaucer's audience to his poetry. But very astute critics have warned us of the fallacious reasoning involved in trying to fathom what original audiences thought about a work of art; such reasoning often employs what Wimsatt calls Vista-Vision Intentionalism, the method of referring to *anything* in the medieval world which will help to confirm a hypothesis.[21]

Thus when I say that we must read *Troilus* not only as a medieval poem, but also as a modern poem, I mean that we must analyze all of its elements in such a way that they make sense to contemporary readers. For what we find in *Troilus* today concerning God, free will, love, friendship, sex, war, character, irony, tragedy, comedy, structure and style will help us to affirm its value as a work which speaks to all ages.

A caveat is in order here. I am not saying that the literary historian should stop searching for the past. Nor am I recommending that we reject the historical approach. It has yielded fruitful results. But it has also produced the kind of inane criticism which, for example, compares Criseyde to Christ. In *Troilus* criticism the preoccupation with the past has been obsessive and excessive. Even if we were to accept the premise that medieval literature, more than any other subject matter, requires a historical perspective, we could not avoid reading it from a modern perspective, since we are moderns. As we have seen, when modern and historical readings coincide, they both serve to enhance the appreciation of Chaucer's artistry. But it is ludicrous to think that any critical mandate can be enforced which proscribes the influence of modern culture. So Sheila Delaney who claims that "the application of modern critical categories to older literature is not necessarily a Procrustean effort," attempts to demonstrate that *Troilus* uses Bertolt Brecht's technique of alienation.[22] Stephenie Yearwood bases her discussion of the poem's narrative techniques on the terminology of the Russian Formalists: Tzvetan Todorov, Jerzy Pelc, and Boris Uspensky.[23] But even if a fortunate scholar were to discover that treasured document in which Chaucer explicates every line of the *Troilus*, readers could repudiate his explanation for various reasons, and formulate their own interpretations based on the evidence of the text. A recognition of this right is one of the important contributions of twentieth-century criticism.

Roger Sharrock judges Speirs' *Chaucer the Maker* to be a failure because "when confronted with Chaucer, the critic is not able to digest himself or to take for granted in his reader a knowledge of the fourteenth-century mind; thus much of his interpretation reads like the substitution of second-hand modern poems for this obscure and intractable material."[24] Many critics through the years have employed what Hirsch aptly calls the fallacy of the Homogeneous Past, the fallacy of assuming that there is such a phenomenon as the Medieval Mind.[25] It is as elusive as the Elizabethan or the Victorian Mind. Speirs' analysis and the modern readings of Ian Robinson, Van Doren, Donaldson, Preston, as well as those offered by feminists and other writers, are welcome additions to the more conventional, historically oriented discussions. Peter Vermeer insists that "anyone who writes on Chaucer should be well informed about his background and his language, should have a sympathetic understanding of the Middle Ages; in other words . . . a good critic cannot restrict himself to the limited perspective of the twentieth century."[26] All of this has been said often enough in medieval studies. But what has not been said often enough is that criticism cannot be restricted to the limited perspective of the past. This is what T. S. Eliot, the poet-critic with an awesome *musée imaginaire*, understood when he wrote:

> What matters most, let us say, in reading an ode of Sappho, is not that I should imagine myself to be an island Greek of twenty-five hundred years ago; what matters is the experience which is the same for all human beings of different centuries and languages capable of enjoying poetry, the spark which can leap across those 2,500 years. So the critic to whom I am most grateful is the one who can make me look at something I have never looked at before, or looked at only with eyes clouded by prejudice, set me face to face with it, and then leave me alone with it. From that point, I must rely upon my own sensibility, intelligence, and capacity for wisdom.[27]

Scholars have taught us a great deal about the sources Chaucer used. But he used more than books to write his poetry; he was certainly influenced by his experiences as a member of the human race. John Livingston Lowes, an exceptional scholar who used the historical approach with great skill and imagination, reminded us "that sources other than the *books*

Chaucer read—sources that lie in his intercourse with men and in his reaction upon the interests, the happenings, the familiar matter of his day—entered likewise into 'that large compasse of his,' and must be taken into account in estimating his work."[28] The first volume of *The Chaucer Library* has been published. This project encompasses the ambitious aim of publishing all the works known to Chaucer. The justification for this undertaking is that "the modern reader of Chaucer must turn to the works known by Chaucer in order to understand how the poet used and transformed his literary materials. . . ."[29] It is always important to know what an author reads, but his art must speak for itself to each generation of readers. One of the most esteemed Chaucerians Charles Muscatine believes that "we need a new Chaucer now—as we need one every generation—a Chaucer who will speak to the concerns of the 1980's and 90's, a Chaucer who will, if nothing else, make sense to college students who are even now turning in increasing numbers away from study of the humanistic classics to secure their futures and allay their terrors with Business Administration and Engineering."[30] Jan Kott has tried to make *Shakespeare Our Contemporary*, but no one has as yet tried to make Chaucer "Our Contemporary," and no one has written a modern full length study of *Troilus* in Muscatine's sense.[31]

The most recent books by McAlpine, *The Genre of Troilus and Criseyde*, and Rowe, *O Love O Charite! Contraries Harmonized in Chaucer's Troilus* are models of how books should be written that utilize a historical approach. Use a source, generally Boethius, add other sources where necessary, and demonstrate the extent of indebtedness. McAlpine and Rowe offer invaluable evidence for those who read *Troilus* as a medieval Christian poem. But the painstaking exegesis of the religious theme in these works has the unfortunate effect of converting a complex and multifaceted poem into a lifeless and humorless sermon.

Muscatine is right. We need a *Troilus* that will speak to all readers in the contemporary world. Chaucer would have understood this need. After all, what else is *Troilus* but his *modern* reading of an old pagan story?[32]

Notes for Chapter I
Introduction

1. *Against Interpretation and Other Essays* (New York, 1966), pp. 3-14; Letter to *TLS*, April 14, 1972, p. 420.

2. *The Languages of Criticism and the Structure of Poetry* (Toronto, 1953), pp. 192-193.

3. *The Act of Interpretation: A Critique of Literary Reason* (Chicago, 1978), pp., 52-61, 168, note 72.

4. *Hamlet and the Philosophy of Criticism* (Cleveland, 1964), p. 316.

5. Weitz, p. 318.

6. *The Language of Art and Art Criticism: Analytic Questions in Aesthetics* (Detroit, 1965), pp. 89-94.

7. *The Truths of Fiction* (London, 1970), p. 83.

8. "On Hypotheses in 'Historical Criticism': Apropos of Certain Contemporary Medievalists" in *The Idea of the Humanities and Other Essays: Critical and Historical* (Chicago, 1967), II, 244.

9. *The Theory of Literary Criticism: A Logical Analysis* (Berkeley, 1974), pp. 194-195.

10. "Is Literary Criticism Possible?" in *Collected Essays* (Denver, 1959), p. 476.

11. "Hamlet on Logic," *PMLA*, 90 (1975), 120-122; " 'I Know My Course': Hamlet's Confidence." *PMLA*, 89 (1974), 477-486.

12. *The Concept of Ambiguity—The Example of James* (Chicago, 1977), pp. 1-26.

13. "Current and Recurrent Fallacies in Chaucer Criticism," *Essays in American and English Literature Presented to Bruce Robert McElderry*, Jr., ed. M. Schulz, W. D. Templeman, C. R. Metzger (Athens, Ohio, 1967), p. 148.

14. *Literary Criticism: An Introductory Reader*, ed. L. Trilling (New Haven, 1970), p. 12.

15. *Making Sense of Literature* (Chicago, 1977), pp. 3, 4-27, 96-126.

16. *Validity in Interpretation* (New Haven, 1967), p. 145.

17. Hirsch, p. 180. See also pp. 173-198, pp. 209-244.

18. *Subjective Criticism* (Baltimore, 1978), p. 41.

19. "Reading Criticism," *PMLA*, 91 (1976), 804; J. L. Borges, *Paris Review*, interview (1967), p. 141, also prefers a critic who feels.

20. Nelson, 803.

21. "Editor's Column," *PMLA*, 91 (1976), 795.

22. See Hartman's letter in *PMLA*, 92 (1977), p. 307, where he states: "Criticism may, despite Frye's concordat, be itself a form of literature."

23. *Anatomy of Criticism* (Princeton, 1957), p. 118.

24. *Poetry and Repression: Revisionism from Blake to Stevens* (New Haven, 1976), p. 27.

25. Bloom, pp. 10, 5, 2.

26. *The Function of Criticism: Problems and Exercises,* 2nd ed. (Denver, 1957), p. 17. See also Frederick C. Crews, "Anaesthetic Criticism, I," *NYRB,* February 26, 1970, pp. 31-35; Graham Hough, *An Essay on Criticism* (London, 1966), p. 3; S. M. Schreiber, *An Introduction to Literary Criticism* (Oxford, Eng., 1965), p. 2.

27. "Literary Criticism," in *The Aims and Methods of Scholarship in Modern Languages and Literature,* ed. J. Thorpe (New York, 1963), pp. 57-69.

28. *Chaucer's Troylus and Cryseyde Compared with Boccaccio's Filostrato,* tr. W. M. Rossetti (London, 1873, 1883), Chaucer Society, First Series, Nos. 44, 65, p. viii.

29. *Chapters on Chaucer* (Baltimore, 1951), p. 100.

30. *Chaucer's Major Poetry,* ed. A. C. Baugh (New York, 1963), p. 81.

31. McCall, "Troilus and Criseyde," *Companion to Chaucer Studies,* ed. B. Rowland (London, 1968), p. 382; Kittredge, *Chaucer and his Poetry* (Cambridge, Mass., 1939), p. 109.

32. *Chaucer in seinen beziehungen zur italieniescher literatur* (Bonn, 1867), pp. 57-58.

33. *Geoffroy Chaucer* (Paris, 1910), pp. 126-127; Etienne G. Sandras, *Étude sur G. Chaucer* (Paris, 1859) pp. 41-50, also judged the *Filostrato* to be superior to the *Troilus.*

34. "Chaucer and the Great Italian Writers of the Trecento," *MC,* 6 (1927), 154.

35. *Chaucer and the English Tradition* (Cambridge, Eng., 1972), pp. 73-85.

36. "Criseyde's Two Half Lovers," *OL,* 16 (1961), 23.

37. Speirs, *Chaucer the Maker* (London, 1951), pp. 64-68; Chute, *Geoffrey Chaucer of England* (New York, 1946), p. 179; Baum, *Chaucer: A Critical Appreciation* (Durham, N.C., 1958), p. 157.

This introduction in somewhat modified form was read at the Modern Language Association Meeting in December, 1978.

Notes for Chapter II
The Historical Hypothesis

1. *The Living Chaucer* (Philadelphia, 1940), p. 20.

2. *The Function of Criticism,* p. 13.

3. "Literary Criticism: Poet, Poem, and Reader" in *Varieties of Religious Experience,* ed. Stanley Burnshaw (New York, 1962), p. 112. See also Robert O. Payne, *The Key of Remembrance: A Study of Chaucer's Poetics* (New Haven, 1963), p. 4.

4. *The Discarded Image: An Introduction to Medieval and Renaissance Literature* (Cambridge, Eng., 1964), pp. 12, 11.

5. "Historical Criticism" in *English Institute Essays,* 1950, ed. A. S. Downer (New York, 1951), p. 4. See also Robertson and B. F. Huppé, *Piers Plowman and*

Scriptural Tradition (New York, 1969), pp. 1-16, and by the same authors, *Fruyt and Chaf: Studies in Chaucer's Allegories* (Princeton, 1963), pp. 3-31.

6.   *Chaucer and the English Tradition*, p. 269.

7.   Robinson, pp. 270, 271, 278, 279.

8.   Robinson, pp. 278-279.

9.   Robinson, p. 277.

10.   Ellis, *The Theory of Literary Criticism*, pp. 118-122.

11.   Ellis, pp. 112-116; Richard Ellmann, "Love in the Catskills," *NYRB*, February 5, 1976, p. 27.

12.   *Theory of Literature* (New York, 1949), p. 34.

13.   "The Sense of the Past" in *The Liberal Imagination: Essays on Literature* (New York, 1957), p. 181.

14.   Ed. *The Book of Troilus and Criseyde by Geoffrey Chaucer* (Princeton, 1926), p. lxxxiv. All references in the context to *Troilus* are to F. N. Robinson's second edition of *The Works of Geoffrey Chaucer* (Boston, 1957). I use Robinson's edition only because I believe that it is the most accessible. See the following impressive works by Root dealing with the manuscripts: *The Manuscripts of Chaucer's Troilus with Collotype Facsimiles of the Various Handwritings*. Chaucer Society, First Series, No. 98 (London, 1914); *The Textual Tradition of Chaucer's Troilus*, Chaucer Society, First Series, No. 99 (London, 1916). See *Research in Progress* in the *Chaucer Review* for information about the projected Variorum Edition.

15.   *The Chaucer Tradition* (Oxford, Eng., 1967), pp. 172, 174; " . . . there do not really exist two versions of *Troilus*, but only traces of the many corrections which Chaucer naturally made in the course of composition" (p. 171).

16.   Cook, "The Revision of Chaucer's *Troilus*: The BETA Text," *ChauR*, 9 (1974), 51-62; F.N. Robinson's review of Root's edition of *Troilus* in *Spec*, 1 (1926), 462; Fisher, ed. *The Complete Poetry and Prose of Geoffrey Chaucer* (New York, 1977), p. 968; Brusendorff, p. 167. Charles A. Owen, Jr. in "Chaucer's Method of Composition," *MLN*, 72 (1957), 164-165, finds confirmation of Root's inferences about Chaucer's method of writing the draft of the *Troilus* in the manuscript of *The Equatorie of the Planetis*, ed. D. Price. See also Owen's "The Significance of Chaucer's Revisions of *Troilus and Criseyde*," *MP*, 55, (1958), 1-5, and Thomas B. Hanson, "The Center of *Troilus and Criseyde*," *ChauR*, 9 (1975), 297-302.

17.   Root, ed. *The Book of Troilus and Criseyde*, pp. xiv-xx, Root and H. N. Russell, "A Planetary Date for Chaucer's *Troilus*, *PMLA*, 39 (1924), 48-63; Lowes, "The Date of Chaucer's *Troilus and Criseyde*," *PMLA*, 23 (1908), 285-306; Tatlock, "The Dates of Chaucer's *Troilus and Criseyde* and *Legend of Good Women, MP*, I (1903-1904), 317-329; "The Date of the 'Troilus' and Minor Chauceriana," *MLN*, 50 (1935), 277-296; Brown, "Another Contemporary Allusion in Chaucer's *Troilus*," *MLN*, 26 (1911), 208-211; G. L. Kittredge, *The Date of Chaucer's Troilus and Other Chaucer Matters*, Chaucer Society, Second Series, No. 42 (London, 1909), pp. 1-61; Ramona Bressie, "The Date of Thomas Usk's 'Testament of Love,' " *MP*, 26 (1928), 28-29.

18.   *A Literary History of England* (New York, 1948), ed. Albert C. Baugh, et alii, p. 255, note, and Baugh, ed. *Chaucer's Major Poetry* (New York, 1963), p. 78.

19.   See *Troilus*, I, 169-172: "Among thise othere folk was Criseyda,/ In

widewes habit blak; but natheles,/ Right as our firste lettre is now an A,/ In beaute first so stood she, makeles."

20.   "The Astronomical Dating of Chaucer's *Troilus*," *JEGP*, 55 (1956), 556-562.

21.   Prologue to the *Fall of Princes*, lines 283-287, ed. H. Bergen, Part I (Washington, 1923), p. 8: "In youthe he made a translacioun/ Off a book, which callid is Trophe,/ In Lumbard tunge, as men may reede & see/ And in our vulgar, longe or that he deide/ Gaf it the name off Troilus & Cresseide." See Root, ed., *The Book of Troilus and Criseyde*, pp. xix, note 19, and p. xl.

22.   See the following for interesting hypotheses concerning the identity of Lollius: Hans J. Epstein, "The Identity of Chaucer's 'Lollius,' " *MLQ*, 3 (1942), 391-400; L. H. Hornstein, "Petrarch's Laelius Chaucer's Lollius?" *PMLA*, 63 (1948), 64-84; Kittredge, "Chaucer's Lollius," *HSCP*, 28 (1917), 47-109; Hugo Lange, "Chaucer's 'Myn Auctour called Lollius' und die Datierung des Hous of Fame," *Anglia*, 43 (1918), 345-351.

23.   "Essay on the Language and Versification of Chaucer," *The Canterbury Tales of Chaucer*, ed. Thomas Tyrwhitt (Edinburgh, 1860), I, lxxxi, note.

24.   For more complete information on Chaucer's use of sources, see the bibliographies of Albert C. Baugh, Lorrayne Y. Baird, Dudley D. Griffith and Eleanor P. Hammond as well as the bibliographies published by the *Chaucer Review*, *PMLA*, and the Modern Humanities Research Association. I list below some of the most well known works on this subject as well as some items that have interested me: Haldeen Braddy, *Chaucer and the French Poet Graunson* (Baton Rouge, La., 1947); John W. Clark, "Dante and the Epilogue of *Troilus*," *JEGP*, 50 (1951), 1-10; J. I. Cope, "Chaucer, Venus, and the 'Seventhe Spere,' " *MLN*, 68 (1952), 245-246; Dean S. Fansler, *Chaucer and the Roman de la Rose* (Gloucester, Mass., 1965); Donald K. Fry, "Chaucer's Zanzis and a Possible Source for *Troilus and Criseyde*, IV, 407-413," *ELN*, 9 (1971), 81-85; Thomas Jay Garbáty, "The *Pamphilus* Tradition in Ruiz and Chaucer," *PQ*, 45 (1967), 457-470; George L. Hamilton, *The Indebtedness of Chaucer's Troilus and Criseyde to Guido delle Colonne's Historia Trojana* (New York, 1903); Arthur E. Hutson, "Troilus's Confession," *MLN*, 69 (1954), 468-470; P. M. Kean, "Chaucer's Dealings with a Stanza of *Il Filostrato* and the Epilogue of *Troilus and Criseyde*," *MAE*, 33 (1964), 36-46; Alfred L. Kellogg, "On the Tradition of Troilus's Vision of the Little Earth," *MS*, 22 (1960), 204-213; G. L. Kittredge, "Chaucer's *Troilus* and Guillaume de Machaut," *MLN*, 30 (1915), 69; Viktor Langhans, "Roman der Rose - Troilus," *Untersuchungen zu Chaucer* (Halle, 1918), pp. 223-228; Robert M. Lumiansky. "The Story of Troilus and Briseida According to Benoit and Guido," *Spec*, 29 (1954), 727-733; Charles Muscatine, "The Feigned Illness in Chaucer's *Troilus and Criseyde*," *MLN*, 63 (1948), 372-377; Charles Muscatine, *Chaucer and the French Tradition: A Study in Style and Meaning* (Berkeley, 1957); Robert A. Pratt, "Chaucer and *Le Roman de Troyle et de Criseida*, *SP*, 53 (1956), 509-539; Root, ed. *The Book of Troilus and Criseyde*, pp. xxxv-li; Claes Schaar, *The Golden Mirror: Studies in Chaucer's Descriptive Technique and its Literary Background* (Lund, 1955); Edgar F. Shannon, *Chaucer and the Roman Poets* (Cambridge, Mass., 1929); Ian C. Walker, "Chaucer and 'Il Filostrato' " *ES*, 49 (1968), 318-326; Ernest H. Wilkins, "Criseide," *MLN*, 24 (1909), 65-67; Ernest H. Wilkins, "*Cantus Troili*," *ELH*, 16 (1949), 167-173; James I. Wimsatt, "Guillaume de Machaut and Chaucer's

Troilus and Criseyde," *MAE,* 45 (1976), 277-293; B. A. Wise, *The Influence of Statius upon Chaucer* (New York, 1967); Karl Young, "Chaucer's Use of Boccaccio's 'Filocolo,' " *MP,* 4 (1906), 169-177, and *The Origin and Development of the Story of Troilus and Criseyde,* Chaucer Society, Second Series, No. 40 (London, 1908).

25. Lewis, "What Chaucer Really Did to *Il Filostrato,*" *E & S,* 17 (1932), 56-75; Cummings, *The Indebtedness of Chaucer's Works to the Italian Works of Boccaccio* (New York, 1965); Meech, *Design in Chaucer's Troilus* (Syracuse, 1959).

26. Rossetti, ed. *Troilus,* Prefatory Remarks, p. iii. F. N. Robinson's edition has 8,239 lines.

27. Cummings, p. 50.

28. Cummings, pp. 121-122.

29. Meech, pp. 426-427. Rudolf Fischer, *Zu den Kunstformen des mittelalterlichen Epos* (Vienna, 1899), pp. 217-370, also compares the *Troilus* and the *Filostrato.*

30. Norman Fruman, *Coleridge, The Damaged Archangel* (New York, 1971); reviewed by Geoffrey H. Hartman in *NYTBR,* March 12, 1972, pp. 1 and 36.

31. Le Marquis de Queux de Saint-Hillaire, ed., Notes and Index by Gaston Raynaud, "Balade 285," *Oeuvres Complètes d'Eustache Deschamps, SATF* (Paris, 1878-1903), II, 138-139. Gretchen Mieszkowski in " 'Pandras' in Deschamps' 'Ballade for Chaucer,' " *ChauR,* 9 (1975), 327-336, argues that "Pandras" in Deschamps' "Ballade for Chaucer" refers to Pandarus and is evidence that Chaucer's *Troilus* was famous in France.

32. *The Allegory of Love: A Study in Medieval Tradition* (New York, 1958), p. 179.

33. *Chaucer the Maker,* p. 28.

34. *rymyng craftily: Meaning in Chaucer's Poetry* (Sydney, Australia, 1973), pp. 85-86.

35. Tyrwhitt, I, lxxxi, note; Root, ed. *The Book of Troilus and Criseyde,* p. xxi.

36. Hartman, p. 36.

37. *The Renaissance Chaucer* (New Haven, 1975), pp. 25-26. See also Miskimin's astute criticism of Lewis' confused remarks on originality in Chaucer, pp. 105-106, note 8. Donald McGrady, "Chaucer and the *Decameron* Reconsidered," *ChauR,* 12 (1977), 15, reminds us of Chaucer's reputation in his own age as a "compiler."

38. "Love in the *Filostrato,*" *ChauR,* 7 (1972), 1-26.

39. *The Date of Chaucer's Troilus,* p. 37.

40. "The Intentional Fallacy" in *The Verbal Icon: Studies in the Meaning of Poetry* (Lexington, Kentucky, 1954), pp. 2-18. See also their earlier article "Intention" in the Revised Edition of the *Dictionary of World Literature,* ed. J. T. Shipley (Patterson, N.J., 1953), pp. 229-232.

41. "Notes Toward a Comic Fiction," *The Theory of the Novel: New Essays,* ed. John Halperin (New York, 1974), p. 74.

42. See the following discussions concerning the intentionalist controversy

in *Issues in Contemporary Literature*, ed. G. T. Polletta (Boston, 1973); Mark Spilka, "The Necessary Stylist: A New Critical Revision," pp. 207-214; Frank Cioffi, "Intention and Interpretation in Criticism," pp. 215-233; Jean Starobinski, "Truth in Masquerade," pp. 233-246; Louis T. Milic, "Against the Typology of Style," pp. 246-254. See also Dorothea Krook, "Intentions and Intentions: The Problem of Intention and Henry James's *The Turn of the Screw"* in J. Halperin's ed. *The Theory of the Novel: New Essays*, pp. 353-372; Hans Georg Gadamer, *Wahrheit und Methode* (Tübingen 1960), pp. 159, 280-282, 290, 370; Hirsch, *Validity in Interpretation*, pp. 245-264; Emilio Roma III, "The Scope of the Intentional Fallacy," *The Monist*, 50 (1966), 250-265; Roy Harvey Pearce, "Historicism Once More," *Twentieth Century Criticism: The Major Statements*, ed. W. J. Hardy and M. Westbrook (New York, 1974), pp. 352-365; George F. Reinecke, "Speculation, Intention, and the Teaching of Chaucer," *The Learned and the Lewed: Studies in Chaucer and Medieval Literature*, ed. L. D. Benson (Cambridge, Mass., 1974), pp. 81-93; Reickert, *Making Sense of Literature*, pp. 56-76; Margolis, *The Language of Art and Art Criticism*, pp. 95-103; Rodway, *The Truths of Fiction*, pp. 84-87.

43. *The Theory of Literary Criticism: A Logical Analysis*, pp. 104-154.

44. Wimsatt, "Genesis: An Argument Resumed," *Day of the Leopard* (New Haven, 1976), pp. 11-39; Beardsley, "Textual Meaning and Authorial Meaning," *Genre*, 1 (1968), 169-181.

45. *The Autobiographical Fallacy in Chaucer and Langland Studies* (London, 1965), pp. 5-6. See also Francis Lee Utley, *The Crooked Rib* (New York, 1970), p. 20.

46. *The Personality of Chaucer* (Norman, Okla. 1968), pp. 6-7.

47. Wagenknecht, p. 8.

48. Wagenknecht, p. 109. Commenting on Baum's remarks in *Chaucer: A Critical Appreciation* on the rape issue , Wagenknecht writes: "What Baum states as conjecture in his 'Note on Cecilia Chaumpaigne,' becomes established fact on p. 133. . ." (p. 108, note 33). A clear case here of the pot calling the kettle black.

49. *A New View of Chaucer* (Durham, N.C., 1965), p. 41.

50. Williams, pp. 41-42.

51. Williams, pp. 66-81.

52. Williams, p. 79.

53. Williams, p. 52. See Margaret Galway's "Joan of Kent and the Order of the Garter," *UBHJ*, 1 (1947), 13-50, for a hypothesis about the relation of Joan of Kent to Criseyde. See also her "The 'Troilus' Frontispiece," *MLR*, 44 (1949), 161-177; Derek Pearsall, "The *Troilus* Frontispiece and Chaucer's Audience," *YES*, 7 (1977), 68-74; John H. Fisher, "The Intended Illustrations in Ms. Corpus Christi 61 of Chaucer's *Troylus and Criseyde* in J. B. Bessinger, Jr. and R. R. Raymo, eds., *Medieval Studies in Honor of Lillian H. Hornstein* (New York, 1976), pp. 111-121; James H. McGregor, "The Iconography of Chaucer in Hoccleve's *De Regimine Principum* and in the *Troilus* Frontispiece," *ChauR*, 11, (1977), 338-350.

54. *The Life and Times of Chaucer* (New York, 1977), p. 279. Of the 493 Chaucer records printed in Martin M. Crow and Clair C. Olson, eds., *Chaucer's Life Records* (Oxford, Eng. 1966), not one refers to Chaucer as an artist.

55. Gardner, p. 121.

56. Gardner, p. 253.

57. Gardner, p. 167.

58. "Chaucerian Tragedy," *ELH*, 19 (1952), reprinted in Richard J. Shoeck and Jerome Taylor, eds., *Chaucer Criticism: Troilus and Criseyde & the Minor Poems* (Notre Dame, Ind., 1961), II, 97.

59. Review of Robertson's *Preface to Chaucer: Studies in Medieval Perspective* (Princeton, 1962): "Grim and Genial," *TLS*, June 11, 1964, p. 510; A. Leigh DeNeef, "Robertson and the Critics," *ChauR*, 2 (1968), 205-234; F. L. Utley, "Robertsonianism Redivivius," *RPh*, 19 (1965), 250-260; *Critical Approaches to Medieval Literature*, ed. Dorothy Bethurum (New York, 1959); M. E. Cotton, "The Artistic Integrity of Chaucer's *Troilus and Criseyde*," *ChauR*, 7 (1972), 37-43. Neil D. Isaacs, "Further Testimony in the Matter of *Troilus*," *SLitI*, 4 (1971), 14, refers to Robertson's use of iconography as "the comic book school of criticism." See also E. T. Donaldson, "Patristic Exegesis in the Criticism of Medieval Literature: The Opposition," *Speaking of Chaucer* (London, 1970), pp. 134-153.

60. Thompson, "Current and Recurrent Fallacies in Chaucer Criticism," p. 156.

61. "Patristic Exegesis: The Defense," *Critical Approaches to Literature*, pp. 31-32. See *Chaucer the Love Poet*, ed. J. Mitchell and W. Provost (Athens, Ga., 1973), p. 99, for Kaske's evasive answer to the question of whether it is possible to say that "Troilus and Criseyde in bed with Pandarus nearby might be compared with Adam and Eve in Paradise and Pandarus as the devil?" Shirley Marchalonis discusses patristic exegesis in "Medieval Symbols and the *Gesta Romanorum*," *ChauR*, 8 (1974), 311-319. As Kaske suggests, she examines one work very carefully, and finds that the Augustinian method of Biblical exegesis "cannot possibly apply to the *Gesta Romanorum*" (318). Kaske in "The Aube in Chaucer's *Troilus*," Schoeck, II, 177, identifies one Biblical allusion in the Aube. See also Saralyn R. Daly, "Criseyde's Blasphemous Aube," *N&Q*, 10 (1963), 442-444; S.G. Kossick, " 'Troilus and Criseyde': The Aubades," *UES*, 9 (1971), 11-13. Jonathan Saville in *The Medieval Erotic Alba: Structure as Meaning* (New York, 1972), p. 214, states: "Chaucer was the first to use the erotic *alba* . . . as a Christian exemplum."

62. "On Hypotheses in 'Historical Criticism,' " p. 257. For invaluable analyses of the hypothesis, see Karl Popper, *The Poverty of Historicism* (Boston, 1957) and *Conjectures and Refutations: The Growth of Scientific Knowledge* (London. 1963). For a different view of the historical approach, see Robert Marsh, "Historical Interpretation and the History of Criticism," *Literary Criticism and Historical Understanding*, ed. Philip Damon (New York, 1967), pp. 1-24.

63. "Lancelot du Lac 2: Le Conte de la Charrette," *Romania*, 12 (1883), 459-534; Theodore Silverstein, "Andreas, Plato, and the Arabs: Remarks on Some Recent Accounts of Courtly Love," *MP*, 47 (1949), 117-126. A Selected Bibliography of the theory of Courtly Love appears in Francis X. Newman, ed., *The Meaning of Courtly Love* (Albany, 1968), pp. 97-102.

64. *Allegory of Love*, p. 13.

65. *The Three Temptations: Medieval Man in Search of the World* (Princeton, 1966), p. 103.

66. Howard, p. 97.

67. Howard, pp. 98-100; Herbert Moller, "The Social Causation of the Courtly Love Complex," *CSSH*, 1 (1959), 162.

68. Paget, *Euphorion: Being Studies of the Antique and the Medieval in the Renaissance* (London. 1885), pp. 346-388; Moller, "The Meaning of Courtly Love," *JAF*, 73 (1960), 39-52.

69. Van de Voort, *Love and Marriage in the English Medieval Romance* (Nashville, 1938); Lippmann, *Das ritterliche Persönlichkeitsideal in der mittelenglischen Literatur des 13. und 14. Jahrhunderts* (Meerane in Sachsen, 1933), pp. 56-72; J. S. P. Tatlock, "The People in Chaucer's *Troilus,*" *PMLA*, 56 (1941), 85-89; Justina Ruiz-de-Conde, *El Amor y el matrimonio secreto en los libros de caballerias* (Madrid, 1948), pp. 122, 153-155; E. T. Donaldson, "The Myth of Courtly Love," *Speaking of Chaucer*, pp. 154-163; Henry Ansgar Kelly, *Love and Marriage in the Age of Chaucer* (Ithaca, 1975), pp. 19-28.

70. "The Concept of Courtly Love as an Impediment to the Understanding of Medieval Texts," in the Newman ed. of *The Meaning of Courtly Love*, p. 17. See also Robertson's "The Doctrine of Charity in Mediaeval Literary Gardens: A Topical Approach through Symbolism and Allegory," *Spec*, 26 (1951), 36-39; "Some Medieval Literary Terminology with Special Reference to Chrétien de Troyes," *SP*, 48 (1951), 691; "The Subject of the *De Amore* of Andreas Capellanus," *MP*, 50 (1952-1953), 145-161; *A Preface to Chaucer*, pp. 391-503. See DeNeef, 232-234, for a bibliography of Robertson's writings.

71. "Clio and Venus: An Historical View of Medieval Love," in Newman, ed. *The Meaning of Courtly Love*, pp. 35-37.

72. Kelly, p. 20.

73. *Pilgrims, Heretics, and Lovers* (New York, 1975), reviewed by C. David Heymann in *NYTBR*, July 13, 1975, p. 7. Edmund Reiss states that Chaucer in *the Book of the Duchess* and *Troilus and Criseyde* and the "Knight's Tale" is concerned with courtly love in "Chaucer's Courtly Love," *The Learned and the Lewed: Studies in Chaucer and Medieval Literature*, ed. L. D. Benson, p. 100. See also J. M. Ferrante and G. D. Economou, eds., *In Pursuit of Perfection: Courtly Love in Medieval Literature* (Port Washington, N.Y., 1975) and N. B. Smith and J. T. Snow, eds., *The Expansions and Transformations of Courtly Literature* (Athens, Ga., 1979).

74. "Must We Abandon the Concept of Courtly Love?" *M&H*, 2 (1972), 299-323.

75. "Chaucer the Man," *PMLA*, 80 (1965), 337. See also his defense of his use of intentionalism in *The Idea of the Canterbury Tales* (Berkeley, 1976). Howard argues that although the *Canterbury Tales* is "unfinished" it is "complete," and he maintains that we can grasp the very idea which was in Chaucer's mind and is revealed in the work. Howard says: " 'Then are you making the outrageous claim that you have seen into the mind of Geoffrey Chaucer?' Well, I am. But I say it isn't so outrageous" (p. 17). Perhaps not, so long as the unwary student does not regard the hypothesis as proven fact.

76. *NYTBR*, January 16, 1977, pp. 4, 5, 28.

Notes for Chapter III
The Philosophy of *Troilus*

1. *Chaucer: A Critical Appreciation*, p. 144.

2. Usener, *Anecdoton Holderi* (Bonn, 1877), pp. 151-152; Rand, *Founders of the Middle Ages* (New York, 1928), pp. 135-136.

3. *Chaucer and the Consolation of Philosophy of Boethius* (New York, 1965), p. 120.

4. Jefferson, p. 130.

5. Jefferson, p. 80.

6. "Destiny in Chaucer's *Troilus*," *PMLA*, 45 (1930), 135. Curry's essay is reprinted in his *Chaucer and the Mediaeval Sciences*, 2nd ed. (New York, 1960), pp. 241-298.

7. Curry, 141.

8. Curry, 149.

9. Curry, 160-161. Dorothy Everett, "Troilus and Criseyde," *Essays in Middle English Literature*, ed. P. Kean (New York, 1955), p. 133, believes that Curry "goes too far" in making the claim that *Troilus* is a tragedy of Fate " 'far in advance of medieval theory and practice.' " Chauncey Wood in *Chaucer and the Country of the Stars: Poetic Uses of Astrological Imagery* (Princeton, 1970), p. 49, contends that the passages which Curry takes seriously are actually funny: "For Chaucer, then, a very solemn comment on destiny as providential agent could be turned promptly to humorous effect, and while Chaucer was no doubt serious when he translated the *Consolation of Philosophy* and when, in the *Treatise on the Astrolabe*, he denied any belief in judicial astrology, he was at one with his age in finding much of the machinations of astrology to be very funny."

10. "Boethius' Influence on Chaucer's *Troilus*," *MP*, 49 (1951-1952), 1-9.

11. "Five-Book Structure in Chaucer's *Troilus*," *MLQ*, 23 (1962), 297-308.

12. *Disembodied Laughter: Troilus and the Apotheosis Tradition: A Reexamination of Narrative and Thematic Contexts* (Berkeley, 1972), p. 67.

13. Steadman, p. 127. See also his "The Age of Troilus," *MLN*, 72 (1957), 89-90.

14. Patch, *On Rereading Chaucer* (Cambridge, Mass., 1954), pp. 113, 115-116, 118-119. Murray F. Markland in *"Troilus and Criseyde*: The Inviolability of the Ending," *MLQ*, 31 (1970), 158, employs the same kind of intentionalism when he writes: ". . . [I]t is easier to visualize a fumbling narrator than a fumbling Chaucer, a narrator whose story has a force he cannot control, rather than a Chaucer grown inept in closing his major completed poem." Patch also discusses Chaucer's philosophy in "Troilus on Predestination," *JEGP*, 17 (1918), 399-422; "Troilus on Determinism," *Spec*, 6 (1931), 225-243; "Chaucer and Lady Fortune," *MLR*, 22 (1927), 377-388. See also Patch's *The Goddess Fortuna in Medieval Literature* (Cambridge, Eng. 1927) and his *The Tradition of Boethius: A Study of His Importance in Medieval Culture* (New York, 1935);

P. M. Kean in *Chaucer and the Making of English Poetry* (London, 1972), I, 120, also denies that Chaucer is a determinist.

15. " 'Sikernesse' and Fortune in *Troilus and Criseyde*," *PQ*, 49 (1970), 160, 163.

16. "An Essay at the Logic of *Troilus and Criseyde*," *CamQ*, 4 (1968), 433, 129-130.

17. "The Problem of Free Will in Chaucer's Narratives," *PQ*, 46 (1967), 443, 444. Wood, *Chaucer and the Country of the Stars*, p. 45, states: "The problem here, however, is that if the stars are in fact both formative and impelling, if indeed, as Curry says, the story is spread against the backdrop of 'the destinal power of the stars,' then the motivation of the story and its backdrop have been poorly chosen, for human action of any kind is ultimately meaningless if it is accomplished in a wholly deterministic universe."

18. "The Boethian God and the Audience of the *Troilus*," *JEGP*, 69 (1970), 433.

19. *Oppositions in Chaucer* (Middletown, Conn., 1975), p. 48. For other analyses of Chaucer and Boethius, see Hardin Craig, "From Gorgias to Troilus," *Studies in Medieval Literature*, ed. M. Leach (Philadelphia, 1961), pp. 97-107; F. C. DeVries, "*Troilus and Criseyde*, Book III, Stanza 251, and Boethius," *ES*, 52 (1971), 502-507; T.P. Dunning, "God and Man in *Troilus and Criseyde*," *English and Medieval Studies Presented to J.R.R. Tolkien*, ed. N. Davis and C.L. Wrenn (London, 1962), pp. 164-182; Lawrence Eldredge, "Boethian Epistemology and Chaucer's *Troilus* in the Light of Fourteenth-Century Thought," *Mediaevalia*, 2 (1976), 50-75; J.E. Gallagher, "Theology and Intention in Chaucer's *Troilus*," *ChauR*, 7 (1972), 44-66; John Gardner, *The Poetry of Chaucer* (Carbondale, Ill. 1977), pp. 96-147; Joseph J. Mogan, Jr., "Further Aspects of Mutability in Chaucer's *Troilus*," *PELL*, 1 (1965), 72-77; Mogan, *Chaucer and the Theme of Mutability* (Paris, 1969); Mogan, "Free Will and Determinism in Chaucer's *Troilus and Criseyde*," *WSLL*, 2 (1969), 131-160; James L. Shanley, "The *Troilus* and Christian Love," *ELH*, 6 (1939), 271-281; John Huber, "Troilus' Predestination Soliloquy," *NM*, 66 (1965), 120-125.

20. "Chaucerian Tragedy," Schoeck, II, 97.

21. "Chaucerian Tragedy," Schoeck, II, 118.

22. "Current and Recurrent Fallacies in Chaucer Criticism," p. 157.

23. "Love and Grace in Chaucer's *Troilus*," *Essays in Honor of Walter Clyde Curry* (Nashville, 1955), p. 68.

24. Slaughter, p. 69.

25. Slaughter, p. 75-76. See also his *Virtue According to Love—in Chaucer* (New York, 1957).

26. "The Troilus and Christian Love," 271-281.

27. "The Two Moralities of Chaucer's *Troilus and Criseyde*," *TRSC*, 44 (1950), 35-46, reprinted in Schoeck, II, 147-159. See Denomy's *The Heresy of Courtly Love* (Gloucester, Mass., 1965), and Marion Green, "Christian Implications of Knighthood and Courtly Love in Chaucer's *Troilus*," *DN*, 30 (1957), 57-92.

28. *Medieval Skepticism and Chaucer* (New York, 1971), p. 82.

29. *Medieval Panorama* (London, 1944), p. 462. See also Gardner's *The Life and Times of Chaucer*, p. 320, note 3.

30. *The Spirit of Protest in Old French Literature*, Columbia University Studies in Romance Philology and Literature (New York, 1917), XXI, 135; Thomas, *Medieval Skepticism and Chaucer*, pp. 83, 14, 19, 12-13, 24-25, 47-48, 44-48, 35-43, 23-24.

31. "Post Face: Le Monachisme médiéval," *Revue d'Ascétique et de Mystique*, 41 (1965), 287.

32. *Geoffrey Chaucer's The Parlement of Foulys*, ed. D. S. Brewer (London, 1960), p. 27.

33. Quoted by Reiss, "*Troilus* and the Failure of Understanding," *MLQ*, 29 (1968), 132-133.

34. Reiss, 141. For a discussion of the astrological crux concerning the "eighth sphere" (called the seventh sphere in most *Troilus* manuscripts), consult Wood, *Chaucer and the Country of the Stars*, pp. 180-189; Root, ed. *The Book of Troilus and Criseyde*, pp. 559-562; Steadman, *Disembodied Laughter*, pp. 1-65; Clarke, "Dante and the Epilogue of *Troilus*," 1-10; Cope, "Chaucer, Venus and the Seventhe Sphere," 245-246; Forrest S. Scott, "The Seventh Sphere: A Note on 'Troilus and Criseyde,' " *MLR*, 51 (1956), 2-5; Kellogg, "On the Tradition of Troilus's Vision," 204-213; M. W. Bloomfield, "The Eighth Sphere: A Note on Chaucer's *Troilus and Criseyde*," *MLR*, 52 (1958), 408-410; John W. Conlee, "The Meaning of Troilus' Ascension to the Eighth Sphere," *ChauR*, 7 (1972), 27-36; Russell A. Peck, "Numerology and Chaucer's *Troilus and Criseyde*," *Mosaic*, 5 (1972), 16-21; Gertrude C. Drake, "The Moon and Venus: Troilus's Havens in Eternity," *PLL*, 11 (1975), 3-17.

35. Reiss, 144.

36. "Sex and Salvation in *Troilus and Criseyde*," *ChauR*, 2 (1968), 246-253.

37. "The Ending of Chaucer's *Troilus*," *Early English and Norse Studies Presented to Hugh Smith*, ed. A. Brown and P. Foote (London, 1963), pp. 26-45, reprinted in *Speaking of Chaucer*. See also Utley, "Stylistic Ambivalence in Chaucer, Yeats, and Lucretius—The Cresting Wave and Its Undertow," *URKC*, 37 (1971), 183-192, and T. J. Garbáty, "*Troilus*, V, 1786-92 and V, 1807-1827: An Example of Poetic Process," *ChauR*, 11 (1977), 299-305.

38. "The Conclusion of *Troilus and Criseyde*," *MAE*, 33 (1964), 47-52.

39. *Chaucer: A Critical Appreciation*, p. 158.

40. Baum, p. 163. Williams, *A New View of Chaucer*, pp. 193-195, offers the "bold but totally unsubstantiated hypothesis" that the epilogue stanzas were composed by an editor from odds and ends he found in several lost manuscripts.

41. Baum, p. 159.

42. Baum, p. 162. Baum, pp. 165-167, discusses the views of W. W. Lawrence, F. N. Robinson, and Kittredge. See also Chesterton, *Chaucer* (London, 1932), pp. 19-20.

43. Baum, pp. 154, 166-167.

44. "The Epilog of Chaucer's *Troilus*," *MP*, 18 (1921), 636.

45. "*Troilus and Criseyde*: A Reconsideration," *Patterns of Love and Courtesy: Essays in Memory of C. S. Lewis*, ed. John Lawlor (London, 1966), p. 106.

46. *Geoffrey Chaucer* (Berlin, 1973), pp. 117-118. Aldous Huxley, *On the Margin* (London, 1956), p. 227, speaks of the defect of *Troilus*—"its hurried and boggled conclusion." See also S. S. Hussey, "The Difficult Fifth Book of 'Troilus

and Criseyde,' " *MLR*, 67 (1972), 721-729, who contends that the *Troilus* manuscripts indicate that Chaucer originally intended the poem to have four parts.

47. See Hoccleve's, *De Regimine Principum*, 11. 2087-2088 in *Hoccleve's Works: The Minor Poems*, I, ed. F. J. Furnivall, *EETS* (London, 1892), p. xxxii and pp. xxx-xxxiv, for passages which reveal Hoccleve's love of Chaucer. In this same connection, see Thomas Usk's *Testament of Love*, Book III, Chapter IV in *Chaucerian and Other Pieces*, ed. W. W. Skeat (London, 1899), VII, 123.

48. "Chaucer and Wyclif," *MP*, 14 (1916), 265.

49. *Studies in Chaucer: His Life and Writings* (New York, 1962), II, 169-426. See Thomas, *Medieval Skepticism and Chaucer*, pp. 60-86.

50. Huxley, *On the Margin*, pp. 221-222; Loomis, "Was Chaucer a Free Thinker?" *Studies in Medieval Literature*, ed. M. Leach, pp. 21-44; Chesterton, *Chaucer*, p. 275, says: "Chaucer was more unmistakably orthodox than Langland. . . ." Loomis, p. 42, concludes that "it is safe to say that, though he was not in our modern sense a free thinker, an agnostic, he displays in his poetry a broad tolerance and even a sympathy with honest doubt." Charles Muscatine writes in *Poetry and Crisis in the Age of Chaucer* (Notre Dame, Ind., 1972), p. 113: "Serious irony can be made finally to expose the instability of this brittle world and by implication to turn our attention to a stable world of faith in God. Chaucer was always a Christian, then, and that solution for Chaucer lay beyond irony."

51. *O Love O Charite! Contraries Harmonized in Chaucer's Troilus* (Carbondale, Ill. 1976), p. 172.

52. *The Poetry of Chaucer*, p. 100; Muscatine, Review, "The Poet's Tale," of Gardner's *The Life and Times of Chaucer* and *The Poetry of Chaucer, NYTBR*, April 24, 1977, p. 39.

53. *"Troilus and Criseyde*: The Art of Amplification," in *Medieval Literature and Folklore Studies: Essays in Honor of Francis Lee Utley*, ed. J. Mandel and B. A. Rosenberg (New Brunswick, N.J., 1970), pp. 169-171.

Notes for Chapter IV
The Formalistic Approach

1. *The Key of Remembrance: A Study of Chaucer's Poetic*, p. 2. Robert B. Burlin claims that he uses *explication de texte* in his *Chaucerian Fiction* (Princeton, 1977), p. vii. But his brief discussion, pp. 113-135, of *Troilus*, which consists essentially of general commentary on each book, hardly constitutes what the New Critics mean by close reading.

2. S. N. Grebstein, ed., *Perspectives in Contemporary Criticism* (New York, 1968), pp. 7, 83-84.

3. Sandras, *Étude sur G. Chaucer*, p. 50; De Sélincourt, *Oxford Lectures on Poetry* (Oxford, Eng., 1934), p. 52; Kittredge, *The Date of Chaucer's Troilus*, p. 56; *Chaucer and his Poetry*, p. 112; Root, *The Poetry of Chaucer*, 2nd ed.

(Boston, 1922), p. 87; Ker, *Epic and Romance*, 2nd ed. (London, 1926), p. 369; Masefield, *Chaucer* (New York, 1931), p. 19; Prokosch, "Geoffrey Chaucer," *The English Novelists: A Survey of the Novel by Twenty Contemporary Novelists*, ed. D. Verschoyle (New York, 1936), p. 15; Speirs, *Chaucer the Maker*, p. 49; A. C. Spearing, *Criticism and Medieval Poetry* (New York, 1964), pp. 96-117; Grossvogel, *Limits of the Novel: Evolution of a Form from Chaucer to Robbe-Grillet* (Ithaca, 1967), pp. 44-73; Marvin Mudrick, "Looking for Kellerman: or, Fiction and the Facts of Life," *The Theory of the Novel*, ed. J. Halperin, p. 286; James I. Wimsatt, "Medieval and Modern in Chaucer's *Troilus and Criseyde*," *PMLA*, 92 (1977) 203-216. But Tatlock in "The People in Chaucer's *Troilus*," *PMLA*, 56 (1941), 2, objected to the view that *Troilus* is a novel.

    4. "*Troilus and Criseyde*: A Most Admirable and Inimitable Epicke Poeme," *E&S*, (1954), 61. Joseph reminds us that the unprinted manuscript of Sir Francis Kynaston's Latin translation of *Troilus* in the Bodleian Library (1636) refers to the work as an "Epicke poem." H. L. Rogers, "The Beginning (and Ending) of Chaucer's *Troilus and Criseyde*," *Festschrift for Ralph Farrell*, ed. A. Stephens, H. L. Rogers, B. Coghlan (Bern, 1977), p. 200, states: ". . . [I]nterpretations of *Troilus* which do not take sufficient account of its epic setting and epic qualities . . . deprive the poem of one of its many large dimensions."

    5. "Elements of Epic Grandeur in the *Troilus*," *ELH*, 6 (1939), 209-210.

    6. "Chaucer's 'Troilus and Criseyde' as Romance," *PMLA* 53 (1938), 38-63. Chesterton, *Chaucer*, pp. 149ff, also discusses *Troilus* as a Romance.

    7. "Dramatic Elements in Chaucer's *Troilus*," *TSLL*, 12 (1970), 312, 319. See also Michael H. Frost, "Narrative Devices in Chaucer's *Troilus and Criseyde*," *Thoth*, 14 (1974), 29-38.

    8. Macey, 323.

    9. "The Trojan Background of the *Troilus*," *ELH*, 9 (1942), 252. See also John P. McCall, "The Trojan Scene in Chaucer's *Troilus*," *ELH*, 29 (1962), 263-275.

    10. Mayo, 256.

    11. *The Medieval Heritage of Elizabethan Tragedy* (Berkeley, 1936), p. 145. On the subject of *Troilus* as a medieval tragedy see Adrienne Lockhart, "Semantic, Moral, and Aesthetic Degeneration in *Troilus and Criseyde*," *ChauR*, 8 (1973), 100-117, and John Lawlor, *Chaucer* (London, 1968), pp. 46-89.

    12. Farnham, p. 137.

    13. Farnham, pp. 159-160.

    14. *The Poet Chaucer* (London. 1949), p. 66.

    15. *The Genre of Troilus and Criseyde* (Ithaca, 1978), pp. 73-74.

    16. McAlpine, pp. 179-180.

    17. McAlpine, pp. 180-181.

    18. *Chaucer: Poet of Mirth and Morality* (Notre Dame, Ind., 1964), pp. 48-49.

    19. *The Noble Voice: A Study of Ten Great Poems* (New York, 1946), p. 276. Willi Erzgräber in "Tragik und Komik in Chaucers *Troilus and Criseyde*," *Festschrift für Walter Hübner*, ed. D. Reisner and H. Gneuss (Berlin, 1964), pp. 139-143, also deals with the comic elements in *Troilus*, but primarily to show how they are transcended by the medieval philosophy at the end of the poem.

See also W. Erzgräber, "Zu Chaucers *Troilus and Criseyde*, Buch IV," ed. M. Bambeck and H. H. Christmann, *Philologica Romanica: Erhard Lomatzsch Giwidmet* (Munich, 1975), pp. 97-117.

20. Van Doren, p. 258.

21. Van Doren, pp. 261-262.

22. Van Doren, pp. 263, 265.

23. Van Doren, p. 277.

24. Van Doren, pp. 281-282. Lawlor, *Chaucer*, pp. 46-89, also makes no reference to the epilogue of *Troilus*, an odd omission.

25. "The Polylithic Romance: with Pages of Illustrations," *Studies in Medieval, Renaissance, American Literature: A Festschrift*, ed. B. F. Colquitt (Fort Worth, Texas, 1971), p. 5. See also Paul Strohm, "Storie, Spelle, Geste, Romance, Tragedie: Generic Distinctions in the Middle English Troy Narratives," *Spec*, 46 (1971), 348-359.

26. *Anatomy of Criticism*, p. 13. Rodway, *The Truths of Fiction*, pp. 18-40, offers a critical analysis of the genre problem.

27. *Die Funktionen des Erzählers in Chaucers epischer Dichtung*, (Tübingen, 1973), pp. 12-13.

28. "Distance and Predestination in *Troilus and Criseyde*," *PMLA*, 72 (1957), 15. See also Robert M. Jordan, "The Narrator in Chaucer's *Troilus*," *ELH*, 25 (1958), 240. But Jordan in his later work, *Chaucer and the Shape of Creation: The Aesthetic Possibilities of Inorganic Structure* (Cambridge, Mass., 1967), p. 67, accepts B. H. Bronson's criticism of his view of the narrator. See note 49.

29. Bloomfield, 21-22.

30. Bloomfield, 18.

31. Bloomfield, 22.

32. "Chaucer's Point of View as Narrator in the Love Poems," *PMLA*, 84 (1959), 516. According to Evan Carton, "Pandarus' Bed and Chaucer's Art," *PMLA*, 94 (1979), Bloomfield's view is absolutely correct.

33. Bethurum, 517.

34. Bethurum, 517-518, 520.

35. Donaldson, *Speaking of Chaucer*, pp. 67-68.

36. Donaldson, pp. 68-69.

37. Donaldson, pp. 99-100.

38. "Chaucer's Tender Trap: The *Troilus* and the 'Yonge, Fresshe Folkes,' " *EM*, 15 (1964), 29.

39. Gaylord, 32.

40. Gaylord, 44-45.

41. Durling, *The Figure of the Poet in Renaissance Epic* (Cambridge, Mass., 1965), pp. 44-66.

42. "The Conclusion to Chaucer's *Troilus and Criseyde*," *EIC*, 13 (1963), 8.

43. Nagarajan, 7.

44. "*Troilus and Criseyde*: The Inviolability of the Ending," *MLQ*, 31 (1970), 156, 158.

45. Markland, 154.

46. Markland, 153, 154, 159.

47. *Paradoxical Patterns in Chaucer's 'Troilus': An Explanation of the Palinode* (Washington, D.C., 1960), p. xix. Sister Frances Dolores Covella, "Audience as Determinant of Meaning in the *Troilus*," *ChauR*, 2 (1968), 235-245, contends that *Troilus* has two epilogues. Donaldson, "The Ending of Chaucer's *Troilus*," *Speaking of Chaucer*, pp. 26-45, and Utley, "Scene-division in Chaucer's *Troilus and Criseyde*," *Studies in Medieval Literature in Honor of Professor Albert C. Baugh*, ed. M. Leach, p. 135, believe that the epilogue consists of 18 stanzas. Peck, "Numerology and Chaucer's *Troilus and Criseyde*," 21, states: . . . "[N]ot only is the epilogue constructed in 12, the number of revelation, but certain stanzas—namely 7, 8, 10 and 12—seem to be strategically numbered in accord with universal patterns, so that in reading through the epilogue we participate in the very rhythm (*numerosa*) of revelation."

48. *rymyng craftily: Meaning in Chaucer's Poetry* , p. 95.

49. *In Search of Chaucer* (Toronto, 1960), p. 26. But this "mistaken" talk continues; see Robert Reilly, "The Narrator and his Audience. A Study of Chaucer's *Troilus*," *U Port R*, 21 (1961), 23-36; Michael R. Peed, "Troilus and Criseyde: The Narrator and the 'olde Bokes,' " *AN&Q*, 12 (1974), 143-146; Rowe, *O Love O Charite! Contraries Harmonized in Chaucer's Troilus*, pp. 152-172; McAlpine, *The Genre of Troilus and Criseyde*, pp. 35-45, 116-147. To Peggy A. Knapp, "The Nature of Nature: Criseyde's 'Slydyng Corage,' " *ChauR*, 13 (1978), 138, the narrator is a "major character."

50. *The Key of Remembrance*, pp. 173, 231.

51. Payne, pp. 181-182.

52. Payne, p. 183.

53. Payne, pp. 186-187. Allen C. Koretsky in "Chaucer's Use of Apostrophe in *Troilus and Criseyde*," *ChauR*, 4 (1970), 244, points out that 8 of the 10 lyrics listed by Payne are apostrophes. Richard A. Lanham, "Opaque Style and Its Uses in *Troilus and Criseide*," *SMC*, 3 (1970), 169-176, discusses Chaucer's use of a rhetorical style. But James J. Murphy in "A New Look at Chaucer and the Rhetoricians," *RES*, 15 (1964), 2, claims that rhetoric did not play an important part in English cultural life and that Chaucer was not indebted to the medieval rhetoricians.

54. *On Rereading Chaucer*, p. 102.

55. *Chapters on Chaucer*, pp. 107-108.

56. *Design in Chaucer's Troilus*, pp. 5, 432, note 5.

57. *Paradoxical Patterns in Chaucer's Troilus*, p. xix.

58. "*Troilus and Criseyde*: A Study in Chaucer's Method of Narrative Construction," *PMLA*, 11 (1896), 307-322.

59. "Scene-division in Chaucer's *Troilus and Criseyde*," pp. 109-136.

60. *Zu den Kunstformen des mittelalterlichen Epos*, p. 9; Meech, p. 432, note 8.

61. "Narrative Structure in Chaucer's *Troilus and Criseyde*," *AnM*, 6 (1965), 13.

62.   *The Structure of Chaucer's Troilus and Criseyde* (Copenhagen, 1974). See also Norman E. Eliason, *The Language of Chaucer's Poetry: An Appraisal of the Verse, Style, and Structure* (Copenhagen, 1972), pp. 161-162.

63.   *Chaucer and the Shape of Creation*, p. 66. On the other hand, George D. S. Henderson, *Gothic* (Harmondsworth, Eng., 1967), p. 200, maintains that the Gothic style is based on an organic principle. D. S. Brewer in the third edition of his *Chaucer* (London, 1973), pp. 165-219, who also believes that Chaucer's style is Gothic, attempts to reconcile the contradictory definitions of Gothic offered by Jordan and Henderson.

64.   Jordan, p. 76.

65.   Jordan, p. 80.

66.   Jordan, pp. 86, 98, 107.

67.   Jordan, p. 107.

68.   Jordan, p. 108. A different view of the imagery of *Troilus* is offered by Samuel Schuman, "The Circle of Nature: Patterns of Imagery in Chaucer's *Troilus and Criseyde*," *ChauR*, 10 (1975), 99-112. See also D. M. Burjorjee, "The Pilgrimage of Troilus's Sailing Heart in Chaucer's *Troilus and Criseyde*," *AnM*, 13 (1972), 14-31.

69.   "Chaucer and the Elusion of Clarity," *E&S*, 25 (1972), 42-43. Note, for example, McKay Sundwall's judgment in "Deiphobus and Helen: A Tantalizing Hint," *MP*, 73 (1975), 156: "Chaucer . . . is the most lucid of poets."

70.   Donaldson, 30-31.

71.   Donaldson, 42.

72.   *Seven Types of Ambiguity*, 3rd ed. (London, 1963), p. 1.

73.   *The Concept of Ambiguity—The Example of James*, p. 25. See pp. 9-26 for her discussion of the views of other writers who have tried to define ambiguity.

74.   *Seven Types of Ambiguity*, pp. 57-68.

75.   Preston states in his *Chaucer* (London, 1952), p. 82, that he finds precise language where Empson finds "multiple meanings."

76.   *Chaucer: The Critical Heritage*, ed. D. S. Brewer (London, 1978), II, 442; Brewer reprints Empson's analysis on pp. 442-452.

77.   "Chaucer's Tender Trap," 27. See also Charles Berryman, "The Ironic Design of Fortune in *Troilus and Criseyde*," *ChauR*, 2 (1967), 2-7; J. K. Hardie, "Structure and Irony in Chaucer's *Troilus and Criseyde*," *PAPA*, 3 (1977), 13-19. David Worcester in *The Art of Satire* (Cambridge, Mass., 1940), pp. 95-102, discusses Chaucer's Socratic irony and Germaine Dempster in *Dramatic Irony in Chaucer* (New York, 1959), pp. 10-26, maintains that Chaucer's irony is based on the principle of Boethian necessity.

78.   "Chaucerian Irony and the Ending of the *Troilus*," *ChauR*, 1 (1967), 215.

79.   "Two Boethian Speeches in *Troilus and Criseyde* and Chaucerian Irony," *Literary Criticism and Historical Understanding*, ed. P. Damon, pp. 85-107. The ideas in this essay appear in Elbow's *Oppositions in Chaucer*, pp. 49-72.

80.   *Chaucer and the French Tradition*, pp. 154, 164-165.

81.   *NYRB*, June 12, 1975, p. 37.

82. *The Double Sorrow of Troilus: A Study of Ambiguities in Troilus and Criseyde* (Oxford, Eng., 1970), p. 1. Rose A. Zimbardo, "Creator and Created: The Generic Perspective of Chaucer's *Troilus and Criseyde*," *ChauR*, 11 (1977), 283-297, deals with cosmic irony in this "Christian" poem.

83. Gordon, pp. 24-60, 125-129.

84. Gordon, p. 133; Adams, "Irony in Troilus' Apostrophe to the Vacant House of Criseyde," *MLQ*, 24 (1963), 61-65; Robertson, "Chaucerian Tragedy," Schoeck, II, 116.

85. "Troilus' Paraclausithyron and Its Setting," *NM*, 73 (1972), 24. See also William Frost, "A Chaucerian Crux," *YR*, 66 (1977), 551-561.

86. Gordon, pp. 70-71.

87. Gordon, pp. 31-33.

88. Gordon, pp. 98-101.

89. Gordon, pp. 100-101.

90. Gordon, pp. 138-139.

91. Gordon, p. 60. See also Sabina Beckman, "Color Symbolism in *Troilus and Criseyde*," *CLAJ*, 20 (1976), 68-74.

92. *Chaucer's Bawdy* (New York, 1972), pp. 12-13.

93. Kökeritz, "Rhetorical Word-play in Chaucer," *PMLA*, 69 (1954), 937-952; Braddy, "Chaucer's Bawdy Tongue," and "Chaucer—Realism or Obscenity?" in *Geoffrey Chaucer: Literary and Historical Studies* (Port Washington, N.Y., 1971), pp. 131-139, 146-158. See also Braddy's "Chaucer's Playful Pandarus," *SFQ*, 34 (1970), 71-81.

94. *Chaucer's Bawdy*, p. 1.

95. *Chaucer*, 3rd. ed., p. 203.

96. *The Old French and Chaucerian Fabliaux: A Study of Their Comic Climax* (Columbia, Mo., 1978), pp. 44-45, 170-171.

Notes for Chapter V
The Psychological Approach

1. *Freudianism and the Literary Mind* (New York, 1959). See also Sigmund Freud, *On Creativity and the Unconscious* (New York, 1958); F. L. Lucas, *Literature and Psychology* (Ann Arbor, 1957).

2. "The Ghost of Henry James: Revised, with a Postscript, 1962" in *Modern Criticism: Theory and Practice*, ed. W. Sutton and R. Foster (New York, 1963), pp. 401-416.

3. Andreas Capellanus, *The Art of Courtly Love*, tr. J. J. Parry (New York, 1941), and the Bibliography on pp. 97-102 in Newman's ed. of *The Meaning of Courtly Love*.

4. Note, for example, Lowes' comment in his *Geoffrey Chaucer* (Oxford, Eng., 1934), p. 142. In the action of *Troilus* "Chaucer is following an accepted literary convention: to wit, the code of courtly or chivalric love."

5. *Courtly Love in Chaucer and Gower* (Gloucester, Mass., 1959), p. 180.

6. "Chaucer's 'Troilus and Criseyde' as Romance," 51 ff.

7. *Allegory of Love*, p. 178.

8. *Love and Marriage in the Age of Chaucer*, p. 176.

9. Kelly, pp. 179, 170-171.

10. Kelly, p. 62.

11. Kelly, p. 240.

12. "The Clandestine Marriage of Troilus and Criseyde," *ChauR*, 8 (1974), 275-276.

13. *"Troilus and Criseyde*: A Study in Chaucer's Method of Narrative Construction," 316.

14. Price, 310-311.

15. *Allegory of Love*, p. 195.

16. *Allegory of Love*, pp. 195-196. Lewis still has his disciples. See Salter, "Troilus and Criseyde: A Reconsideration," pp. 86-87, and Lawlor, *Chaucer*, pp. 47 ff.

17. *Courtly Love in Chaucer and Gower*, pp. 153-154.

18. *Chaucer's Troilus: A Study in Courtly Love* (Gloucester, Mass., 1958), p. 262.

19. "The Hero of the *Troilus*," *Spec*, 37 (1962), 567; Bronson, *In Search of Chaucer*, p. 117. E. G. Stanley, *"About Troilus*," *E&S*, 29 (1976), 84-106, defends Troilus mainly by comparing him to his prototype in Boccaccio.

20. *Chaucer: ses modèles, ses sources, sa religion* (Lille, 1931), p. 53. Stephen A. Barney in "Troilus Bound," *Spec*, 47 (1972), 445-458, also has a very high opinion of Troilus who is a "Romantic Promethean . . . a man of purity of heart and of speculative intellect. . . " (458).

21. David, 568.

22. David, 569.

23. David, 573.

24. David, 576-577.

25. David, 577, 579. See also his *The Strumpet Muse* (Bloomington, Ind., 1976), pp. 27-36.

26. "Chaucer's Troilus of Book IV," *PMLA*, 79 (1964), 546.

27. Wenzel, 546.

28. Wenzel, 544.

29. David, 573, 568-569.

30. *Love and Marriage in the Age of Chaucer*, p. 240.

31. "The Clandestine Marriage of Troilus and Criseyde," 273.

32. *The Genre of Troilus and Criseyde*, p. 31. Gerould, *Chaucerian Essays* (Princeton, 1952), p. 91; Rutherford, "Pandarus as Lover: 'A Joly Wo' or 'Loves Shotes Keene?' " *AnM*, 13 (1972), 10; Patch, "Troilus on Predestination," 419; Patch's review of K. Malone's *Chapters on Chaucer*, *MLN*, 68 (1953), 556-557; Patch, *On Rereading Chaucer*, pp. 83-101; Whiting, "Troilus and Pilgrims in Wartime," *MLN*, 60 (1945), 49; Tatlock, *The Mind and Art of Chaucer*, p. 43;

June H. Martin, *Love's Fools: Aucassin, Troilus, Calisto, and the Parody of the Courtly Lover* (London, 1972), pp. 55-56; Donaldson, "The Elusion of Clarity," 34-36.

33. *The Noble Voice*, p. 266.

34. Van Doren, pp. 271-272.

35. Van Doren, p. 273.

36. Van Doren, pp. 265-266.

37. "Troilus: A Medieval Psychoanalysis," *AnM*, 2 (1961), 82, 88. Martin, *Love's Fools*, p. 53, who claims that Chaucer parodies courtly love in the characterization of Troilus, states: "While Troilus may be biologically 'the perfect specimen,' I think there is some question as to whether he is equally fit psychologically." Robert Pitfield, M.D., "Chaucer's Nervous Depression," *JNMD*, 82 (1935), 30-32, assures us that "The Book of the Duchess" "records the symptoms of Chaucer's depression and his insomnia. . . . His 'fantasyes' were probably the expression of a psychoneurosis." This was all caused by a "chronic infection, bad teeth or tonsils, syphilis. . . . No one can possibly know. . . . It is futile to speculate further in the matter." Futile indeed!

38. Georgia R. Crampton, "Action and Passion in Chaucer's *Troilus*," *MAE*, 43 (1974), 26; Julia Ebel, "Troilus and Oedipus: The Genealogy of an Image," *ES*, 55 (1974), 15-21; F. Xavier Baron, "Chaucer's Troilus and Self-Renunciation in Love," *PLL*, 10 (1974), 14; F. L. Utley, "Chaucer's Troilus and St. Paul's Charity," *Chaucer and Middle English Studies in Honor of Rossell Hope Robbins*, ed. B. Rowland (London, 1974), pp. 272-287.

39. Kirby, *Chaucer's Troilus: A Study in Courtly Love*, pp. 106-118; Lewis, *Allegory of Love*, pp. 192-193; Young, *The Origin and Development of the Story of Troilus and Criseyde*, pp. 45ff; Lowes, *Geoffrey Chaucer*, pp. 142-143.

40. *Allegory of Love*, p. 191.

41. *Oxford Lectures on Poetry*, p. 57.

42. *The Noble Voice*, pp. 273-274, 277.

43. "Chaucerian Tragedy," Schoeck, II, 99. Peter Christmas refers to Pandarus' "cruelty" and "brutality" in his "*Troilus and Criseyde*: The Problems of Love and Necessity," *ChauR*, 9 (1975), 290, revealing once again how Pandarus must be viewed as a "bad man" in order to make the religious ending "seem inevitable and aesthetically justifiable." Laurens J. Mills, *One Soul in Bodies Twain* (Bloomington, Ind., 1937), pp. 62-63, also believes that Pandarus lacks virtue.

44. "Pandarus a Devil?" *PMLA*, 71 (1956), 275-279.

45. "Friendship in Chaucer's *Troilus*," *ChauR*, 3 (1969), 249. See also Gaylord's "Uncle Pandarus as Lady Philosophy," *PMASAL*, 47 (1961), 511-595. Leah R. Freiwald, "Swich Love of Frendes: Pandarus and Troilus," *ChauR*, 6 (1971), 120-129, agrees with Gaylord.

46. "Chaucer's Pandarus and the Medieval Ideal of Friendship," *JEGP*, 69 (1970), 419. See also Charles A. Muscatine, "The Feigned Illness in Chaucer's *Troilus and Criseyde*," 372-377.

47. R. G. Cook, 420-422.

48. *Geoffroy Chaucer*, pp. 119-121.

49. "Chaucer's Pandarus," *WHR*, 4 (1950), 348. E. E. Slaughter, "Chaucer's Pandarus: Virtuous Uncle and Friend," *JEGP*, 48 (1949), 186-195, also believes that Pandarus is an ideal friend.

50. Neff, 347.

51. De Sélincourt, *Oxford Lectures*, p. 56; Neff, 345; Lowes, *Geoffrey Chaucer*, pp. 144-145.

52. "Chaucer: (1) *Troilus and Criseyde*," 92-93.

53. Speirs, 99.

54. Matthew Corrigan, "Chaucer's Failure with Woman: The Inadequacy of Criseyde," *WHR*, 23 (1969), 109.

55. *Chaucer's Troilus: A Study in Courtly Love*, p. 237.

56. *A Preface to Chaucer*, pp. 498-499.

57. *Allegory of Love*, p. 183.

58. *Allegory of Love*, p. 185; Lawlor, *Chaucer*, pp. 76, 87-88, agrees that Criseyde's "fears are real. . . ." See also Elizabeth R. Hatcher, "Chaucer and the Psychology of Fear: Troilus in Book V," *ELH*, 40 (1973), 307-324, who denies that Chaucer *intended* to view Criseyde as a slut. However, she admits that Gretchen Mieszkowski in *The Reputation of Criseyde: 1155-1500* (Hamden, Conn., 1971), pp. 71-153, demonstrates that in Chaucer's time Criseyde was considered "a type of the fickle woman" (p. 130). H. R. Hays in *The Dangerous Sex: The Myths of Feminine Evil* (New York, 1964), pp. 123-133, gives a summary of changing attitudes towards Criseyde. Arundell del Re, *The Secret of the Renaissance and Other Essays and Studies* (Tokyo, 1930), p. 67, describes Criseyde as a girl "who has been married, yet remains virginal and pure. This virginal quality distinguishes her at every step of the story. . . ." Robert A. Jelliffe, in *Troilus and Criseyde: Studies in Interpretation* (Folcroft, Pa., 1971), p. 64, says that Chaucer wanted us to love Criseyde, so he gave her a soul.

59. *Allegory of Love*, pp. 189-190. Robert B. Bechtel in "The Problem of Criseide's Character," *SUS*, 7 (1963), 117, offers the following chauvinistic remark: "And is not fear one of the most commonly accepted traits of womanhood?" Therefore, Criseyde, since she is a woman, must be fearful!

60. *The Noble Voice*, pp. 266-267, 269.

61. "Literature and Sexuality: Book III of Chaucer's *Troilus*," *MR*, 8 (1967), 446.

62. "The Central Episode in Chaucer's *Troilus*," *PMLA*, 76 (1962), 382.

63. *Love and Marriage in the Age of Chaucer*, p. 287.

64. Kelly, pp. 288-289.

65. *Geoffrey Chaucer: Literary and Historical Studies*, p. 131. Ann S. Haskell in "The Doppelgängers in Chaucer's *Troilus*," *NM*, 72 (1971), 728-729, states that Pandarus is Troilus' Doppelgänger, and that Pandarus and Troilus "constitute the complete lover," a "yin and yang duality." She writes: " . . . [Pandarus] has remained with [Criseyde] long after she has bedded down with her physiological lover, and returns to be with her again before she gets out of bed. Having fulfilled his specific parts of the relationship, Troilus has left and Pandarus has returned to take up his part of the romance with his characteristic vigor. . . . [I]n this coy scene of their 'pleye' . . . [Pandarus'] vicariousness approaches first-hand experience." Of this scene Rowe writes in

O Love O Charite! Contraries Harmonized, pp. 55-56: "The impulse to see more sex here than mere kissing does not misread entirely the spirit of this scene, however much it misrepresents what actually takes place." Carton, "Pandarus' Bed and Chaucer's Art," 57, describes this "post-nuptial encounter" as "the consummate instance of evasive language. . . . No amount of receptivity to its sexual suggestiveness will *give* us the incest, but any amount should make us reexamine interpretations of the poem that can only survive by flatly rejecting such a possibility." The prevalent willingness to confront the issue of sexual play in the "post-nuptial encounter" between Criseyde and Pandarus makes W. F. Bolton's unreservedly religious view of this scene seem archaic. See his "Treason in *Troilus*," *Archiv*, 203 (1967), 262.

66. "Pandarus and the Fate of Tantalus," *OL*, 24 (1969), 11, 9-10.

67. *Chaucer's Bawdy*, pp. 78, 115, 164.

68. "An Essay at the Logic of *Troilus and Criseyde*," 142-143.

69. *Chaucer and the English Tradition*, pp. 81-82.

70. *Chaucer's Bawdy*, pp. 103-105. See also his "*Troilus and Criseyde*, II, 582-587: A Note," *ChauR*, 5 (1970), 137-139, and Margaret Jennings, "Chaucer's Troilus and the Ruby," *NSQ*, 23 (1976), 533-537.

71. "Literature and Sexuality: Book III of Chaucer's *Troilus*," 445, 453.

72. *Chaucer's Bawdy*, p. 215. H. M. Smyser, "The Domestic Background of *Troilus and Criseyde*," *Spec*, 31 (1956), 308, does not mention this meaning.

73. "An Essay at the Logic of *Troilus and Criseyde*," 142-143.

74. Skeat, ed. *Complete Works of Geoffrey Chaucer* (Oxford, Eng., 1894), VI, 236; Root ed., *Troilus*, p. 544; F. N. Robinson, 2nd ed. of Chaucer's Poetry, pp. 451, 1104; Lowes, *Geoffrey Chaucer*, p. 152; A. C. Cawley, "A Note on Chaucer's Prioress and Criseyde," *MLR*, 43 (1948), 76; Baugh, ed. of Chaucer's Poetry, p. 195; D. S. and L. E. Brewer, eds. *Troilus and Criseyde* (London, 1969), p. 125.

75. Krapp, tr., *Chaucer's Troilus and Cressida* (New York, 1939), p. 272; Smith, "Chaucer's Prioress and Criseyde," *WVUPP*, 6 (1949), 7-8; Shelly, *The Living Chaucer*, p. 126.

76. *Chaucer*, pp. 78-80.

77. *Chaucer's Bawdy*, p. 64; Fisher, ed., *Complete Poetry and Prose of Geoffrey Chaucer*, p. 249, note for l. 780.

78. Corsa, "Dreams in *Troilus and Criseyde*," *AI*, 27 (1970), 54; Hagopian, "Chaucer as Psychologist in *Troilus and Criseyde*," *L&P*, 5 (1955), 5-11. Marshall W. Stearns, "A Note on Chaucer's Use of Aristotelian Psychology," *SP*, 43 (1946), 15-21, deals with a few images that Chaucer might have borrowed from Aristotle.

79. "Is This a Mannes Herte?" *L&P*, 16 (1966), 189.

80. Gallagher, "Criseyde's Dream of the Eagle: Love and War in *Troilus and Criseyde*," *MLQ*, 36 (1975), 115-132; Corsa, "Dreams," 57-58. Hatcher, "Chaucer and the Psychology of Fear," 318, note 20, and Spearing, *Criticism and Medieval Poetry*, pp. 105-107, also comment on Freud and Criseyde's dream. See also Preston, *Chaucer*, pp. 83-84; Beryl Rowland, *Blind Beasts: Chaucer's Animal World* (Kent, Ohio, 1971), pp. 79-86. Donald R. Howard in "Experience, Language, and Consciousness: *Troilus and Criseyde*, II, 596-931," *Medieval Literature and Folklore Studies: Essays in Honor of Frances Lee Utley*, ed. J.

Mandel and B. A. Rosenberg, p. 189, says that "perhaps indeed the eagle is love itself. . . ."

81. Corsa, "Dreams," 58. Renoir in "Criseyde's Two Half Lovers," 239-255, uses Jungian terminology, *anima-animus*, to explain Criseyde's passivity.

82. Corsa, "Dreams," 61. Rowland, "Pandarus and the Fate of Tantalus," 12-13, believes that the boar symbolizes Pandarus' desire for Criseyde while McAlpine, *The Genre of Troilus and Criseyde*, p. 172, argues that the boar is the jealous Troilus.

83. "Dreams," 63.

84. "Dreams," 65.

85. Eds. *Troilus and Criseyde*, p. xxxiv.

86. "Myth as Paradigm in *Troilus and Criseyde*," *PLL*, 3 (1967), 29; Sundwall in "Deiphobus and Helen: A Tantalizing Hint," 151-156, treats the same subject, but does not mention Kelly's article.

87. "Friendship in Chaucer's *Troilus*," 258-260. For a different and adulatory view of Hector, see K. S. Kiernan, "Hector the Second: The Lost Face of Troilustratus," *AnM*, 16 (1975), 52-62.

88. Mizener, "Character and Action in the Case of Criseyde," *PMLA*, 54 (1939), 65-66; Willene P. Taylor, "Supposed Antifeminism in Chaucer's *Troilus and Criseyde* and Its Retraction in *The Legend of Good Women*," *XUS*, 9 (1970), 6-7; Bayley, *The Characters of Love: A Study in the Literature of Personality* (New York, 1960), pp. 72, 82, 83; Durham, "Love and Death in *Troilus and Criseyde*," *ChauR*, 3 (1968), 1-11; Payne, *The Key of Remembrance*, pp. 182-183; Muscatine, *Chaucer and the French Tradition*, pp. 133-165. But Lawlor, *Chaucer*, pp. 87-88, insists that Criseyde, like Emma Bovary, is a "real woman." To Knapp, "The Nature of Nature: Criseyde's 'Slydyng Corage,' " 136, Criseyde is both a real woman and an image of nature's patterns.

89. *The Difficulty of Medieval Poetry*, Sussex International Tape, Side B, "Troilus and Criseyde."

90. "Chaucer's Failure with Woman: The Inadequacy of Criseyde," 119. Compare Corrigan's view with Donald R. Howard's contention in "Experience, Language, and Consciousness: *Troilus and Criseyde*, II, 596-931," 175, that in *Troilus*, II, 596-931, Chaucer "does what few men have ever done in literature or life—he sees into the mind of a woman."

91. "Chaucer and Literary Criticism," *DQR*, 4 (1974), 106.

92. "*Troilus and Criseyde*: A Reconsideration," pp. 88, 106.

93. Godwin, *Life of Chaucer*, 2nd ed. (London, 1804), I, 472; Saintonge, "In Defense of Criseyde," *MLQ*, 15 (1954), 312. See Thomas A. Van, "Chaucer's *Troilus and Criseyde*," *Expl*, 34 (1975) Item 20, who compares Criseyde to Christ.

94. "Chaucer's Women and Women's Chaucer," *The Authority of Experience: Essays in Feminist Criticism*, ed. Arlyn Diamond and Lee R. Edwards (Amherst, 1977), pp. 60-61. See also Utley, *The Crooked Rib*, p. 5.

95. "Time and the Narrator in Chaucer's *Troilus and Criseyde*," 26.

96. "The Doppelgängers in Chaucer's *Troilus*," 732.

97. " 'Slydynge of Corage': Chaucer's Criseyde as Feminist and Victim,"

The Authority of Experience: Essays in Feminist Criticism, ed. Arlyn Diamond and Lee R. Edwards, pp. 57-58.

98. Fries, 58.

99. "Chaucer's Good Woman," *ChauR,* 2 (1967), 90.

100. *The Dangerous Sex,* p. 128. See Hans Käsmann, " 'I wolde excuse hire yit for routhe': Chaucers Einstellung zu Criseyde," *Chaucer und seine zeit: Symposium für Walter F. Schirmer,* ed. Arno Esch (Tübingen, 1968), pp. 97-122.

101. *rymyng craftily: Meaning in Chaucer's Poetry,* pp. 65-76. On Chaucer's use of proverbs see Bartlett J. Whiting, *Chaucer's Use of Proverbs* (Cambridge, Mass., 1934), pp. 7, 49, 74-75; R. M. Lumiansky, "The Function of the Proverbial Monitory Elements in Chaucer's *Troilus and Criseyde,*" *TSE,* 2 (1950), 5-48.

102. "A Defense of Chaucer's Diomede," *CF,* 16 (1962), 112. Archibald M. Hill, "Diomede: The Traditional Development of a Character," *UMPLL,* 8 (1932), 1-25, and Laila Gross, "The Two Wooings of Criseyde," *NM,* 74 (1972), 120, both agree that Diomede is a simple, uncomplicated character. Isaacs, "Further Testimony in the Matter of *Troilus,*" 21-22, refers to Diomede's relationship to Criseyde as "complex" involving a "sophisticated love affair." Henry H. Peyton, III, "Diomed, the Large Tongued Greek," *In,* 6 (1974), 1, contends that Diomede represents "the spirit of Greek superiority."

103. "A Defense of Chaucer's Diomede," 122.

104. "The Role of Calkas in *Troilus and Criseyde,*" *MAE,* 36 (1967), 150; Robert M. Lumiansky, "Calchas in the Early Versions of the *Troilus,*" *TSE,* 4 (1954), 5-20, notes that Calchas is the same character in Boccaccio.

105. *rymyng craftily,* pp. 50-56.

106. Knight, pp. 56-69. Kiernan, "Hector the Second," 52-62, also exaggerates the role of Hector and writes about him as if he were the real hero of *Troilus.*

107. Knight, pp. 59-65. See also Sister Marcy C. Borthwick, "Antigone's Song as 'Mirour' in Chaucer's *Troilus and Criseyde,*" *MLQ,* 22 (1961), 227-235. Note that Kittredge in "Antigone's Song of Love," *MLN,* 25 (1910), 158, describes Antigone's song as an example of "adaptive mastery" which Chaucer based on Machaut's *Le Paradis d'Amour.*

108. "The Roles of Calkas, Helen and Cassandra in Chaucer's *Troilus,*" *In,* 7 (1975), 10-12. See also Peyton's "Three Minor Characters in Chaucer's *Troilus:* Hector, Antigone and Deiphebus," *In,* 8 (1975), 47-53.

109. "Characters and Crowds in Chaucer's *Troilus,*" *N&Q,* 13 (1966), 50-52.

Notes for Chapter VI
Conclusion

1. "Chaucer's Sense of History," *JEGP,* 51 (1952), 308.

2. Baum, *Chaucer's Verse* (Durham, N.C., 1961); Knight, *The Poetry of the*

Canterbury Tales (Sydney, Australia, 1973), and *rymyng craftily*; Southworth, *The Prosody of Chaucer and his Followers* (Oxford, Eng., 1962); I. Robinson, *Chaucer's Prosody: A Study of the Middle English Verse Tradition* (Cambridge, Eng., 1971).

3. "Scanning the Prosodists: An Essay in Metacriticism," *ChauR*, 11 (1976), 22-82. Gaylord's exasperation surfaces when he comments on Southworth's scansion of Chaucer's "metrically various" lines which require that the final *e* should not be pronounced. Gaylord asks, p. 39: "What the devil is the meter of which they are a variation?"

4. Reiss, "Chaucer's Courtly Love," 97, note 7. Gardner, *The Poetry of Chaucer*, p. 345, note 2. Compare these comments with Peter M. Vermeer's negative, yet polite criticism in "Chaucer and Literary Criticism," 97-110. Although most of his discussion is given over to a diatribe against Robinson's unhistorical approach, Vermeer ends by praising Robinson profusely as an "excellent critic."

5. Benjamin R. Bessent, "The Puzzling Chronology of Chaucer's *Troilus*," *SN*, 41 (1968), 99-111; Wendy A. Bie, "Dramatic Chronology in *Troilus and Criseyde*," *ELN*, 14 (1976), 9-13; John M. Ganim, "Tone and Time in Chaucer's *Troilus*, *ELH*, 43 (1976) 141-153; Laila Gross, "Time and the Narrator in Chaucer's *Troilus and Criseyde*," *McNr*, 19 (1968), 16-26; Joseph A. Longo, "The Double Time Scheme in Book II of Chaucer's *Troilus and Criseyde*," *MLQ*, 22 (1961), 37-40; Henry W. Sams, "The Dual Time-Scheme in Chaucer's *Troilus*," *MLN*, 56 (1941), 94-100.

6. Ed. *Chaucer's Poetry: An Anthology for the Modern Reader* (New York, 1958), p. 965.

7. Graydon, "Defense of Criseyde," *PMLA*, 44 (1929), 177; French, "A Defense of Troilus," *PMLA*, 44 (1929), 1246-1251; J. M. Beatty, Jr., "Mr. Graydon's Defense of Criseyde," *SP*, 26 (1929), 470-481.

8. Ellis, *The Theory of Literary Criticism*, p. 11; Heller, *The Disinherited Mind: Essays in Modern German Literature and Thought*, 3rd ed. (London, 1971), p. ix.

9. Ed. *Chaucer's Poetry*, p. vi.

10. "The Historical Criticism We Need," *Chaucer at Albany*, ed. Rossell Hope Robbins (New York, 1975), p. 189.

11. "Chaucer and Modernism: An Essay in Criticism," *Chaucer at Albany*, pp. 212-213.

12. *Poetic Freedom and Poetic Truth: Chaucer, Shakespeare, Marlowe, Milton* (Oxford, Eng., 1976), pp. 30-31.

13. Hawkins, p. 31.

14. *Scientific Explanation* (New York, 1960), pp. 12ff.

15. Hawkins, p. 33.

16. "Teaching *Troilus and Criseyde*," *SoRa*, 5 (1972), 13.

17. "The Unity of *Troilus and Criseyde*," *CR*, 14 (1971), 17.

18. *Paradoxical Patterns in Chaucer's Troilus*, p. 26, note 2.

19. *Milton's God*, pp. 198-199.

20. "The Sense of the Past," *The Liberal Imagination*, p. 181.

21. *Day of the Leopard*, p. 34; Hawkins, p. 23, reminds us that some very

respectable critics have objected to criticism based on the reactions of original audiences: William Empson, *Milton's God*; Helen Gardner, *The Business of Criticism* (Oxford, Eng., 1959); Robert Ornstein, *The Moral Vision of Jacobean Tragedy* (Madison, 1960); Wilbur Sanders, *The Dramatist and the Received Idea* (Cambridge, Eng., 1968). For a typical example of a work which deals with Chaucer's audience, see Dieter Mehl, "The Audience of *Troilus and Criseyde*," *Chaucer and Middle English Studies*, ed. B. Rowland, pp. 173-189.

22. "Techniques of Alienation in *Troilus and Criseyde*," *The Uses of Criticism*, ed. A. P. Foulkes (Frankfurt, 1976), p. 94.

23. "The Rhetoric of Narrative Rendering in Chaucer's *Troilus*," *ChauR*, 12 (1977), 27-37. See also J.A. Burrow, *Ricardian Poetry: Chaucer, Gower, Langland and the Gawain Poet* (London, 1971), pp. 131-132.

24. "Second Thoughts: C. S. Lewis on Chaucer's *Troilus*," *EIC*, 8 (1958), 124.

25. "Criticism versus Historicism," paper read at the Modern Language Association Meeting, December, 1963, quoted by Wimsatt in *Day of the Leopard*, p. 37, note 50.

26. "Chaucer and Literary Criticism," 108.

27. "The Frontiers of Criticism," *On Poetry and Poets* (New York, 1957), p. 131.

28. "The Dry Sea and the Carrenare," *MP*, 3 (1905-1906), 46.

29. Advertisement of the University of Georgia Press, 1977.

30. Review, "A Poet's Tale," of Gardner's *Life and Times of Chaucer* and *The Poetry of Chaucer*, p. 13.

31. *Shakespeare Our Contemporary*, tr. B. Taborski (New York, 1966).

32. Susan Schibanoff in "Argus and Argyve: Etymology and Characterization in Chaucer's *Troilus*," *Spec*, 51 (1976) 658, notes that Chaucer as a poet interpreter was both historical and anachronistic.

As this book was in the process of being printed, I had the good fortune to read a newly published issue of *New Literary History*, 10 (1979) on the subject of "Medieval Literature and Contemporary Theory." It contains articles by Hans Robert Jauss, Paul Zumthor, Rainer Warning, and Maria Corti (translated from the original versions in German, French, and Italian). They deal with the subject of the alterity and modernity of medieval literature. Also discussed in these and other essays is the question of whether the new structural linguistics, semiotics, and phenomenological and sociological theories of our age can be fruitfully utilized in the study of medieval works. Eugene Vance in his "Mervelous Signals: Poetics, Sign Theory, and Politics in Chaucer's *Troilus*" (293-337), uses the modern linguistic terminology of Roman Jakobson, J.R. Searles, and J.L. Austin. Vance's "new" approach leads him to a very "old" conclusion, namely, the *contemptus mundi* interpretation of *Troilus* with the main characters cast in the role of sinners and Diomede "of tonge large" debased as a "cunnilinguist." But these are, for the most part, provocative essays which treat important critical issues debated in European circles. As Paul Zumthor wisely observes, neither naive historicism nor blind modernism will help us to resolve the dilemma of "l'éloignement du moyen âge," but we must recognize that " 'To read' a medieval text can in effect only signify for us the following: to render it comprehensible for the mind and sensibility of the twentieth century, conditioned by its own culture" (p. 371).

BIBLIOGRAPHY

Adams, John F. "Irony in Troilus' Apostrophe to the Vacant House of Criseyde." *MLQ*, 24 (1963), 61-65.

Adamson, Jane. "The Unity of *Troilus and Criseyde*." *CR*, 14 (1971), 17-37.

Aers, David. "Woman in Medieval Society." *ChauR*, 13 (1979), 177-200.

apRoberts, Robert P. "The Boethian God and the Audience of the *Troilus*." *JEGP*, 69 (1970), 425-436.

apRoberts, Robert P. "The Central Episode in Chaucer's *Troilus*." *PMLA*, 76 (1962), 373-385.

apRoberts, Robert P. "Criseyde's Infidelity and the Moral of the Troilus." *Spec*, 44 (1969), 383-402.

apRoberts, Robert P. "Love in the *Filostrato*." *ChauR*, 7 (1972), 1-26.

apRoberts, Robert P. "Notes on *Troilus and Criseyde*." *MLN*, 57 (1942), 92-97.

Arntz, Sister Mary Luke. " 'That Fol of Whos Folie Men Ryme.' " *AN&Q*, 3 (1965), 151-152.

Baird, Lorrayne, Y. *A Bibliography of Chaucer 1964-1973*. Boston: G. K. Hall, 1977.

Barney, Stephen A. "Troilus Bound." *Spec*, 47 (1972), 445-458.

Baron, F. Xavier. "Chaucer's Troilus and Self-Renunciation in Love." *PLL*, 10 (1974), 5-14.

Bartel, Neva, A. "Child of Night." *BSUF*, 6 (1965), 45-50.

Bass, Eben. "The Jewels of *Troilus*." *CE*, 23 (1961), 145-147.

Basu, Kajal. "The Moral Confusion in Chaucer's *Troilus and Criseyde*." *IJES*, 4 (1963), 25-47.

Baugh, Albert C. *Chaucer*. Goldentree Bibliographies in Language and Literature. New York: Appleton-Century-Crofts, 1968.

Baugh, Albert C., ed. *Chaucer's Major Poetry*. New York; Appleton-Century-Crofts, 1963.

Baugh, Albert C. "Fifty Years of Chaucer Scholarship." *Spec*, 26 (1951), 650-672.

Baugh, Albert C., et alii, eds. *A Literary History of England*. New York, Appleton-Century-Crofts, 1948.

Baum, Paul F. *Chaucer: A Critical Appreciation*. Durham, N. C.: Duke University Press, 1958.

Baum, Paul F. *Chaucer's Verse*. Durham, N. C.: Duke University Press, 1961.

Bayley, John. *The Characters of Love: A Study in the Literature of Personality*. New York: Basic Books, 1960.

Beardsley, Monroe C. *Aesthetics: Problems in the Philosophy of Criticism*. New York: Harcourt Brace Jovanovich, 1958.

Beardsley, Monroe C. "Textual Meaning and Authorial Meaning." *Genre*, 1 (1968), 169-181.

Beatty, Joseph M. "Mr. Graydon's 'Defense of Criseyde.' " *SP*, 26 (1929), 470-481.

Bechtel, Robert B. "The Problem of Criseide's Character." *SUS*, 7 (1963), 109-118.

Beckman, Sabina. "Color Symbolism in *Troilus and Criseyde*." *CLAJ*, 20 (1976), 68-74.

Benson, Larry D. "A Reader's Guide to Writings on Chaucer." *Writers and Their Background: Geoffrey Chaucer*, ed. D. S. Brewer. Athens, Ohio: Ohio University Press, 1975, pp. 321-351.

Benton, John F. "Clio and Venus: An Historical View of Medieval Love." *The Meaning of Courtly Love*, ed. F. X. Newman, Albany: State University of New York Press, 1968, pp. 19-42.

Berryman, Charles. "The Ironic Design of Fortune in *Troilus and Criseyde*." *ChauR*, 2 (1967), 2-7.

Bessent, Benjamin R. "The Puzzling Chronology of Chaucer's *Troilus*." *SN*, 41 (1968), 99-111.

Bethurum, Dorothy. "Chaucer's Point of View as Narrator in the Love Poems." *PMLA*, 84 (1959), 511-520.

Bethurum, Dorothy, ed. *Critical Approaches to Medieval Literature*. New York: Dover, 1959.

Bie, Wendy A. "Dramatic Chronology in *Troilus and Criseyde*." *ELN*, 14 (1976), 9-13.

Birney, Earle. "The Beginnings of Chaucer's Irony." *PMLA*, 54 (1939), 637-655.

Birney, Earle. "Is Chaucer's Irony a Modern Discovery?" *JEGP*, 41 (1942), 303-319.

Bleich, David. *Subjective Criticism*. Baltimore, Md.: Johns Hopkins University Press, 1978.

Bloom, Harold. *Poetry and Repression: Revisionism from Blake to Stevens*. New Haven: Yale University Press, 1976.

Bloomfield, Morton W. "Chaucer's Sense of History." *JEGP*, 51 (1952), 301-313.

Bloomfield, Morton W. "Distance and Predestination in *Troilus and Criseyde*." *PMLA*, 72 (1957), 14-26.

Bloomfield, Morton W. "The Eighth Sphere: A Note on Chaucer's *Troilus and Criseyde*." *MLR*, 52 (1958), 408-410.

Bloomfield, Morton W. "Troilus' Paraclausithyron and Its Setting." *NM*, 73 (1972), 15-24.

Boethius. *The Theological Tractates: The Consolation of Philosophy*, tr. E. K. Rand and H. F. Stewart. Cambridge, Mass.: Harvard University Press, 1962.

Bolton, Whitney F. "Treason in *Troilus*." *Archiv*, 203 (1967), 255-262.

Bonnard, G. "A Note on Chaucer's *Troilus and Criseyde*, V. 1637." *RES*, V (1929), 323-324.

Booth, Wayne C. *The Rhetoric of Irony.* Chicago: University of Chicago Press, 1974.

Borthwick, Sister Mary C. "Antigone's Song as 'Mirour' in Chaucer's *Troilus and Criseyde.*" *MLQ*, 22 (1961), 227-235.

Boughner, Daniel C. "Elements of Epic Grandeur in the *Troilus.*" *ELH*, 6 (1939), 201-210.

Bowers, R. H. "The 'Suttell and Dissayvabull' World of Chaucer's *Troilus.*" *N&Q*, 202 (1957), 278-279.

Braddy, Haldeen. *Chaucer and the French Poet Graunson.* Baton Rouge, La.: Louisiana State University Press, 1947.

Braddy, Haldeen. "Chaucer's Playful Pandarus." *SFQ*, 34 (1970), 71-81.

Braddy, Haldeen. *Geoffrey Chaucer: Literary and Historical Studies.* Port Washington, N. Y.: Kennikat Press, 1971.

Braithwaite, Richard B. *Scientific Explanation.* New York: Harper and Row, 1960.

Brenner, Geoffrey. "Narrative Structure in Chaucer's *Troilus and Criseyde.*" *AnM*, 6 (1965), 5-18.

Bressie, Ramona. "The Date of Thomas Usk's 'Testament of Love.' " *MP*, 26 (1928), 17-29.

Brewer, Derek S. "The Ages of Troilus, Criseyde and Pandarus." *SELit*, 1 (1972), 3-13.

Brewer, Derek S. *Chaucer*, 3rd ed. London: Longman, 1973.

Brewer, Derek S., ed. *Chaucer and Chaucerians: Critical Studies in Middle English Literature.* London: Thomas Nelson, 1966.

Brewer, Derek S. *Chaucer in his Time.* London: Thomas Nelson, 1963.

Brewer, Derek S. *Chaucer: The Critical Heritage.* 2 vols. London: Routledge & Kegan Paul, 1978.

Brewer, Derek, S. "The Criticism of Chaucer in the Twentieth Century." *Chaucer's Mind and Art*, ed. A. C. Cawley. Edinburgh: Oliver & Boyd, 1969, pp. 3-28.

Brewer, Derek S. *Geoffrey Chaucer's The Parlement of Foulys.* London: Thomas Nelson, 1960.

Brewer, Derek S. "Gothic Chaucer." *Writers and Their Background: Geoffrey Chaucer*, ed. D. Brewer. Athens, Ohio: Ohio University Press, 1975, pp. 1-32.

Brewer, Derek S. "Love and Marriage in Chaucer's Poetry." *MLR*, 49 (1954), 461-464.

Brewer, Derek S. and Brewer, L. E. Elisabeth, eds. *Troilus and Criseyde* (abridged). London: Routledge & Kegan Paul, 1969.

Brewer, Derek S., ed. *Writers and their Background: Geoffrey Chaucer.* Athens, Ohio: Ohio University Press, 1975.

Broatch, James W. "The Indebtedness of Chaucer's *Troilus* to Benoit's *Roman.*" *JEGP*, 2 (1898), 14-28.

Bromwich, David. "Review of L. R. Thompson's and R. H. Winnick's

Robert Frost: The Later Years, 1938-1963." NYTBR, January 16, 1977, pp. 4, 5, 28.

Bronson, Bertrand H. *In Search of Chaucer*. Toronto: University of Toronto Press, 1960.

Brookhouse, Christopher. "Chaucer's Impossibilia." *MAE*, 34 (1965), 40-42.

Brooks, Cleanth. "Literary Criticism: Poet, Poem and Reader." *Varieties of Religious Experience*, ed. Stanley Burnshaw. New York: New York University Press, 1962.

Brown, Carleton. "Another Contemporary Allusion in Chaucer's *Troilus." MLN*, 26 (1911), 208-211.

Brusendorff, Aage. *The Chaucer Tradition*. 1925; reprint ed. Oxford: Clarendon Press, 1967.

Bühler, Curt F. "Notes on the Campsall Manuscript of Chaucer's *Troilus and Criseyde* Now in the Pierpont Morgan Library." *Spec*, 20 (1945), 457-460.

Burjorjee, D. M. "The Pilgrimage of Troilus's Sailing Heart in Chaucer's *Troilus and Criseyde." AnM*, 13 (1972), 14-31.

Burlin, Robert B. *Chaucerian Fiction*. Princeton: Princeton University Press, 1977.

Burnley, J. D. "Proude Bayard: 'Troilus and Criseyde,' I.218." *N&Q*, 23 (1976), 148-152.

Burrow, J. A. *Ricardian Poetry: Chaucer, Gower, Langland and the Gawain Poet*. London: Routledge & Kegan Paul, 1971.

Byrd, David G. "Blanche Fever: The Grene Sickness," *BSUF*, 19 (1978), 56-64.

Campbell, Jackson J. "A New *Troilus* Fragment." *PMLA*, 73 (1958), 305-308.

Capellanus, Andreas. *The Art of Courtly Love*, tr. J. J. Parry. New York: Columbia University Press, 1941.

Carpenter, Nan C. "Chaucer's *Troilus and Criseyde*, III, 624-628." *Expl*, 30 (1972), Item 51.

Carson, Mother Angela, " 'To Synge a Fool a Masse.' " *AN&Q*, (1968), 135-136.

Carton, Evan. "Pandarus' Bed and Chaucer's Art." *PMLA*, 94 (1979), 47-61.

Cassidy, F. G. " 'Don Thyn Hood' in Chaucer's *Troilus." JEGP*, 57 (1958), 739-742.

Cawley, Arthur C., ed. *Chaucer's Mind and Art*. Edinburgh: Oliver & Boyd, 1969.

Cawley, Arthur C. "A Note on Chaucer's Prioress and Criseyde." *MLR*, 43 (1948), 74-77.

Chesterton, G. K. *Chaucer*. London: Faber and Faber, 1932.

Christmas, Peter. "*Troilus and Criseyde*: The Problems of Love and Necessity." *ChauR*, 9 (1975), 285-296.

Chute, Marchette. *Geoffrey Chaucer of England*. New York: E. P. Dutton, 1946.

Cioffi, Frank. "Intention and Interpretation in Criticism." *Issues in Contemporary Literary Criticism*, ed. Gregory T. Polletta. Boston: Little Brown, 1973, pp. 215-233.

Clark, John W. "Dante and the Epilogue of *Troilus*." *JEGP*, 50 (1951), 1-10.

Coghill, Nevill. *The Poet Chaucer*. London: Oxford University Press, 1949.

Conlee, John W. "The Meaning of Troilus' Ascension to the Sphere." *ChauR*, 7 (1972), 27-36.

Cook, Albert S. "The Character of Criseyde." *PMLA*, 22 (1907), 531-547.

Cook, Albert S. "Chaucer's *Troilus and Criseyde* 3.1-38." *Archiv*, 119 (1907), 40-54.

Cook, Daniel. "The Revision of Chaucer's *Troilus*: The BETA Text." *ChauR*, 9 (1974), 51-62.

Cook, Robert G. "Chaucer's Pandarus and the Medieval Ideal of Friendship." *JEGP*, 69 (1970), 407-424.

Cope, Jackson, I. "Chaucer, Venus, and the 'Seventhe Spere.' " *MLN*, 68 (1952), 245-246.

Corrigan, Matthew. "Chaucer's Failure with Woman: The Inadequacy of Criseyde." *WHR*, 23 (1969), 107-120.

Corsa, Helen Storm. *Chaucer: Poet of Mirth and Morality*. Notre Dame, Ind.: University of Notre Dame Press, 1964.

Corsa, Helen Storm. "Dreams in Troilus and Criseyde." *AI*, 27 (1970), 52-65.

Corsa, Helen Storm. "Is this a Mannes Herte?" *L&P*, 16 (1966), 184-191.

Cotton, M. E. "The Artistic Integrity of Chaucer's *Troilus and Criseyde*." *ChauR*, 7 (1972), 37-43.

Coulton, G. G. *Medieval Panorama*. Cambridge: Cambridge University Press, 1944.

Covella, Sister Frances Dolores, "Audience as Determinant of Meaning in the *Troilus*." *ChauR*, 2 (1968), 235-245.

Craig, Hardin. "From Gorgias to Troilus." *Studies in Medieval Literature in Honor of Albert C. Baugh*, ed. MacEdward Leach. Philadelphia: University of Pennsylvania Press, 1961, pp. 97-107.

Crampton, Georgia. "Action and Passion in Chaucer's *Troilus*." *MAE*, 43 (1974), 22-36.

Crane, Ronald S. *The Languages of Criticism and the Structure of Poetry*. Toronto: University of Toronto Press, 1953.

Crane, Ronald S. "On Hypotheses in 'Historical Criticism': Apropos of Certain Contemporary Medievalists." *The Idea of the Humanities and Other Essays: Critical and Historical*. Chicago: University of Chicago Press, 1967, II, 236-260.

Crawford, William R. *Bibliography of Chaucer 1954-63*. Seattle: University of Washington Press, 1967.

Crews, Frederick C. "Anaesthetic Criticism, I." *NYRB*, February 26, 1970, pp. 31-35.

Crow, Martin M. and Olson, Clair C., eds. *Chaucer Life-Records*. Oxford: Clarendon Press, 1966.

Cummings, Hubertis M. *The Indebtedness of Chaucer's Works to the Italian Works of Boccaccio: A Review and Summary*. 1916; reprint ed. New York: Haskell House, 1965.

Curry, Walter Clyde. "Destiny in Chaucer's *Troilus*." *PMLA*, 45 (1930), 129-168.

Daly, Saralyn R. "Criseyde's Blasphemous Aube." *N&S*, 10 (1963), 442-444.

David, Alfred. "The Hero of the Troilus." *Spec*, 37 (1962), 566-581.

David, Alfred. *The Strumpet Muse: Art and Morals in Chaucer's Poetry*. Bloomington: Indiana University Press, 1976.

Davis, Norman. "The *Litera Troili* and English Letters." *RES*, 16 (1965), 233-244.

Davis, Walter A. *The Act of Interpretation: A Critique of Literary Reason*. Chicago: University of Chicago Press, 1978.

Day, Mabel. "Chaucer's *Troilus and Criseyde*, V. 1637." *RES*, 6 (1930), 73.

Delaney, Sheila. "The Techniques of Alienation in 'Troilus and Criseyde.' " *The Uses of Criticism*, ed. A. P. Foulkes. Frankfort: Lang, 1976, pp. 77-95.

Dempster, Germaine. *Dramatic Irony in Chaucer*. 1932; reprint ed. New York: Humanities Press, 1959.

DeNeef, A. Leigh. "Robertson and the Critics." *ChauR*, 2 (1968), 205-234.

Denomy, Alexander J. *The Heresy of Courtly Love*. 1947; reprint ed. Gloucester, Mass.: Peter Smith, 1965.

Denomy, Alexander J. "The Two Moralities of Chaucer's *Troilus and Criseyde*." *PTRSC*, 44 (1950), 35-46.

Deschamps, Eustache. *Oeuvres Completes de Eustache Deschamps*, ed. le Marquis de Saint-Hilaire et G. Reynaud. 11 Vols. Paris: SATF, 1878-1903, II.

De Sélincourt, E. *Oxford Lectures on Poetry*. Oxford: Clarendon Press, 1934.

D'Evelyn, Charlotte. "Pandarus a Devil?" *PMLA*, 71 (1956), 275-279.

Devereux, James A. "A Note on *Troilus and Criseyde*, Book III, Line 1309." *PQ*, 44 (1965), 550-552.

DeVries, F. C. "*Troilus and Criseyde*, Book III, Stanza 251, and Boethius." *ES*, 52 (1971), 502-507.

Diamond, Arlyn. "Chaucer's Women and Women's Chaucer." *The Authority of Experience: Essays in Feminist Criticism*, ed. A.

Diamond and L. R. Edwards. Amherst: University of Massachusetts Press, 1977, pp. 60-83.

Di Pasquale, Pasquale, Jr. " 'Sickernesse' and Fortune in *Troilus and Criseyde.*" *PQ*, 49 (1970), 152-162.

Dodd, William G. *Courtly Love in Chaucer and Gower.* 1913; reprint ed. Gloucester, Mass.: Peter Smith, 1959.

Donaldson, E. Talbot. "Chaucer's Three 'P's': Pandarus, Pardoner and Poet." *MQR*, 14 (1975), 282-301.

Donaldson, E. Talbot, ed. *Chaucer's Poetry: An Anthology for the Modern Reader.* New York: Ronald Press, 1958.

Donaldson, E. Talbot. "Chaucer's Three 'P's': Pandarus Pardoner and Poet." *MQR*, 14 (1975), 282-3pmm

Donaldson, E. Talbot. "The Ending of Chaucer's *Troilus.*" *Early English and Norse Studies Presented to Hugh Smith*, ed. A. Brown and P. Foote. London: Methuen, 1963, pp. 26-45.

Donaldson, E. Talbot. *Speaking of Chaucer.* London: Athlone, 1970.

Doob, Penelope B.R. "Chaucer's 'Corones Tweyne' and the Lapidaries." *ChauR*, 7 (1972), 85-96.

Drake, Gertrude C. "The Moon and Venus: Troilus's Havens in Eternity." *PLL*, 11 (1975), 3-17.

Dronke, Peter. "The Conclusion of *Troilus and Criseyde.*" *MAE*, 33 (1964), 47-52.

Dunning, T. P. "God and Man in *Troilus and Criseyde.*" *English and Medieval Studies Presented to J. R. R. Tolkien*, ed. N. Davis, and C. L. Wrenn. London: Allen and Unwin, 1962, pp. 164-182.

Durham, Lonnie J. "Love and Death in *Troilus and Criseyde.*" *ChauR*, 3 (196), 1-11.

Durling, Robert M. *The Figure of the Poet in Renaissance Epic.* Cambridge: Harvard University Press, 1965.

Ebel, Julia. "Troilus and Oedipus: The Genealogy of an Image." *ES*, 55 (1974), 15-21.

Edmunds, Paul E. "A Defense of Chaucer's Diomede." *CF*, 16 (1962), 110-123.

Elbow, Peter H. *Oppositions in Chaucer.* Middletown, Conn.: Wesleyan University Press, 1975.

Elbow, Peter H. "Two Boethian Speeches in *Troilus and Criseyde* and Chaucerian Irony." *Literary Criticism and Historical Understanding*, ed. Philip Damon. New York: Columbia University Press, 1967, pp. 85-107.

Eldredge, Laurence. "Boethian Epistemology and Chaucer's *Troilus* in the Light of Fourteenth-Century Thought." *Mediaevalia*, 2 (1976), 50-75.

Eliason, Norman E. *The Language of Chaucer's Poetry: An Appraisal of the Verse, Style, and Structure.* Copenhagen: Rosenkilde and Bagger, 1972.

Eliot, T. S. *On Poetry and Poets*. New York: Farrar, Straus, & Cudahy, 1957.

Ellis, Deborah. " 'Calle It Gentilesse': A Comparative Study of Two Medieval Go-Betweens." *Comitatus*, 8 (1977), 1-13.

Ellis, John M. *The Theory of Literary Criticism: A Logical Analysis.* Berkeley: University of California Press, 1974.

Ellmann, Richard. "Love in the Catskills." *NYRB*, February 5, 1976, pp. 27-28.

Empson, William. *Milton's God*. London: Chatto & Windus, 1961.

Empson, William. " 'The Voice of the Underdog': Review of Wayne C. Booth's *A Rhetoric of Irony*." *NYTBR*, June 12, 1975, pp. 37-39.

Empson, William. *Seven Types of Ambiguity*, 3rd ed. London: Chatto and Windus, 1963.

Epstein, Hans J. "The Identity of Chaucer's 'Lollius.' " *MLQ*, 3 (1942), 391-400.

Erzgräber, Willi. "Tragik und Komik in Chaucers *Troilus and Criseyde*." *Festschrift für Walter Hübner*, ed. Dieter Riesner and Helmut Gneuss. Berlin: Erich Schmidt, 1964, pp. 139-163.

Erzgräber, Willi. "Zu Chaucers *Troilus and Criseyde*, Buch IV," *Philologica Romanica: Erhard Lomatzsch Giwidmet*, ed. Manfred Bambeck and Hans C. Christmann. Munich: W. Fink, 1975, pp. 97-117.

'Espinasse, Margaret. "Chaucer's 'Fare-Carte.' " *N&Q*, 23 (1976), 295-296.

Evans, L. G. "A Biblical Allusion in *Troilus and Criseyde*." *MLN*, 74 (1959), 584-587.

Everett, Dorothy. "*Troilus and Criseyde*." *Essays in Middle English Literature*, ed. P. Kean. New York: Oxford University Press, 1959, pp. 115-138.

Fansler, Dean Spruill. *Chaucer and the Roman de la Rose*. 1914; reprint ed. Gloucester, Mass.: Peter Smith, 1965.

Farina, Peter M. "Two Notes on Chaucer." *LangQ*, 10 (1972), 23-26.

Farnham, Anthony E. "Chaucerian Irony and the Ending of the *Troilus*." *ChauR*, 1 (1967), 208-216.

Farnham, Willard. *The Medieval Heritage of Elizabethan Tragedy.* Berkeley: University of California Press, 1936.

Ferrante, J. M. and Economou, G. D., eds., *In Pursuit of Perfection: Courtly Love in Medieval Literature*. Port Washington, N. Y.: Kennikat Press, 1975.

Fischer, Rudolph. *Zu den Kunstformen des mittelalterlichen Epos.* Vienna: Wilhelm Broümuller, 1899.

Fisher, John Hurt, ed. *The Complete Poetry and Prose of Geoffrey Chaucer*. New York: Holt, Rhinehart & Winston, 1977.

Fisher, John Hurt. "The Intended Illustrations in Ms. Corpus Christi 61 of Chaucer's *Troilus and Criseyde*." *Medieval Literature in Honor of Lillian Herlands Hornstein*, ed. J. B. Bessinger, Jr. and R. R. Raymo. New York: New York University Press, 1976, pp. 111-121.

Fowler, David C. "An Unusual Meaning of 'win' in Chaucer's *Troilus and Criseyde*." *MLN*, 69 (1954), 313-315.

Fowler, David C. "Love in Chrétien's Lancelot." *RR*, 63 (1972), 5-14.

Frank, Robert W., Jr. "*Troilus and Criseyde*: The Art of Amplification." *Medieval Literature and Folklore Studies: Essays in Honor of Francis Lee Utley*, ed. J. Mandel and B. A. Rosenberg. New Brunswick, N. J.: Rutgers University Press, 1970, pp. 155-171.

Freiwald, Leah R. "Swich Love of Frendes: Pandarus and Troilus." *ChauR*, 6 (1971), 120-129.

French, J. Milton. "A Defense of Troilus." *PMLA*, 44 (1929), 1246-1251.

Freud, Sigmund. *On Creativity and the Unconscious*. New York: Harper & Row, 1958.

Friedman, John B. "'Pandarus' Cushion and the 'pluma Sardanapalli.' " *JEGP*, 75 (1976), 41-55.

Fries, Maureen. " 'Slydynge of Corage': Chaucer's Criseyde as Feminist and Victim." *The Authority of Experience: Essays in Feminist Criticism*, ed. Arlyn Diamond and Lee R. Edwards. Amherst: University of Massachusetts Press, 1977, pp. 45-59.

Frost, Michael H. "Narrative Devices in Chaucer's *Troilus and Criseyde*." *Thoth*, 14 (1974), 29-38.

Frost, William. "A Chaucerian Crux." *YR*, 66 (1977), 551-561.

Fruman, Norman. *Coleridge, The Damaged Archangel*. New York: George Braziller, 1971.

Fry, Donald K. "Chaucer's Zanzis and a Possible Source for *Troilus and Criseyde*, IV, 407-13." *ELN*, 9 (1971), 81-85.

Frye, Northrop. *Anatomy of Criticism*. Princeton: Princeton University Press, 1957.

Frye, Northrop. "Literary Criticism." *The Aims and Methods of Scholarship in Modern Languages and Literature*, ed. James Thorpe. New York: Modern Language Association of America, 1963, pp. 57-69.

Gadamer, Hans Georg. *Wahrheit und Methode: Grundzüge einer philosophischen Hermeneutik*. Tübingen: Mohr, 1960.

Gallagher, Joseph E. "Criseyde's Dream of the Eagle: Love and War in *Troilus and Criseyde*." *MLQ*, 36 (1975), 115-132.

Gallagher, Joseph E. "Theology and Intention in Chaucer's *Troilus*." *ChauR*, 7 (1972), 44-66.

Galway, Margaret. "Joan of Kent and the Order of the Garter." *UBHJ*, 1 (1974), 13-50.

Galway, Margaret. "The 'Troilus' Frontispiece." *MLR*, 44 (1949), 161-177.

Ganim, John M. "Tone and Time in Chaucer's *Troilus*." *ELH*, 43 (1976), 141-153.

Garbáty, Thomas J. "The Pamphilus Tradition in Ruiz and Chaucer." *PQ*, 45 (1967), 457-470.

Garbáty, Thomas J. *"Troilus,* V, 1786-1792 and V, 1807-1827: An Example of Poetic Process." *ChauR*, 11 (1977), 299-305.

Gardner, Helen. *The Business of Criticism.* London: Oxford University Press, 1959.

Gardner, John. *The Life and Times of Chaucer.* New York: Alfred A. Knopf, 1977.

Gardner, John. *The Poetry of Chaucer.* Carbondale: Southern Illinois University Press, 1977.

Gaylord, Alan T. "Chaucer's Tender Trap: The *Troilus* and the 'Yonge Fresshe Folkes.' " *EM*, 15 (1964), 25-42.

Gaylord, Alan T. "Friendship in Chaucer's *Troilus.*" *ChauR*, 3 (1969), 239-264.

Gaylord, Alan T. "Gentillesse in Chaucer's *Troilus.*" *SP*, 61 (1964), 19-34.

Gaylord, Alan T. "Scanning the Prosodists: An Essay in Metacriticism." *ChauR*, 11 (1976), 22-82.

Gaylord, Alan T., "Uncle Pandarus as Lady Philosophy," *PMASAL*, 47 (1961), 522-95.

Gill, Sister Ann Barbara, *Paradoxical Patterns in Chaucer's Troilus: An Explanation of the Palinode.* Wash., D.C.: Catholic University of America Press, 1960.

Gillmeister, Heiner. "Chaucer's *Kan Ke Dort (Troilus,* II, 1752), and the 'Sleeping Dogs' of the Trouvères." *ES*, 59 (1978), 310-323.

Gnerro, Mark L. " 'Ye Haselwodes Shaken!'—Pandarus and Divination." *N&Q*, 207 (1962), 164-165.

Godwin, William. *Life of Geoffrey Chaucer, the early English poet.* 4 Vols. 2nd ed. London: R. Phillips, 1804, I.

Goffin, R. D. " 'Here and howne' in 'Troilus and Criseyde.' " *MLR*, 90 (1945), 208-210.

Gordon, Ida L. *The Double Sorrow of Troilus: A Study of Ambiguities in Troilus and Criseyde.* Oxford: Clarendon Press, 1970.

Gordon, Ida L. "The Narrative Function of Irony in Chaucer's *Troilus and Criseyde.*" *Medieval Miscellany Presented to Eugene Vinaver by Pupils, Colleagues, and Friends,* ed. F. Whitehead, A. H. Diverres, and S. E. Sutcliffe. New York: Barnes and Noble, 1965, pp. 146-156.

Gordon, Ida L. "Processes of Characterization in Chaucer's *Troilus.*" *Studies in Medieval Literature and Languages in Memory of Frederick Whitehead,* ed. W. Rothwell, W. R. J. Barron, D. Blamires, and L. Thorpe. New York: Barnes and Noble, 1973, pp. 117-131.

Gordon, Robert K. *The Story of Troilus as told by Benoit de Sainte-Maure, Giovanni Boccaccio, Geoffrey Chaucer, and Robert Henryson.* London: Dent, 1934.

Graydon, Joseph S. "Defense of Criseyde." *PMLA*, 44 (1929), 160-163.

Grebstein, Sheldon N., ed. *Perspectives in Contemporary Criticism.* New York: Harper & Row, 1968.

Green, Marion. "Christian Implications of Knighthood and Courtly Love in Chaucer's *Troilus.*" *DN*, 30 (1957), 57-92.

Green, Richard F. "*Troilus* and the Game of Love." *ChauR*, 13 (1979), 201-220.

Greenfield, Stanley B. "The Role of Calkas in *Troilus and Criseyde.*" *MAE*, 36 (1967), 141-51.

Griffin, Nathaniel E. and Myrick, Arthur B. *The Filostrato of Giovanni Boccaccio: A Translation with Parallel Text.* Philadelphia: University of Pennsylvania Press, 1929.

Griffin, N. E. "Chaucer's Portrait of Criseyde." *JEGP*, 20 (1921), 39-46.

Griffith, Dudley D. *Bibliography of Chaucer*, 1908-1953. Seattle: University of Washington Press, 1955.

" 'Grim and Genial': Review of D. W. Robertson's *Preface to Chaucer.*" *TLS*, June 11, 1964, p. 510.

Gross, Laila. "Time and the Narrator in Chaucer's *Troilus and Criseyde.*" *McNr*, 19 (1968), 16-26.

Gross, Laila. "The Two Wooings of Criseyde." *NM*, 74 (1972), 113-125.

Grossvogel, David I. *Limits of the Novel: Evolution of a Form from Chaucer to Robbe-Grillet.* Ithaca: Cornell University Press, 1967.

Gunn, Alan M. S. "The Polylithic Romance: With Pages of Illustrations." *Studies in Medieval, Renaissance, American Literature: A Festschrift*, ed. Betsy F. Colquitt. Forth Worth, Texas: Christian University Press, 1971, pp. 1-18.

Hagopian, John V. "Chaucer as Psychologist in *Troilus and Criseyde.*" *L&P*, 5 (1955), 5-11.

Hagopian, John V. "Chaucer's *Troilus and Criseyde*, III. 1744-71." *Expl*, 10 (1951), item 2.

Hamilton, George L. *The Indebtedness of Chaucer's Troilus and Criseyde to Guido delle Colonne's Historia Trojana.* New York: Columbia University Press, 1903.

Hammond, Eleanor P. *Chaucer: A Bibliographical Manual.* 1908; reprint ed. New York: Peter Smith, 1933.

Hanson, Thomas B. "The Center of Troilus and Criseyde." *ChauR*, 9 (1975), 297-302.

Hanson, Thomas B. "Criseyde's Brows Once Again." *N&Q*, 18 (1971), 285-286.

Hardie, Keith J. "Structure and Irony in Chaucer's *Troilus and Criseyde.*" *PAPA*, 3 (1977), 13-19.

Hartman, Geoffrey H. "Letter." *PMLA*, 92 (1977), 307.

Hartman, Geoffrey H. "Review of Norman Fruman's *Coleridge, The Damaged Archangel.*" *NYTBR*, March 12, 1972, pp. 1 and 36.

Harvey, Patricia A. "ME. 'Point' (*Troilus and Criseyde* III, 695)." *N&Q*, 15 (1968), 243-244.

Haselmayer, Louis A., Jr. "The Portraits in *Troilus and Criseyde.*" *PQ,* 17 (1938), 220-223.

Haskell, Ann S. "The Doppelgängers in Chaucer's *Troilus.*" *NM,* 72 (1971), 723-734.

Hatcher, Elizabeth R. "Chaucer and the Psychology of Fear: Troilus in Book V." *ELH,* 40 (1973), 307-324.

Hays, H. R. *The Dangerous Sex: The Myth of Feminine Evil.* New York: G. P. Putnam's Sons, 1964.

Hawkins, Harriett. *Poetic Freedom and Poetic Truth: Chaucer, Shakespeare, Marlowe, Milton.* Oxford: Clarendon Press, 1976.

Heidtmann, Peter. "Sex and Salvation in *Troilus and Criseyde.*" *ChauR,* 2 (1968), 246-253.

Heller, Erich. *The Disinherited Mind: Essays in Modern German Literature and Thought,* 3rd ed. London: Bowes and Bowes, 1971.

Helterman, Jeffrey. "Masks of Love in *Troilus and Criseyde.*" *CL,* 26 (1974), 14-31.

Henderson, George D. S. *Gothic.* Harmondsworth, Eng.: Penguin, 1967.

Heymann, C. David. "Review of Claude Marks' *Pilgrims, Heretics and Lovers.*" *NYTBR,* July 13, 1975, p. 7.

Hill, Archibald A. "Diomede: The Traditional Development of a Character." *UMPLL,* 8 (1932), 1-25.

Hill, Archibald, A. "Ilium, the Palace of Priam." *MP,* 30 (1932-1933), 94-96.

Hirsch, E. D., Jr. *Validity in Interpretation.* New Haven: Yale University Press, 1967.

Hoccleve, Thomas. *Hoccleve's Works, the Minor Poems, I,* ed. F. J. Furnivall, *EETS.* London: Oxford University Press, 1892.

Hoffman, Frederick J. *Freudianism and the Literary Mind.* New York: Grove Press, 1959.

Hoffman, Nancy Y. "The Great Gatsby: *Troilus and Criseyde* Revisited." *Fitzgerald/Hemingway Annual,* ed. M. J. Bruccoli and C. E. Frazer Clark. Washington, D. C.: NCR Microcards Editions, 1971, pp. 148-158.

Hornstein, Lillian Herlands. "Petrarch's Laelius Chaucer's Lollius?" *PMLA,* 63 (1948), 64-84.

Hough, Graham. *An Essay on Criticism.* London: Duckworth, 1966.

Howard, Donald R. "Chaucer the Man." *PMLA,* 80 (1965), 337-343.

Howard, Donald R. "Experience, Language, and Consciousness: *Troilus and Criseyde,* II, 596-931." *Medieval Literature and Folklore Studies: Essays in Honor of Francis Lee Utley,* ed. J. Mandel and B. A. Rosenberg. New Brunswick, N. J.: Rutgers University Press, 1970, pp. 173-192.

Howard, Donald R. *The Idea of the Canterbury Tales.* Berkeley: University of California Press, 1976.

Howard, Donald R. "Literature and Sexuality: Book III of Chaucer's *Troilus.*" *MR,* 8 (1967), 442-456.

Howard, Donald R. *The Three Temptations: Medieval Man in Search of the World.* Princeton: Princeton University Press, 1966.

Howard, Edwin J. *Geoffrey Chaucer.* New York: Twayne, 1964.

Huber, John. "Troilus' Predestination Soliloquy." *NM*, 66 (1965), 120-125.

Hussey, S. S. *Chaucer: An Introduction.* London: Methuen, 1971.

Hussey, S. S. "The Difficult Fifth Book of *Troilus and Criseyde.*" *MLR*, 67 (1972), 721-729.

Hutson, Arthur E. "Troilus' Confession." *MLN*, 69 (1954), 458-470.

Huxley, Aldous. *On the Margin.* London: Chatto & Windus, 1956.

Isaacs, Neil D. "Further Testimony in the Matter of *Troilus.*" *SLitI*, 4 (1971), 11-27.

Isaacs, Neil D. "On Six and Sevene: *Troilus*, IV.622." *AN&Q*, 5 (1967), 85-86.

Jefferson, Bernard L. *Chaucer and the Consolation of Philosophy of Boethius.* 1917; reprint ed. New York: Haskell House, 1965.

Jelliffe, Robert A. *Troilus and Criseyde: Studies in Interpretation.* 1956; reprint ed. Folcroft, Pa.: Folcroft Library Editions, 1971.

Jennings, Margaret. "Chaucer's *Troilus* and the Ruby." *N&Q*, 23 (1976), 533-537.

Johnston, Everett C. "The Pronoun of Address in Chaucer's *Troilus.*" *LangQ*, 1 (1962), 17-20.

Jordan, Robert M. *Chaucer and the Shape of Creation: The Aesthetic Possibilities of Inorganic Structure.* Cambridge: Harvard University Press, 1967.

Jordan, Robert M. "The Narrator in Chaucer's Troilus." *ELH*, 25 (1958), 237-257.

Joseph, Bertram. "*Troilus and Criseyde*—A Most Admirable and Inimitable Epicke Poeme." *E&S*, 7 (1954), 42-61.

Kane, George. *The Autobiographical Fallacy in Chaucer and Langland Studies.* London: H. K. Lewis, 1965.

Kararah, Azza. "An Approach to *Troilus and Criseyde.*" *AUBFA*, 18 (1963), 1-19.

Kaske, R. E. "The Aube in Chaucer's *Troilus.*" *Chaucer Criticism, Troilus and Criseyde, & the Minor Poems.* 2 vols., ed. Richard J. Schoeck and Jerome J. Taylor. Notre Dame, Ind.: University of Notre Dame Press, 1961, I, 167-179.

Kaske, R. E. "Patristic Exegesis: The Defense." *Critical Approaches to Literature*, ed. D. Bethurum. New York: Dover, 1959, pp. 27-82.

Käsmann, Hans. " 'I wolde excuse hire yet for routhe': Chaucers Einstellung zu Criseyde." *Chaucer und Seine Zeit: Symposion für Walter F. Schirmer*, ed. Arno Esch. Tübingen: Max Niemeyer, 1968, pp. 97-122.

Kean, Patricia M. *Chaucer and the Making of English Poetry.* 2 Vols. London: Routledge & Kegan Paul, 1972. I.

Kean, Patricia M. "Chaucer's Dealings with a Stanza of *Il Filostrato* and the Epilogue of *Troilus and Criseyde.*" *MAE*, 33 (1964), 36-46.

Kellogg, Alfred L. "On the Tradition of Troilus's Vision of the Little Earth." *MS*, 22 (1960), 204-213.

Kelly, Edward H. "Myth as Paradigm in *Troilus and Criseyde.*" *PLL*, 3 (1967), 28-30.

Kelly, Henry Ansgar. *Love and Marriage in the Age of Chaucer.* Ithaca: Cornell University Press, 1975.

Ker, William P. *Epic and Romance*, 2nd ed. London: MacMillan, 1926.

✓ Kiernan, Kevin S. "Hector the Second: The Lost Face of Troilustratus." *AnM*, 16 (1975), 52-62.

Kirby, Thomas A. "As Good Chepe." *MLN*, 48 (1933), 527-528.

Kirby, Thomas A. "A Note on '*Troilus*,' II, 1298." *MLR*, 29 (1934), 67-68.

✓ Kirby, Thomas A. *Chaucer's Troilus: A Study in Courtly Love.* 1940; reprint ed. Gloucester, Mass.: Peter Smith, 1958.

Kissner, Alfons. *Chaucer in seinen beziehungen zur italienischer literatur.* Bonn: Marcus, 1867.

Kittredge, George Lyman. "Antigone's Song of Love." *MLN*, 25 (1910), 158.

Kittredge, George Lyman. *Chaucer and his Poetry.* Cambridge: Harvard University Press, 1939.

Kittredge, George Lyman. "Chaucer and Some of his Friends." *MP*, 1 (1903), 1-18.

Kittredge, George Lyman. "Chaucer's Lollius." *HSCP*, 28 (1917), 47-109.

Kittredge, George Lyman. "Chaucer's *Troilus* and Guillaume de Machaut." *MLN*, 30 (1915), 69.

Kittredge, George Lyman. *The Date of Chaucer's Troilus and Other Chaucer Matters.* Chaucer Society, Second Series, No. 42. London: Kegan Paul, 1909.

Kittredge, George Lyman. *Observations on the Language of Chaucer's Troilus.* Chaucer Society, Second Series, No. 28. London: Kegan Paul, Trench, Trübner, 1891.

Kleinstück, Johannes. "Chaucer's *Troilus* und die höfische Liebe." *Archiv*, 193 (1956), 1-14.

Knapp, Peggy A. "Boccaccio and Chaucer on Cassandra." *PQ*, 56 (1977), 413-417.

Knapp, Peggy A. "The Nature of Nature: Criseyde's 'Slydyng Corage.' " *ChauR*, 13 (1978), 133-140.

Knight, Stephen. *rymyng craftily: Meaning in Chaucer's Poetry.* Sydney, Australia: Angus and Robertson, 1973.

Kökeritz, Helge. "Rhetorical World-Play in Chaucer." *PMLA*, 69 (1954), 937-952.

Koretsky, Allen C. "Chaucer's Use of the Apostrophe in *Troilus and Criseyde.*" *ChauR*, 4 (1970), 242-266.

Kossick, S. G. " 'Troilus and Criseyde': the Aubades." *UES*, 9 (1971), 11-13.

Kott, Jan. *Shakespeare Our Contemporary*, tr. B. Taborski. New York: Doubleday, 1966.

Krapp, George Philip, Jr., tr. *Chaucer's Troilus and Cressida*. New York: Limited Editions Club, 1939.

Kreuzer, James R. "The Zanzis Quotation in Chaucer's *Troilus and Criseyde*, IV, 415." *N&Q*, 202 (1957), 237.

Kornbluth, Alice F. "Another Chaucer Pun." *N&Q*, 204 (1959), 243.

Krook, Dorothea. "Intentions and Intentions: The Problem of Intention and Henry James's *The Turn of the Screw*." *The Theory of the Novel: New Essays*, ed. John Halperin. New York: Oxford University Press, 1974, pp. 353-372.

Lackey, Allen D. "Chaucer's *Troilus and Criseyde*, IV, 295-301." *Expl*, 32 (1973), Item 5.

Lange, Hugo. "Chaucer's 'Myn Auctour Called Lollius' und die Datierung des 'Hous of Fame.' " *Anglia*, 42 (1918), 345-351.

Langhans, Viktor. *Untersuchungen zu Chaucer*. Halle: Max Niemeyer, 1918.

Lanham, Richard A. "Opaque Style and Its Uses in *Troilus and Criseide*." *SMC*, 3 (1970), 169-176.

Larsen, Swen A. "The Best of Chaucer's 'Connyng': *Troilus and Criseyde*, II. 3-4." *N&Q*, 194 (1949), 332.

Lawlor, John. *Chaucer*. London: Hutchinson University Library, 1968.

Leclercq, Jean. "Post Face: Le Monachisme Médiéval." *Revue d' Ascétique et de Mystique*, 41 (1965), 287.

Legouis, Émile. *Geoffroy Chaucer*. Paris: Blood, 1910.

Lewis, C. S. *The Allegory of Love: A Study in Medieval Tradition*. New York: Oxford University Press, 1958.

Lewis, C. S. *The Discarded Image: An Introduction to Medieval and Renaissance Literature*. Cambridge: Cambridge University Press, 1964.

Lewis, C. S. "What Chaucer Really Did to *Il Filostrato*." *E&S*, 17 (1932), 56-75.

Lippmann, Kurt L. *Das ritterliche Persönlichkeitsideal in der mittelenglischen Literatur des 13. und 14. Jahrhunderts*. Meerane in Sachsen, 1933.

Lockhart, Adrienne. "Semantic, Moral, and Aesthetic Degeneration in *Troilus and Criseyde*." *ChauR*, 8 (1973), 100-117.

Longo, Joseph A. "The Double Time Scheme in Book II of Chaucer's *Troilus and Criseyde*." *MLQ*, 22 (1961), 37-40.

Loomis, Roger Sherman. "Was Chaucer a Free Thinker?" *Studies in Medieval Literature in Honor of Albert C. Baugh*, ed. MacEdward Leach. Philadelphia: University of Pennsylvania Press, 1961, pp. 21-44.

Looten, Camille. *Chaucer: ses modèles, ses sources, sa religion.* Lille: L'Economat des Facultés Catholiques, 1931.

Lounsbury, Thomas R. *Studies in Chaucer: His Life and Writings.* 3 Vols. 1892; reprint ed. New York: Russell & Russell, 1962, II.

Lowes, John Livingston. "The Date of Chaucer's *Troilus and Criseyde.*" *PMLA,* 23 (1908), 285-306.

Lowes, John Livingston. "The Dry Sea and the Carrenare." *MP,* 3 (1905-1906), 1-46.

Lowes, John Livingston. *Geoffrey Chaucer.* Oxford: Clarendon: Indiana University Press, 1934.

Lucas, F. L. *Literature and Psychology.* Ann Arbor: University of Michigan Press, 1957.

Lüdeke, Henry. *Die Funktionen des Erzählers in Chaucers epischer Dichtung.*" 1928; reprint ed. Tübingen: Max Niemeyer, 1973.

Lumiansky, Robert M. "Calchas in the Early Versions of the *Troilus.*" *TSE,* 4 (1954), 5-20.

Lumiansky, Robert M. "The Function of the Proverbial Monetary Elements in Chaucer's *Troilus and Criseyde.*" *TSE,* 2 (1950), 5-48.

Lumiansky, Robert M. "The Story of Troilus and Briseida According to Benoit and Guido." *Spec,* 29 (1954), 727-733.

Lydgate, John. The *Fall of Princes,* ed. H. Bergen, Part I. Washington, D. C.: The Carnegie Institute of Washington, 1923.

Macey, Samuel L. "Dramatic Elements in Chaucer's *Troilus.*" *TSLL,* 12 (1970), 301-323.

Madden, William A. "Chaucer's Retraction and Medieval Canons of Seemliness." *MS,* 17 (1955), 173-184.

Magoun, F. P., Jr. "Chaucer's Summary of Statius' *Thebaid* II-XII." *Traditio,* 11 (1955), 409-420.

Magoun, F. P., Jr. " 'Hymselven lik a pilgrym to desgise': *Troilus,* V.1577." *MLN,* 59 (1941), 176-178.

Maguire, John B. "The Clandestine Marriage of *Troilus and Criseyde.*" *ChauR,* 8 (1974), 275-276.

Malarkey, Stoddard. "The 'Corones Tweyne': An Interpretation." *Spec,* 38 (1963), 473-478.

Malone, Kemp. *Chapters on Chaucer.* Baltimore, Md.: Johns Hopkins Press, 1951.

Manlove, Colin. " 'Rooteles moot grene soone deye': The Helplessness of Chaucer's Troilus and Criseyde." *E&S,* 31 (1978), 1-22.

Manly, John Matthews. "Chaucer and the Rhetoricians." *Chaucer Criticism: The Canterbury Tales,* ed. Richard Schoeck and Jerome Taylor. 2 Vols. Notre Dame, Ind.: University of Notre Dame Press, 1960, I, 268-290.

Manzalaoui, M. "Roger Bacon's 'in convexitate' and Chaucer's 'in convers' (*Troilus and Criseyde,* V. 1810)." *N&Q,* 209 (1964), 165-166.

Marchalonis, Shirley. "Medieval Symbols and the *Gesta Romanorum.*" *ChauR,* 8 (1974), 311-319.

Margolis, Joseph. *The Language of Art and Art Criticism: Analytic Questions in Aesthetics*. Detroit: Wayne State University Press, 1965.

Marken, Ronald. "Chaucer and Henryson: A Comparison." *Discourse*, 7 (1964), 381-387.

Markland, Murray F. "Pilgrims Errant: The Doubleness of *Troilus and Criseyde*." *RS*, 33 (1965), 64-77.

Markland, Murray F. "*Troilus and Criseyde*: The Inviolability of the Ending." *MLQ*, 31 (1970), 147-159.

Marks, Claude. *Pilgrims, Heretics, and Lovers*. New York: Macmillan, 1975.

Marsh, Robert. "Historical Interpretation and the History of Criticism." *Literary Criticism and Historical Understanding*, ed. Philip Damon. New York: Columbia University Press, 1967, pp. 1-24.

Martin, June H. *Love's Fools: Aucassin, Troilus, Calisto, and the Parody of the Courtly Lover*. London: Tamesis Books, 1972.

Martin, Robert B. "Notes Toward a Comic Fiction." *The Theory of the Novel: New Essays*, ed. John Halperin. New York: Oxford University Press, 1974, pp. 71-90.

Masefield, John. *Chaucer*. New York: Macmillan, 1926.

Masi, Michael. "Troilus: A Medieval Psychoanalysis." *AnM*, 11 (1970), 81-88.

Masui, Michio. "The Development of Mood in Chaucer's *Troilus*: An Approach." *Studies in Language and Literature in Honour of Margaret Schlauch*, ed. Brahmer, Mieczyslaw, Stanislaw Helsztyński and Julian Krźyzanowski. New York: Russell & Russell, 1971, pp. 245-254.

Masui, Michio. "A Mode of Word-Meaning in Chaucer's Language of Love." *SELit*, Eng. No. (1967), 113-126.

Matthews, Lloyd J. "Chaucer's Personification of Prudence in *Troilus* (V.743-749): Sources in the Visual Arts and Manuscript Scholia." *ELN*, 13 (1976), 249-255.

Mayhew, A. L. " 'Dulcarnon' in Chaucer." *N&Q*, 11 (1910), 505-506.

Mayo, Robert D. "The Trojan Background of the *Troilus*." *ELH*, 9 (1942), 245-256.

McAlpine, Monica E. *The Genre of Troilus and Criseyde*. Ithaca: Cornell University Press, 1978.

McCall, John P. "Five-Book Structure in Chaucer's *Troilus*." *MLQ*, 23 (1962), 297-308.

McCall, John P. "The Trojan Scene in Chaucer's *Troilus*." *ELH*, 29 (1962), 263-275.

McCall, John P. "Troilus and Criseyde." *Companion to Chaucer Studies*, ed. Beryl Rowland. London: Oxford University Press, 1968, pp. 370-384.

McCall, John P., and Rudisill, George, Jr. "The Parliament of 1386 and Chaucer's Trojan Parliament." *JEGP*, 58 (1959), 276-288.

McCormick, W. S. "Another Chaucer Stanza?" *An English Miscellany Presented to Dr. Furnivall.* Oxford: Clarendon Press, 1901, pp. 296-300.

McGrady, Donald. "Chaucer and the *Decameron* Reconsidered." *ChauR*, 12 (1977), 1-15.

McGregor, James H. "The Iconography of Chaucer in Hoccleve's *De Regimine Principum* and in the *Troilus* Frontispiece." *ChauR*, 11 (1977), 338-350.

McNally, John J. "Chaucer's Topsy-Turvy Dante." *SMC*, 2 (1966), 104-110.

Medieval Literature and Contemporary Theory. New Literary History, 10 (1979), 181-416.

Meech, Sanford B. *Design in Chaucer's Troilus.* New York: Syracuse University Press, 1959.

Mehl, Dieter. "The Audience of Chaucer's *Troilus and Criseyde.*" *Chaucer and Middle English Studies in Honor of Rossell Hope Robbins*, ed. Beryl Rowland. London: Unwin, 1974, pp. 173-189.

Mehl, Dieter. *Geoffrey Chaucer: Eine Einführung in seine erzählenden Dictungen.* Berlin: Erich Schmidt, 1973.

Mieszkowski, Gretchen. " 'Pandras' in Deschamps' 'Ballade for Chaucer.' " *ChauR*, 9 (1975), 327-336.

Mieszkowski, Gretchen. *The Reputation of Criseyde, 1155-1500.* Transactions of the Connecticut Academy of Arts and Sciences, 43 (1971), pp. 71-153. Hamden, Conn.: Archon Books, 1971.

Milic, Louis T. "Against the Typology of Styles." *Issues in Contemporary Literary Criticism*, ed. Gregory T. Polletta. Boston: Little, Brown, 1973, pp. 246-254.

Miller, Ralph N. "Pandarus and Procne." *SMC*, 7 (1964), 65-68.

Mills, Laurens J. *One Soul in Bodies Twain.* Bloomington, Ind.: Principia Press, 1937.

Miskimin, Alice S. *The Renaissance Chaucer.* New Haven: Yale University Press, 1975.

Mizener, Arthur. "Character and Action in the Case of Criseyde." *PMLA*, 54 (1939), 65-81.

Mogan, Joseph Jr. *Chaucer and the Theme of Mutability.* Paris: Mouton, 1969.

Mogan, Joseph, Jr. "Free Will and Determinism in Chaucer's *Troilus and Criseyde.*" *WSLL*, 2 (1969), 131-160.

Mogan, Joseph Jr. "Further Aspects of Mutability in Chaucer's *Troilus.*" *PELL*, 2 (1965), 72-77.

Moller, Herbert. "The Meaning of Courtly Love." *JAF*, 73 (1960), 39-52.

Moller, Herbert. "The Social Causation of the Courtly Love Complex." *CSSH*, 1 (1959), 137-163.

Morse, David. "Letter." *TLS*, April 14, 1972, p. 420.

Mudrick, Marvin. "Chaucer's Nightingales." *HudR*, 10 (1957), 88-95.

Mudrick, Marvin. "Looking for Kellerman: or, Fiction and the Facts of

Life." *The Theory of the Novel: New Essays*, ed. John Halperin. New York: Oxford University Press, 1974, pp. 270-304.

Murphy, James J. "A New Look at Chaucer and the Rhetoricians." *RES*, 15 (1964), 1-20.

Murray, John J. "Hamlet and Logic." *PMLA*, 90 (1975), 120-121.

Muscatine, Charles. *Chaucer and the French Tradition: A Study in Style and Meaning*. Berkeley: University of California Press, 1957.

Muscatine, Charles. "The Feigned Illness in Chaucer's *Troilus and Criseyde.*" *MLN*, 63 (1948), 372-377.

Muscatine, Charles. *Poetry and Crisis in the Age of Chaucer*. Notre Dame, Ind.: University of Notre Dame Press, 1972.

Muscatine, Charles. "A Poet's Tale: A Review of John Gardner's *The Life and Times of Chaucer* and *The Poetry of Chaucer.*" *NYTBR*, April 24, 1977, pp. 13, 38, 39.

Mustanoja, Tauno F. "*Troilus and Criseyde*, IV, 607: 'of Fered.' " *NM*, 56 (1955), 174-177.

Nagarajan, S. "The Conclusion to Chaucer's *Troilus and Criseyde.*" *EIC*, 13 (1963), 1-8.

Neff, Sherman B. "Chaucer's Cressida, 'lufsom lady dere.' " *UCS*, 2 (1945), 45-51.

Neff, Sherman B. "Chaucer's Pandarus." *WHR*, 4 (1950), 343-348.

Nelson, Cary. "Reading Criticism." *PMLA*, 91 (1976), 801-805.

Newman, Francis X. ed. *The Meaning of Courtly Love*. Albany: State University of New York Press, 1968.

Newton, Judith M. "Chaucer's *Troilus*: Sir Francis Kynaston's Latin Translation with a Critical Edition of His English and Latin Annotations." *DA*, 28 (1968), 5026A. University of Illinois, 1967.

O'Connor, John V. "The Astronomical Dating of Chaucer's *Troilus.*" *JEGP*, 55 (1956), 556-562.

Olmert, Michael. "Troilus and a Classical Pander: TC3:729-30." *Chaucer Newsletter*, 1 (1979), 18-19.

O'Neill, W. M. "The Bente Moone." *AUMLA*, 43 (1975), 50-52.

Ornstein, Robert. *The Moral Vision of Jacobean Tragedy*. Madison: University of Wisconsin Press, 1960.

Overbeck, Pat T. "Chaucer's Good Woman." *ChauR*, 2 (1967), 75-94.

Owen, Charles A., Jr. "Chaucer's Method of Composition." *MLN*, 72 (1957), 164-165.

Owen, Charles A., Jr. "Mimetic Form in the Central Love Scene of *Troilus and Criseyde.*" *MP*, 67 (1969), 125-132.

Owen, Charles A., Jr. "The Problem of Free Will in Chaucer's Narrative." *PQ*, 46 (1967), 433-456.

Owen, Charles A., Jr. "The Significance of Chaucer's Revision of *Troilus and Criseyde.*" *MP*, 55 (1958), 1-5.

Paget, Violet. *Euphorion: Being Studies of the Antique and the Medieval in the Renaissance*. London: T. F. Unwin, 1885.

Paris, Gaston. "Lancelot du Lac 2: Le Conte de la Charrette." *Romania*, 12 (1883), 459-534.

Patch, Howard R. "Chaucer and Lady Fortune." *MLR*, 22 (1927), 377-388.

Patch, Howard R. *The Goddess Fortuna in Medieval Literature*. Cambridge: Harvard University Press, 1927.

Patch, Howard R. *On Rereading Chaucer*. Cambridge: Harvard University Press, 1954.

Patch, Howard R. "A Review of Kemp Malone's *Chapters on Chaucer*." *MLN*, 68 (1953), 556-557.

Patch, Howard R. *The Tradition of Boethius: A Study of His Importance in Medieval Culture*. New York: Oxford University Press, 1935.

Patch, Howard R. "Troilus on Determinism." *Spec*, 6 (1931), 225-243.

Patch, Howard R. "Troilus on Predestination." *JEGP*, 17 (1918), 399-422.

Patch, Howard R. "Two Notes on Chaucer's *Troilus*." *MLN*, 70 (1955), 8-12.

Payne, Robert O. "The Historical Criticism We Need." *Chaucer at Albany*, ed. Rossell Hope Robbins. New York: Burt Franklin, 1975.

Payne, Robert O. *The Key of Remembrance: A Study of Chaucer's Poetic*. New Haven: Yale University Press, 1963.

Pearce, Roy Harvey. "Historicism Once More." *Twentieth Century Criticism: The Major Statements*, ed. W. J. Hardy and M. Westbrook. New York: Free Press, 1974, pp. 352-365.

Pearsall, Derek. "The *Troilus* Frontispiece and Chaucer's Audience." *YES*, 7 (1977), 68-74.

Pearsall, Derek and Salter, Elizabeth. *The Difficulty of Medieval Poetry*. Sussex International Tape, Side B, "Troilus and Criseyde."

Peck, Russell A. "Numerology and Chaucer's *Troilus and Criseyde*." *Mosaic*, 5 (1972), 1-29.

Peed, Michael R. "*Troilus and Criseyde*: The Narrator and the 'Old Bokes.'" *AN&M*, 12 (1974), 143-146.

Peyton, III, Henry H. "Diomed the Large Tongued Greek." *In*, 6 (1974), 1-6.

Peyton, III, Henry H. "The Role of Calkas, Helen, and Cassandra in Chaucer's *Troilus*." *In*, 7 (1975), 8-12.

Peyton, III, Henry H. "Three Minor Characters in Chaucer's *Troilus*: Hector, Antigone, and Deiphebus." *In*, 8 (1975), 47-53.

Pitfield, Robert, M.D. "Chaucer's Nervous Depression." *JNMD*, 82 (1935), 80-82.

Popper, Karl. *Conjectures and Refutations: The Growth of Scientific Knowledge*. London: Routledge & Kegan Paul, 1963.

Popper, Karl. *The Poverty of Historicism*. Boston: Beacon Press, 1957.

Pratt, Robert A. "Chaucer and *Le Roman de Troyle et de Criseida*." *SP*, 53 (1956), 509-539.

Pratt, Robert A. "Chaucer's 'Natal Jove' and 'Seint Jerome . . . agayn Jovinian.'" *JEGP*, 61 (1962), 244-248.

Pratt, Robert A. "A Geographical Problem in *Troilus and Criseyde*." *MLN*, 61 (1946), 541-543.

Praz, Mario. "Chaucer and the Great Italian Writers of the Trecento." *MC*, 6 (1927), 18-157.

Preston, Raymond. *Chaucer*. London: Sheed and Ward, 1952.

Price, Thomas R. "*Troilus and Criseyde*: A Study in Chaucer's Method of Narrative Construction." *PMLA*, 11 (1896), 307-322.

Prokosch, Frederic. "Geoffrey Chaucer." *The English Novelists: A Survey of the Novel by Twenty Contemporary Novelists*, ed. D. Verschoyle. New York: Harcourt Brace, 1936, pp. 3-16.

Provost, William. *The Structure of Chaucer's Troilus and Criseyde*. Copenhagen: Rosenkilde and Bagger, 1974.

Provost, William and Mitchell, Jerome, eds. *Chaucer the Love Poet*. Athens, Ga.: University of Georgia Press, 1973.

Rand, E. K. *Founders of the Middle Ages*. New York: Dover, 1928.

Reed, W. A. "On Chaucer's *Troilus and Criseyde* I, 228." *JEGP*, 20 (1921), 397-398.

Reichert, John. *Making Sense of Literature*. Chicago: University of Chicago Press, 1977.

Reilly, Robert. "The Narrator and his Audience: A Study of Chaucer's *Troilus*." *U Port R*, 21 (1961), 23-36.

Reinecke, George F. "Speculation, Intention, and the Teaching of Chaucer." *The Learned and the Lewed: Studies in Chaucer and Medieval Literature*, ed. L. D. Benson. Cambridge: Harvard University Press, 1974, pp. 81-93.

Reiss, Edmund. "Chaucer's Courtly Love." *The Learned and the Lewed: Studies in Chaucer and Medieval Literature*, ed. L. D. Benson. Cambridge: Harvard University Press, 1974, pp. 95-111.

Reiss, Edward. "Troilus and the Failure of Understanding." *MLQ*, 29 (1968), 131-144.

Renoir, Alain. "Another Minor Analogue to Chaucer's Pandarus." *N&Q*, 203 (1958), 421-422.

Renoir, Alain. "Criseyde's Two Half Lovers." *OL*, 16 (1961), 239-255.

Renoir, Alain. "Thebes, Troy, Criseyde and Pandarus: An Instance of Chaucerian Irony." *SN*, 32 (1960), 14-17.

Rimmon, Shlomith. *The Concept of Ambiguity—The Example of James*. Chicago: University of Chicago Press, 1977.

Robbie, May G. "Three-Faced Pandarus." *CEJ*, 3 (1967), 47-54.

Robertson, D. W., Jr. "Chaucerian Tragedy." *ELH*, 19 (1952), 1-37.

Robertson, D. W., Jr. "The Concept of Courtly Love as an Impediment to the Understanding of Medieval Texts." *The Meaning of Courtly Love*, ed. F. X. Newman. Albany: State University of New York Press, 1968, pp. 1-18.

Robertson, D. W., Jr. "The Doctrine of Charity in Mediaeval Literary

Gardens: A Topical Approach through Symbolism and Allegory."
Spec, 26 (1951), 24-49.

Robertson, D. W., Jr., and Huppé, B. F. *Fruyt and Chaf: Studies in Chaucer's Allegories*. Princeton: Princeton University Press, 1963.

Robertson, D. W., Jr. "Historical Criticism." *English Institute Essays*, 1950, ed. A. S. Downer. New York: Columbia University Press, 1951.

Robertson, D. W., Jr., and Huppé, B. F. *Piers Plowman and Scriptural Tradition*. New York: Octagon Books, 1969.

✓ Robertson, D. W., Jr. *A Preface to Chaucer: Studies in Medieval Perspective*. Princeton: Princeton University Press, 1962.

Robertson, D. W., Jr. "Some Medieval Literary Terminology with Special Reference to Chrétien de Troyes." *SP*, 48 (1951), 669-692.

Robertson, D. W., Jr. "The Subject of the *De Amore* of Andreas Capellanus." *MP*, 50 (1952-53), 145-161.

Robinson, F. N. "Review of R. K. Root's edition of *Troilus and Criseyde*." *Spec*, 1 (1926), 461-467.

Robinson, F. N., ed. *The Works of Geoffrey Chaucer*, 2nd ed. Boston: Houghton Mifflin, 1957.

Robinson, Ian. *Chaucer and the English Tradition*. Cambridge: Cambridge University Press, 1971.

Robinson, Ian. *Chaucer's Prosody: A Study of the Middle English Verse Tradition*. Cambridge: Cambridge University Press, 1971.

Rodway, Allan. *The Truths of Fiction*. London: Chatto & Windus, 1970.

Rogers, H. L. "The Beginning (and Ending) of Chaucer's *Troilus and Criseyde*." *Festschrift for Ralph Farrell*, ed. Anthony Stephens, H. L. Rogers, and Brian Coghlan. Bern: Lang, 1977, pp. 185-200.

Rollins, Hyder E. "The Troilus-Cressida Story from Chaucer to Shakespeare." *PMLA*, 32 (1917), 383-429.

Roma, III, Emilio. "The Scope of the Intentional Fallacy." *The Monist*, 50 (1966), 250-265.

Root, Robert K., ed. *The Book of Troilus and Criseyde by Geoffrey Chaucer*. Princeton: Princeton University Press, 1926.

Root, Robert K. *The Manuscripts of Chaucer's Troilus with Collotype Facsimiles of the Various Handwritings*. Chaucer Society, First Series, No. 98. London: K. Paul, Trench, Trübner, 1914.

Root, Robert K. and Russell, H. N. "A Planetary Date for Chaucer's *Troilus*." *PMLA*, 39 (1924), 48-63.

Root, Robert K. *The Poetry of Chaucer*, 2nd ed. Boston: Houghton Mifflin, 1922.

Root, Robert K. *The Textual Tradition of Chaucer's Troilus*. Chaucer Society, First Series, No. 99. London: K. Paul, Trench, Trübner, 1916.

Rosenzweig, Saul. "The Ghost of Henry James: Revised with a Postscript, 1962." *Modern Criticism: Theory and Practice*, ed. W. Sutton and R. Foster. New York: Odyssey Press, 1963, pp. 401-416.

Ross, Thomas W. *Chaucer's Bawdy*. New York: E. P. Dutton, 1972.

Ross, Thomas W. "*Troilus and Criseyde*, II, 582-587: A Note." *ChauR*, 5 (1970), 137-139.

Rossetti, William M., tr. *Chaucer's Troylus and Crysede Compared with Boccaccio's Filostrato*. Chaucer Society, First Series, Nos. 44, 65. London: N. Trübner, 1873-1883.

Rowe, Donald W. *O Love O Charite! Contraries Harmonized in Chaucer's Troilus*. Carbondale: Southern Illinois University Press, 1976.

Rowland, Beryl. *Blind Beasts: Chaucer's Animal World*. Kent, Ohio: Kent State University Press, 1971.

Rowland, Beryl. "Contemporary Chaucer Criticism." *English*, 22 (1973), 3-10.

Rowland, Beryl. "Pandarus and the Fate of Tantalus." *OL*, 24 (1969), 3-16.

Ruiz-de-Conde, Justina. *El Amor y el Matrimonio secreto en los libros de Caballerias*. Madrid: Aguilar, 1948.

Russell, Nicholas. "Characters and Crowds in Chaucer's *Troilus*." *N&Q*, 13 (1966), 50-52.

Rutherford, Charles S. "Pandarus as Lover: 'A Joly Wo' or 'Loves Shotes Keene?' " *AnM*, 13 (1972), 5-13.

Saintonge, Constance. "In Defense of Criseyde." *MLQ*, 15 (1954), 312-320.

Salter, Elizabeth and Parkes, M.B. Introduction to Chaucer's *The Corpus Christi College Cambridge MS 61 facsimile* of *Troilus and Criseyde*. Cambridge, Eng.: D. S. Brewer, 1978.

Salter, Elizabeth. "*Troilus and Criseyde*: A Reconsideration." *Patterns of Love and Courtesy: Essays in Memory of C. S. Lewis*, ed. John Lawlor. London: Edward Arnold, 1966, pp. 86-106.

Sams, Henry W. "The Dual Time-Scheme in Chaucer's *Troilus*." *MLN*, 56 (1941), 94-100.

Sanders, Wilbur. *The Dramatist and the Received Idea*. Cambridge: Cambridge University Press, 1968.

Sandras, Etienne Gustave. *Étude sur G. Chaucer*. Paris: Auguste Durand, 1859.

Saville, Jonathan. *The Medieval Erotic Alba: Structure as Meaning*. New York: Columbia University Press, 1972.

Schaar, Claes. *The Golden Mirror: Studies in Chaucer's Descriptive Technique and its Literary Background*. Lund: C. W. K. Gleerup, 1955.

Schaar, Claes. *Some Types of Narrative in Chaucer's Poetry*. Lund: C. W. K. Gleerup, 1954.

Schaar, Claes. "Troilus' Elegy and Criseyde's." *SN*, 29 (1962), 185-191.

Schelp, Hanspeter. "Die Tradition der Alba und die Morgenszene in Chaucers *Troilus and Criseyde* III, 1415 ff." *GRM*, 46 (1956), 251-261.

Schibanoff, Susan. "Argus and Argyve: Etymology and Characterization in Chaucer's *Troilus*." *Spec*, 51 (1976), 647-658.

Schibanoff, Susan. "Chaucer and 'Stewart's' Pandarus and the Critics." *SSL*, 13 (1978), 92-99.

Schibanoff, Susan. "Criseyde's 'Impossible' *Aubes*." *JEGP*, 76 (1977), 326-333.

Schibanoff, Susan. "Prudence and Artificial Memory in Chaucer's *Troilus*." *ELH*, 42 (1975), 507-517.

Schmidt, Dieter. "Das Anredepronomen in Chaucers *Troilus and Criseyde*." *Archiv*, 212 (1975), 120-124.

Schoeck, Richard J. and Taylor, Jerome, eds. *Chaucer Criticism: Troilus and Criseyde & the Minor Poems*. 2 vols. Notre Dame, Ind.: University of Notre Dame Press, II.

Schreiber, S. M. *An Introduction to Literary Criticism*. Oxford, Eng.: Pergamon Press, 1965.

Schuman, Samuel. "The Circle of Nature: Patterns of Imagery in Chaucer's *Troilus and Criseyde*." *ChauR*, 10 (1975), 99-112.

Scott, Forrest S. "The Seventh Sphere; A Note on 'Troilus and Criseyde.' " *MLR*, 51 (1956), 2-5.

Shanley, James. "The *Troilus* and Christian Love." *ELH*, 6 (1939), 271-281.

Shannon, Edgar Finlay. *Chaucer and the Roman Poets*. Cambridge: Harvard University Press, 1929.

Sharrock, Roger. "Second Thoughts: C. S. Lewis on Chaucer's *Troilus*." *EIC*, 8 (1958), 123-137.

Shelly, Percy V.D. *The Living Chaucer*. Philadelphia: University of Pennsylvania Press, 1940.

Shepherd, G. T. "Troilus and Criseyde." *Chaucer and Chaucerians: Critical Studies in Middle English Literature*, ed. D. S. Brewer. London: Nelson, 1966, pp. 65-87.

Siddiqui, Naimuddin M. "*Troilus and Cressida*: Treatment of the Theme by Chaucer and Shakespeare." *OJES*, 4 (1964), 105-114.

Silverstein, Theodore. "Andreas, Plato, and the Arabs: Remarks on Some Recent Accounts of Courtly Love." *MP*, 47 (1949), 117-126.

Sims, David. "An Essay at the Logic of *Troilus and Criseyde*." *CamQ*, 4 (1968), 124-149.

Skeat, W. W., ed. *Complete Works of Geoffrey Chaucer*. 7 Vols. Oxford: Clarendon Press, 1894, VI.

Skulsky, Harold. "Hamlet and Logic." *PMLA*, 90 (1975), 121-122.

Skulsky, Harold. " 'I Know My Course': Hamlet's Confidence." *PMLA*, 89 (1974), 477-486.

Slaughter, Eugene E. "Chaucer's Pandarus: Virtuous Uncle and Friend." *JEGP*, 48 (1949), 186-195.

Slaughter, Eugene E. "Love and Grace in Chaucer's *Troilus*." *Essays in Honor of Walter Clyde Curry. Vanderbilt Studies in the Humanities*, II. Nashville: Vanderbilt University Press, 1955, pp. 61-76.

Slaughter, Eugene E. *Virtue According to Love—in Chaucer.* New York: Bookman Associates, 1957.

Smith, Fred Manning. "Chaucer's Prioress and Criseyde." *WVUPP*, 6 (1949), 1-11.

Smith, Nathaniel B. and Snow, Joseph T., eds. *The Expansion and Transformations of Courtly Literature.* Athens, Ga.: University of Georgia Press, 1980.

Smithers, G. V. "Ten Cruces in Middle English Texts, [TCIV.207-210]." *EGS*, 3 (1949-1950), 65-81.

Smyser, Hamilton M. "The Domestic Background of *Troilus and Criseyde.*" *Spec*, 31 (1956), 297-315.

Sommer, George J. "The Attitudes of the Narrator in Chaucer's *Troilus and Criseyde.*" *NY-Pa. MLA Newsletter*, 1 (1968), 1-5.

Sontag, Susan. *Against Interpretation and Other Essays.* New York: Farrar, Straus and Giroux, 1966.

Southworth, James G. *The Prosody of Chaucer and his Followers.* Oxford: Basil Blackwell, 1962.

Spargo, John W. "Chaucer's 'Kandedort.' " *MLN*, 64 (1949), 264-266.

Spearing, Anthony C. *Criticism and Medieval Poetry.* New York: Barnes and Noble, 1964.

Speirs, John. *Chaucer the Maker.* London: Faber and Faber, 1951.

Speirs, John. "Chaucer: (1) *Troilus and Criseyde.*" *Scrutiny*, 11 (1942), 84-108.

Spilka, Mark. "The Necessary Stylist: A New Critical Revision." *Issues in Contemporary Literary Criticism*, ed. Gregory T. Polletta. Boston: Little, Brown, 1973, pp. 207-214.

Spitzer, Leo. "Kanke(r) dort, 'A State of Suspense, a Difficult Position.' " *MLN*, 64 (1949), 502-504.

Spurgeon, Caroline, F. E. *Five Hundred Years of Chaucer Criticism and Allusion, 1357-1900.* 7 parts, Chaucer Society, 1914-1924; 3 vols. Cambridge, 1925; reprint ed. New York: Russell, 1961.

Stanley, E. G. "About Troilus." *E&S*, 29 (1976), 84-106.

Stanley, E. G. "Stanza and Ictus: Chaucer's Emphasis in *Troilus and Criseyde.*" *Chaucer und seine Zeit; Symposion für Walter F. Schirmer*, ed. Arno Esch. Tübingen: Max Niemeyer, 1968, pp. 123-148.

Stanley-Wrench, Margaret, tr. *Troilus and Criseyde.* Fontwell, Arundel (Sussex): Centaur Press, 1965.

Starobinski, Jean. "Truth in Masquerade." *Issues in Contemporary Literary Criticism*, ed. Gregory T. Polletta. Boston: Little, Brown, 1973, pp. 233-246.

Steadman, John M. "The Age of Troilus." *MLN*, 72 (1957), 89-90.

Steadman, John M. *Disembodied Laughter: Troilus and the Apotheosis Tradition: A Reexamination of Narrative and Thematic Contexts.* Berkeley: University of California Press, 1972.

Stearns, Marshall W. "A Note on Chaucer's Use of Aristotelian Psychology." *SP*, 43 (1946), 15-21.

Stevens, Martin. "Chaucer and Modernism: An Essay in Criticism." *Chaucer at Albany*, ed. Rossell Hope Robbins. New York: Burt Franklin, 1975.

Stevens, Martin. "Juliet's Nurse: Love's Herald." *PLL* 2 (1966), 196-206.

Stevens, Martin. "The Winds of Fortune in the *Troilus.*" *ChauR*, 13 (1979), 285-307.

Strauss, Jennifer. "Teaching *Troilus and Criseyde.*" *SoRa*, 5 (1972), 13-20.

Strohm, Paul. "Storie, Spelle, Geste, Romaunce, Tragedie: Generic Distinctions in the Middle English Troy Narratives." *Spec*, 46 (1971), 348-359.

Stroud, Theodore A. "Boethius' Influence on Chaucer's *Troilus.*" *MP*, 49 (1951-1952), 1-9.

Sturtevant, Peter A. "Chaucer's *Troilus and Criseyde*, III, 890." *Expl*, 28 (1969), Item 5.

Sundwall, McKay. "Criseyde's Rein." *ChauR*, 11 (1976), 156-163.

Sundwall, McKay. "Deiphobus and Helen: A Tantalizing Hint." *MP*, 73 (1975), 151-156.

Sundwall, McKay. "*The Destruction of Troy*, Chaucer's *Troilus and Criseyde*, and Lydgate's *Troy Book.*" *RES*, 26 (1975), 313-317.

Tate, Allen. *Collected Essays*. Denver: Alan Swallow, 1959.

Tatlock, John S. P. "Chaucer and Wyclif." *MP*, 14 (1916), 257-268.

Tatlock, John S. P. "Dante and Guinizelli in Chaucer's *Troilus.*" *MLN*, 35 (1920), 443.

Tatlock, John S. P. "The Date of the 'Troilus' and Minor Chauceriana." *MLN*, 50 (1935), 277-296.

Tatlock, John S. P. "The Dates of Chaucer's *Troilus and Criseyde* and *Legend of Good Women.*" *MP* (1903-1904), 317-329.

Tatlock, John S. P. *The Development and Chronology of Chaucer's Works*, 1907; reprint ed. Gloucester, Mass.: Peter Smith, 1964.

Tatlock, John S. P. "The Epilog of Chaucer's *Troilus.*" *MP*, 18 (1921), 625-659.

Tatlock, John S. P. *The Mind and Art of Chaucer*. Syracuse: Syracuse University Press, 1950.

Tatlock, John S. P. "The People in Chaucer's *Troilus.*" *PMLA*, 56 (1941), 85-104.

Taylor, Ann. "Criseyde's 'Thought' in *Troilus and Criseyde*, (II, 598-812)." *An&Q*, 17 (1978), 18-19.

Taylor, Ann. "On *Troilus and Criseyde*, III, 736-742." *AN&Q*, 13 (1974), 24-25.

Taylor, Davis. "The Terms of Love: A Study of Troilus's Style." *Spec*, 51 (1976), 69-90.

Taylor, Willene P. "Supposed Antifeminism in Chaucer's *Troilus and*

Criseyde and Its Retraction in *The Legend of Good Women.*" *XUS,* 9 (1970), 1-18.

Thomas, Mary Edith. *Medieval Skepticism and Chaucer.* 1950; reprint ed. New York: Cooper Square, 1971.

Thompson, Ann. "*Troilus and Criseyde* and *Romeo and Juliet.*" *YES,* 6 (1976), 26-37.

Thompson, Meredith. "Current and Recurrent Fallacies in Chaucer Criticism." *Essays in American and English Literature Presented to Bruce Robert McElderry, Jr.,* ed. Max F. Schulz, William D. Templeman, Charles R. Metzger. Athens, Ohio: Ohio University Press, 1967, pp. 141-164.

Thomson, Patricia. "The 'Canticus Troili': Chaucer and Petrarch." *CL,* 11 (1959), 313-328.

Trilling, Lionel. *The Liberal Imagination: Essays on Literature.* New York: Doubleday, 1957.

Trilling, Lionel. "What is Criticism." *Literary Criticism: An Introductory Reader,* ed. Lionel Trilling. New York: Holt, Rhinehart & Winston, 1970.

Tyrwhitt, Thomas. "Essay on the Language and Versification of Chaucer." *The Canterbury Tales of Chaucer,* ed. Thomas Tyrwhitt. 5 Vols. Edinburgh: James Nichol, 1860. I, xxxviii-xcv.

Usener, Hermann. *Anecdoton Holderi.* Bonn: Georgi, 1877.

Usk, Thomas. *Testament of Love, Chaucerian and other Pieces,* ed. W. W. Skeat. London: Oxford University Press, 1899, VII.

Utley, Francis Lee. "Chaucer's *Troilus* and St. Paul's Charity." *Chaucer and Middle English Studies in Honor of Rossell Hope Robbins,* ed. Beryl Rowland. London: Unwin, 1974, pp. 272-287.

Utley, Francis Lee. *The Crooked Rib* (New York: Octagon Books, 1970).

Utley, Francis Lee. "Must We Abandon the Concept of Courtly Love?" *M&H,* 2 (1972), 299-323.

Utley, Francis Lee. "Robertsonianism Redivivius." *RPh,* 19 (1965), 250-260.

Utley, Francis Lee. "Scene-division in Chaucer's *Troilus and Criseyde.*" *Studies in Medieval Literature in Honor of Albert C. Baugh,* ed. MacEdward Leach. Philadelphia: University of Pennsylvania Press, 1961, pp. 109-138.

Utley, Francis Lee. "Stylistic Ambivalence in Chaucer, Yeats, and Lucretius—The Cresting Wave and Its Undertow." *KCUR,* 37 (1971), 174-198.

Van, Thomas A. "Chaucer's Pandarus as an Earthly Maker." *SHR,* 12 (1978), 89-97.

Van, Thomas A. "Chaucer's *Troilus and Criseyde.*" *Expl,* 34 (1975), Item 20.

Van, Thomas A. "Criseyde's Indirections." *AN&Q,* 13 (1974), 34-35.

Van, Thomas A. "Imprisoning and Ensnarement in *Troilus* and the *Knight's Tale.*" *PLL*, 7 (1971), 3-12.

Van de Voort, Donnell. *Love and Marriage in the English Medieval Romance.* Privately Printed: Nashville, 1938.

Van Doren, Mark. *The Noble Voice: A Study of Ten Great Poems.* New York: Henry Holt, 1946.

Vermeer, Peter M. "Chaucer and Literary Criticism." *DQR*, 4 (1974), 97-110.

Wagenknecht, Edward, ed. *Chaucer: Modern Essays in Criticism.* New York: Oxford University Press, 1959.

Wagenknecht, Edward. *The Personality of Chaucer.* Norman: University of Oklahoma Press, 1968.

Wager, William. "Fleshly Love in Chaucer's *Troilus.*" *MLR*, 34 (1939), 62-66.

Walcutt, Charles C. "The Pronoun of Address in *Troilus and Criseyde.*" *PQ*, 14 (1935), 282-287.

Walker, Jan C. "Chaucer and 'Il Filostrato.' " *ES*, 49 (1968), 318-326.

Warrington, John, ed. *Troilus and Criseyde.* Rev. introd. M. Mills. London: Dent, 1974.

Watts, Ann Chalmers. "Chaucerian Selves—Especially Two Serious Ones." *ChauR*, 4 (1970), 229-241.

Weitz, Morris. *Hamlet and the Philosophy of Criticism.* Cleveland: World, 1964.

Wellek, René, and Warren, Austin. *Theory of Literature.* New York: Harcourt, Brace, 1949.

Wentersdorf, K. P. "Chaucer and the Lost Tale of Wade." *JEGP*, 65 (1966), 274-286.

Wenzel, Siegfried. "Chaucer's Troilus of Book IV." *PMLA*, 79 (1964), 542-547.

Weston-Smith, Miranda, and Duncan, Ronald, eds. *The Encyclopedia of Ignorance.* New York: Pergamon Press, 1977.

Whiting, Bartlett Jere. *Chaucer's Use of Proverbs.* Cambridge: Harvard University Press, 1934.

Whiting, Bartlett Jere. "Troilus and Pilgrims in Wartime." *MLN*, 60 (1945), 47-49.

Whitman, Frank H. "*Troilus and Criseyde* and Chaucer's Dedication to Gower." *TSL*, 18 (1973), 1-11.

Wilkins, Ernest H. "Cantus Troili." *ELH*, 16 (1949), 167-173.

Wilkins, Ernest H. "Criseide." *MLN*, 24 (1909), 65-67.

Williams, George. *A New View of Chaucer.* Durham, N. C.: Duke University Press, 1965.

Williams, George. "The *Troilus and Criseyde* Frontispiece Again." *MLR*, 57 (1962), 173-178.

Wimsatt, James I. "Guillaume de Machaut and Chaucer's *Troilus and Criseyde.*" *MAE*, 45 (1976), 277-293.

Wimsatt, James I. "Medieval and Modern in Chaucer's *Troilus and Criseyde.*" *PMLA*, 92 (1977), 203-216.

Wimsatt, W. K., Jr. *Day of the Leopard.* New Haven: Yale University Press, 1976.

Wimsatt, W. K., Jr. and Beardsley, Monroe C. "Intention." *Dictionary of World Literature*, Revised Edition, ed. J. T. Shipley. Patterson, N.J.: Littlefield Adams, 1953, pp. 229-232.

Wimsatt, W. K., Jr. and Beardsley, Monroe C. *The Verbal Icon: Studies in the Meaning of Poetry.* Lexington: University of Kentucky Press, 1954.

Windeatt, Barry. " 'Love that oughte ben secree' in Chaucer's *Troilus.* " *ChauR*, 14 (1979), 116-131.

Winters, Yvor. *The Function of Criticism: Problems and Exercises*, 2nd ed. Denver: Alan Swallow, 1957.

Wise, Boyd A. *The Influence of Statius upon Chaucer.* 1911; reprint ed. New York: Phaeton Press, 1967.

Witlieb, Bernard L. "Chaucer's Elysian Fields (*Troilus*, IV, 789f)." *N&Q*, 16 (1969), 250-251.

Wood, Chauncey. *Chaucer and the Country of the Stars: Poetic Uses of Astrological Imagery.* Princeton: Princeton University Press, 1970.

Wood, Chauncey. "On Translating Chaucer's *Troilus and Criseyde*, Book III, Lines 12-14." *ELN*, 11 (1973), 9-14.

Wood, Mary Norton. *The Spirit of Protest in Old French Literature.* Columbia University Studies in Romance Philology and Literature, XXI. New York: Columbia University Press, 1917.

Worcester, David. *The Art of Satire.* Cambridge: Harvard University Press, 1940.

Yearwood, Stephenie. "The Rhetoric of Narrative Rendering in Chaucer's *Troilus.*" *ChauR*, 12 (1977), 27-37.

Young, Arthur M. *Troy and Her Legend.* Pittsburgh: University of Pittsburgh Press, 1948.

Young, Karl. "Aspects of the Story of Troilus and Criseyde." *UWSLL*, 2 (1918), 379-394.

Young, Karl. "Chaucer's Renunciation of Love in Troilus." *MLN*, 40 (1925), 270-276.

Young, Karl. "Chaucer's *Troilus and Criseyde* as Romance." *PMLA*, 53 (1938), 38-63.

Young, Karl. "Chaucer's Use of Boccaccio's 'Filocolo.' " *MP*, 4 (1906), 169-177.

Young, Karl. *The Origin and Development of the Story of Troilus and Criseyde.* Chaucer Society, Second Series, No. 40. London: Kegan Paul, 1908.

Zimbardo, Rose A. "Creator and Created: The Generic Perspective of Chaucer's *Troilus and Criseyde.*" *ChauR*, 11 (1977), 283-297.

INDEX